"I have bent back at least 20 pages in *Storytelling: Imagination and Faith* to use in my Sunday storytelling exercises. As a matter of fact, on a recent Sunday I used the one about the chief who left his village leaving his three sons in charge. The congregation loved it....Congratulations on a very, very fine, important, and useful book."

Andrew M. Greeley

"Preachers and church educators always ask, 'Where can I get some stories?' The answer is Bill Bausch's book. Here is a work on narrative theology which combines theory and practice. It brings together philosophical insights into the storytelling process and stories galore!"

John Shea

"By providing examples for every theory and theory for every example, the book itself becomes an excellent teacher. It completes and fleshes out much contemporary writing on story, and puts the best sources in our hands in just one volume."

Maria Harris
Andover Newton Theological School

"This book is about the use of stories, both sacred and profane, as our way of rediscovering gospel values and living the Christian faith....The book has all the marks of a pastor conversant with contemporary trends in theology as well as with ways of making pastoral application of this theology.

Richard M. Gula
The Living Light

"No wonder *Storytelling* is in its sixth printing now. It deserves many more....Altogether, this is a superb book."

Richard L. McCandless

"Of more help to catechists than the actual stories presented in the book is the whole background and analysis of what story is and why story is important. Fr. Bausch discusses what makes a good story, he traces the storytelling history in our Christian tradition, he analyzes Jesus' stories, and he examines our own story in relation to the sacred story."

Philip Ross Beaudoin
The Catechist's Connection

"To Father Bausch, Scripture is a whole anthology of stories. The reaction to cold, analytical thinking, he says, has been to rediscover the value of storytelling as a means to arrive at profound, heartfelt truth. The imaginative is making itself felt more every day and...there is a wealth of stories, sacred and profane, to help adults 'rediscover the gospel values' and to find our 'completeness in Christ.'"

Thomas More Book Club News

"This is a stimulating and practical book for those who long to open people to powerful images of God's grace and human responses to it....Bausch shows the importance of including storytelling that engages not only the cognitive capacities and committed obedience of our communities but also their imagination, laughter, whimsy, and dreams."

Elizabeth Nordquist
Weavings

"I can recommend *Storytelling: Imagination and Faith* as a book that will both enlighten and entertain you....Father William J. Bausch is a storyteller who will cast a spell over you, so do not begin his book until you have enough time to savor it."

Frank J. McNulty

WILLIAM J. BAUSCH

STORYTELLING

Imagination
and
Faith

TWENTY-THIRD PUBLICATIONS
Mystic, Connecticut

Other, Related Books by William J. Bausch

Telling Stories, Compelling Stories:
35 Stories of People of Grace

Timely Homilies:
The Wit and Wisdom of an Ordinary Pastor

More Telling Stories, Compelling Stories

Eighth printing 1993

Twenty-Third Publications
185 Willow Street
P.O. Box 180
Mystic, CT 06355
(203) 536-2611
800-321-0411

ISBN 0-89622-199-7
Library of Congress Catalog Card Number 83-51515

For Charles, Colette,
Charlie, Rita, Jim, Kathryn, Dick:
First and Enduring Chapters
In My Story

Credits

Contents

Introduction:
It's
Story Time

"Once upon a time" is no time and every time. It is the standard phrase that introduces us to other worlds and to our own world, that connects humanity to a common story and storyteller. That is why storytelling and story listening are so congenial, for, in one way or another, we are hearing about ourselves. John and Mary Harrell in *To Tell of Gideon* go so far as to say that "storytelling is so natural to human beings it suggests a definition: we are the creatures who think in stories." But you would never know it.

We are trained to think rather in propositions. Analytical thinking in our computer age is the ideal, an ideal that is amply rewarded. In the religious tradition in which I am writing, Roman Catholicism, creeds and catechisms have dominated our thought patterns, especially since the lives of the saints have fallen on hard times. Yet, in all areas of life, it seems that there is a reaction setting in. More and more we hear about the imaginative. More and more the art of storytelling is making itself felt and is undergoing a revival in our day.

The National Association for the Preservation and Perpetuation of Storytelling in Jonesboro, Tennessee lists more than 170 professional storytellers in its directory. This does not include the countless part-time amateurs and the countless storytellers who are so by nature and nurture. Why this revival in the secular realm?

Some suggest that the revival is a reaction to television, which lacks any personal contact. Perhaps it is a reaction to the loneliness so many people feel in their lives. Perhaps it is linked to the renewal of interest in traditional values. Maybe, too, in a society where more and more words are "processed" by computer printouts, the story gains more popularity because it engages the mind and permits a savoring of words.

Whatever the reasons for story's revival in the secular world, there are many reasons for its revival in the religious world as we shall see. And fundamentally all of the reasons are going to boil down to William James' remark made almost a century ago, "I do believe that feeling is the deeper source of religion, and that philosophic and theological formulas are secondary products, like translations of a text into another tongue." Indeed, there is a distinct interest in story today; the phrase "theology of story" is becoming more common. And the interest is not just in so-called religious tales, but in tales of all sorts; not just in the normative stories enshrined in our scriptures and oral traditions, but also in folklore and fairy tale as well. There is a new awareness of what Rosemary Haughton wrote in *Tales From Eternity*:

> Fairy stories are never deliberately symbolic, yet they embody mankind's shrewdest and most realistic insights into human nature. We can use them to orientate ourselves in the present, and discover which way to go. They can help us to do this because they also link us to our Christian past, link the Christian past to its pagan prehistory, and link it also to its equally "pagan" subcultures. They throw a bridge from us to our contemporaries who are not Christians and to our successors in the faith and in the world. With the help of the typical figures which embody its perennial philosophy we may rediscover the gospel values which have become obscured and uncertain under the influence of recent cultural changes. We may set about developing a Christian life which, faced with unique challenges, is human, contemporary, uncompromising and hopeful. Fairy tales can open our minds to the human, and make us able to hear more sharply the demand for the transformation of the human into its own completeness in Christ.[1]

To "rediscover the gospel values" and to find our "completeness in Christ" in stories, sacred and profane, are what this book is all about. This is why I first entered *Nathan's Legacy* as the title because, in spite of all current evidence to the contrary, we stand in his tradition. Nathan is the Jewish prophet who told a secular story to catch the conscience of the King. "Then the Lord sent Nathan to David. He came to him and said to him, 'Once upon a time there were two men in a certain city, the one rich and the other poor'" (2 Samuel 12).

Nor is Nathan alone. He, the rest of the prophets, and in fact all the sacred writers, as we shall see, thought and wrote in terms of stories. Our heritage is one of story and our master, Jesus, was known for his stories. There is no doubt that through Jesus we are Nathan's people nor that the stories of our tradition are "Cezanne's apple" — the reference here being to Paul Tillich's famous statement that "An apple of Cezanne has more presence of ultimate reality than a picture of Jesus by Hoffman." True enough. It is story and all related art forms that touch us at our deepest levels and convince us of truth.

> How do we change the vision of people? It is love that art and religion have most in common. The artist convinces us of the truth by dealing with us holistically. Artists try to make us feel the truth. Good art gets the truth inside us on a level deeper than the surface of our minds. On this level, truth is most irresistible. The mind may not only resist the truth but may even accept it and keep it at a personal distance. Logical convictions are not necessarily existential imperatives. The artist makes us nostalgic for the beauty we have missed, the life we have forfeited, the meaning which somehow eluded our grasp. Art haunts us with the spectre of a lost humanity and bids us return to paradise.[2]

As we pursue these thoughts, however, there are two important points to make. The first is that in this book I shall be giving a great deal of emphasis to the imaginative and the story. This is deliberate. It is a counteraction to the undue emphasis placed for so long on the rational and the logical in religion. However, I have no desire to set up an opposition between reason and imagination. Both the intellectual and the intuitive must be affirmed. There is no intention of creating a disdain for the logical, the rational, and the analytical. I do not want to be caught in John Dewey's remark, "Only the psychology that has separated things which in reality belong together holds that scientists and philosophers think while poets and painters follow their feelings."

In churchy terminology the tension between thought and feeling is expressed as the tension between creed and story:

There is a tension between creed and story. The former is too precise for the latter. The latter is too variegated and too rich for the former. Both are inevitable in a religious heritage, though their different perspectives lead to the possibility of conflict — not merely conflict between different creeds based on different interpretations of the primary story, but also conflicts between creed believers and story believers. A belief system without creed may be too amorphous to survive in a propositional culture like our own. But a belief system without a story may lack human vitality. Both story and creed are simple. The former is a direct result of the experience. Story is nothing more than an attempt to resonate and represent that experience, while creed, far removed from experience, is a result of philosophical refinement and purification and distillation of the experience.[3]

The second point refers to a hidden premise. Even though it is not apparent nor the term ever mentioned, I am writing from the perspective of a parish priest. This is to say that beneath all the words and chapters in this book lies the conviction that the parish is the fundamental place of story for the average person. It is here that the Larger Story is proclaimed in the various liturgies and paraliturgies. It is here that our personal stories are counterpointed against this Larger Story, where we whisper them in the sacraments of reconcilation, birth them in baptism, affirm them in confirmation, celebrate them in the eucharist, and so on. The parish is the space and place in which storytelling and story healing take place for most people. This is the hidden agenda implicit in this book.

The book's outline is fairly direct. We shall start out by examining the whole shift from the doctrinal proposition we have known in our church in the past to what is called narrative theology. From this we proceed to examine the thirteen characteristics of story in general and its six paradoxes. Next we briefly trace our storytelling history in our Christian tradition, moving from there to see scripture itself primarily as a story, a whole anthology of them as a matter of fact. From here we look at the stories Jesus told with all of their impact, challenge, and invitation. Then there is our story counterpointed against the sacred story itself and, finally, there is a word on spirituality and story. Such is the general outline of this book.

There are a little under a hundred anecdotes, illustrations, poems, jokes, and stories in this book. Early on I made the decision, I hope agreeable to the reader, not to separate them from the rest of the book in indented or small type. For one thing, it would grate on the eye too much since there are so many of them. But, more importantly, I did not want the stories to be seen as illustrations of the text. The stories *are* the text. All the rest is commentary.

But what about the stories themselves? Here I had to choose those that were not only pertinent and illustrative but also reasonably brief. This means that I had to pass over many, many fine and more profound stories. So the choice is, within these limitations, strictly personal and idiosyncratic, especially in my tendency to turn to children's stories. Since this is a book intended for the general, popular audience, I wanted to be sure that we wouldn't all get a headache trying to figure out some marvelous but dense tale.

There are two final points to be made. One is that it will be evident that, although I borrow from other traditions, especially from the Jewish one, I am writing from a Catholic perspective. The second point is one of gratitude. There is a heavy indebtedness to Reverend John Shea whose pioneering work in *Stories of God* and *Stories of Faith*, plus his lectures at Boston College, have set us all to thinking about our story past. I am especially indebted to him for using some of his outline topics in Chapters 7, 8, and 10 and his guidance in thought development. There is also a debt owed to Methodist minister, Reverend Belden Lane. To him I am indebted for the outline topics in Chapter 4 and partly in Chapter 2. To both these men I wish to openly express my gratitude.

I must further express my gratitude to the people of St. Mary's, Colts Neck, N.J., who allowed me to practice on them with a course on the theology and spirituality of story, to Noreen Juliano who patiently typed the manuscript, and to all the world's storytellers and story listeners who remind us daily that we are indeed the inheritors of Nathan's legacy.

The Emergence
of Narrative
Theology

1

W hen the Israelites heard the first word of the Law in the Ten Commandments, so the old rabbinical story goes, they swooned. Their souls left them. So the word returned to God and cried out "O Soverign of the Universe, You live eternally and your Law lives eternally. But you have sent me to the dead. They are all dead!" Thereupon God had mercy and made his word more palatable.[1] This story has two points. First that the word of God is indeed powerful. It is his very self and "who can endure his presence"? Secondly, to make his word-presence more palatable, God hit upon a solution: he retold it in stories.

Why? Is there something in stories that of their very nature express the way and mind of God more than any other expression? Is it because story is an intractable "knowledge-energy" that links one person to another, one generation to another and ultimately all to God? Is story in fact — spoken, written, enacted, painted, sculpted, drawn, sung — an echo of our origin, a tradition-bond to our beginnings, a resonance of something pristine? Jewish tradition openly says yes.

☐When the great Rabbi Israel Shem Tov saw misfortune threatening the Jews, it was his custom to go into a certain part of the forest to meditate. There he would light a fire, say a special prayer, and the miracle would be accomplished and the misfortune averted. Later, when his disciple, the celebrated Magid of Mezritch, had occasion, for the same reason, to intercede with heaven, he would go to the same place in the forest and say: "Master of the Universe, listen! I do not know how to light the fire, but I am still able to say the prayer," and again the miracle would be accomplished. Still later, Rabbi Moshe-leib of Sasov, in order to save his people once more, would go into the forest and say, "I do not know how to light the fire. I do not know the prayer, but I know the place and this must be sufficient." It was sufficient and the miracle was accomplished. Then it fell to Rabbi Israel of Rizhyn to overcome misfortune. Sitting in his armchair, his head in his hands, he spoke to God: "I am unable to light the fire, and I do not know the prayer, and I cannot even find the place in the forest. All I can do is to tell the story, and this must be sufficient." And it was sufficient. God made man because he loves stories.[2]□

All this seems to say that God's story and our stories are somehow original experiences. Maybe that's where our "image and likeness" resides: we're paragraphs to the same story. In due time, however, something happened to our mutual stories. It was inevitable and indeed necessary. People, gifted with intelligence by that same story-God, began to reflect on our mutual stories. In due time they began to draw conclusions and finally (and rightly) they codified such conclusions into propositions, systems, and creeds. The result has been what we call systematic theology. Be it quickly noted, however, that such theology is not the raw experience of our stories itself. It is an intellectual sorting out of the experiences in order to talk about them philosophically. This is a good and needed thing and gives the professionals the necessary categories and vocabulary to talk to one another and to teach us. Nevertheless, there are two severe drawbacks to such a development, drawbacks that only recently we are trying to overcome. One is that any such systematizing must necessarily be done in current modes of thought and is based on the suppositions of past or current philosophies — and these are limited and conditioned. Codifed systematic theology is wedded to a specific system and this affects its conclusions and expressions. Secondly, all systematic theologies, to this extent, are closed off to others with different assumptions and groundings, and so are only a piece of the whole. So, for both these reasons the systematic theologies are limited, dated, partial.

Then, too, there is the growing dissatisfaction with any logical, philosophizing approach that leaves out a more holistic pattern of our story. Amos Wilder in his important book *Theopoetic: Theology and the Religious Imagination* tells us that it is rather at the level of the imagination that the issues of religion and world experiences must be handled. He challenges what he calls our "long addiction to the discursive, the rationalistic and the prosaic." He calls for a greater use of the imagination, for it is "a necessary component of all profound knowing and celebration . . . it is at the level of imagination that any full engagement with life takes place." He criticizes "the stultifying axiom that genuine truth or insight or wisdom must be limited to that which can be stated in discursive prose, in denotative language, stripped as far as possible of all connotative suggestion, in 'clear ideas,' in short, in statement or description of a scientific character."[3]

Thomas Driver says the same thing in *Patterns of Grace*:

A number of theologians recently have become interested in the importance of stories. They sense that all our logical, scientific, and theological discourse is secondary. I share this belief. I have long thought that theology is to religious narrative as literary criticism is to literature— commentary upon a more basic form of expression. . . . I am one of a number of theologians today who believes that theology has, in the course of time, removed itself too far from its roots in narrative. I find myself not only agreeing that theology originates in stories (and should itself tell more of them), but also thinking that all knowledge comes from a mode of understanding that is dramatic. Far from merely illustrating truths we already know some other way, the dramatic imagination is the means whereby we get started in any knowledge whatever.[4]

Sallie McFague adds her voice: "Where theology becomes overly abstract, conceptual and systematic, it separates thought and life, belief and practice, words and their embodiment, making it more difficult, if not impossible, for us to believe in our hearts what we confess with our lips."[5]

The result of all this is the tendency today to appreciate systematic theology, but to realize that it is only commentary on the original event ("secondary process thinking"). The tendency is to get closer to the way the raw event was first transmitted: by way of myth, metaphor, and story. This is because, sooner or later, if we work far enough behind the theology, we're going to get down to the story. "Well," we'll say, "what *originally* happened was that this man or woman had an experience in the desert . . . there was this vision, this voice. . . ." We're going to get into narrative language that will not only explain but compel and challenge as well. "In many and various ways God spoke of old to our fathers by the prophets; but in these last days he has spoken to us by a Son . . ." (Hebrews 1:1-2). And how did the Son speak to us? He told stories.

It should be further noted here that when Jesus did speak in stories he was not engaging in a unique method of teaching. He was in fact simply following the common practices of his culture, which was a story culture. As Scripture scholar Eugene LaVerdiere says:

> Notice how the Gospels are filled with stories and sayings. It's one thing to understand the context of the stories Jesus told. It's quite another to understand how stories functioned in ancient life.
>
> When we ask a question, we expect a direct answer. We don't expect to be told a story. . . . And yet, a story was an appropriate way of responding in Jesus' context. No one appears in the least puzzled. How can we appreciate this without a good grasp of a culture in which stories play an enormous role?[6]

Incidentally, not only are the theologians having second thoughts about the ability of systematic theology to tell the whole story of faith, but so are the liturgists. They are slowly moving away from what has been a too literal and too logical reform of text and rubric to a greater use of the metaphorical, the story, the imaginative. Liturgist Jake Empereur, for example, suggests that the liturgical experience ought to be displayed less in terms of levels of logic than in terms of levels of the imagination, following John Dominic Crossan's four stages of the magical, the literal, the metaphoric, and the paradoxical. He writes:

> The poetic aspect of the liturgy is now recognized as intrinsic and all pervasive in language, ritual and environment. It is not to be accepted as mere decoration. . . . Hopefully the age of reason in liturgy has passed. The purpose of storytelling as well as any other form of fantasy is to break the imperialism of the one-dimensional meaning in the liturgy.[7]

Theologian Ken Meltz reflects the same thought when he says, "Our liturgical renewal has not fully succeeded because it has lost sight of what could be called the 'affective' dimension of liturgy."

To the extent, then, that we go back to the "first" ways that God spoke through his prophets (in sign, symbol, metaphor, and anecdote) and by his Son (in parables), to that extent we are moving into what is called narrative theology or the theology of storytelling. It is going back to the original language to hear it, not as a text or as a science dissertation, but as poetry and story and all the other categories people use who strain to express the inexpressible. Or, to put it another way, narrative theology is a takeoff on John Robinson's remark that "the approach to truth for our generation starts from life rather than dogma." And life is made up of wild dreams, half-seen visions, impulses, and nameless shadows we relate in our stories. All theologies, therefore, must somehow tap into and reflect life and point to story, and all stories are ultimately theological.

> All stories are meant to be "theological." Humankind needs theological stories because human beings are fundamentally interpersonal and because, if the Christian God's promise is true, then humankind is fundamentally related to God as person. Since story is the only means by which the interpersonal reality of humankind can be expressed in its cognitive and affective fullness and since our relationship to God is fundamentally interpersonal, it follows that storytelling and story listening provide the most appropriate means of enabling us to live in this relationship.[8]

Nor must we suppose that it is just the certified "sacred" stories of a particular canon like the Bible that we must tap, although the biblical stories remain normative, but all human stories have meaning underneath the meaning (a good definition of myth) that evoke subtle or overt responses from us. Which is why today we read theology as literature and acknowledge that literature is a vehicle for theology.[9]

It is interesting to note, by the way, that the Jewish tradition tended to follow the course of storytelling rather than creed and doctrine. The Jewish rabbis were quite restrained in writing down any kind of finished, systematic theology. They refrained from hammering their insights and thoughts into creeds. They simply expounded on the great daily reality of God as they perceived him and they tended to speak of this immediacy rather than some future theological development. Therefore, they kept the homiletic and storytelling quality of expression about God and Israel's experience with him in everyday life. And they allowed the story to grow and to be retold a hundred different ways as people needed the story. To this extent Judaism largely comes down to us in sayings, sermons, and stories rather than in books of theology; and, as I said, in an ongoing re-formulation like a constant spring that feeds an ever-changing river. Thus:

☐A pagan once asked Rabbi Joshua ben Qarehah "Why, of all things, did God choose the humble thornbush as the place from which to speak with Moses?"

The rabbi replied: "If He had chosen a carob tree or a mulberry bush, you would have asked me the same question. Yet it is impossible to let you go away empty-handed. That is why I am telling you that God chose the humble thornbush—to teach you that there is no place on earth bereft of the Divine Presence, not even a thornbush."[10]☐

And this story finds its retelling in the story of Calvary. It prompts the remark that one of the essential meanings of that terrible and horrendous scene of a man hanging on a tree is that there is no place where the divine presence will not dwell. Calvary's tree is Moses' thornbush.

A spiritual and racial descendant of Rabbi Joshua ben Qarehah expresses the same reality in another retelling, the hanging of a young boy in a Nazi concentration camp on his tree:

☐The SS seemed more preoccupied, more disturbed than usual. To hang a young boy in front of thousands of spectators was no light matter. The head of the camp read the verdict. All eyes were on the child. He was lividly pale, almost calm, biting his lips. The gallows threw its shadow over him. . . . The three victims mounted together onto the chairs. The three necks were placed at the same moment within the nooses. "Long live liberty!" cried the two adults.

But the child was silent.

"Where is God? Where is He?" someone behind me asked. At a sign from the head of the camp, the three chairs tipped over. Total silence throughout the camp. On the horizon the sun was setting. "Bare your heads!" yelled the head of the camp. His voice was raucous. We were weeping.

"Cover your heads."

Then the march past began. The two adults were no longer alive. Their tongues hung swollen, blue-tinged. But the third rope was still moving; being so light, the child was still alive. . . .

For more than half an hour he stayed there, struggling between life and death, dying in slow agony under our eyes. And we had to look at him full in the face. He was still alive when I passed in front of him. His tongue was still red, his eyes not yet glazed. Behind me, I heard the same man asking: "Where is God now?" And I heard a voice within me answer him: "Where is He? Here He is—He is hanging here on this gallows. . ."[11] □

Three versions of the same story, and all far more powerful than any "bottom line" text or any creed. "He suffered under Pontius Pilate, died and was buried" is a good catechetical summary but no substitute for the original metaphors of darkening skies, falling rocks, ghostly appearances, and the primal scream of forsakenness. Systematic theology rightfully philosophizes on these ultimate mysteries and sheds light on them, but it is the story that carries power, that asks, "What do you think?" or better, "How does it move you? What truth did you encounter? Do you see hope in your own death here?"

There are other factors that have led us back to narrative theology. One is the shift to what is called "low" christology from "high" christology, which sees Jesus as very high up, God's only-begotten Son, the Second Person of the Blessed Trinity, the pre-existent One who dropped into this world like someone from another planet to bring to us certain revealed truths. This is the Jesus who walks on water, performs miracles, speaks long Johannine sentences. This is the imperial Pancrator. But if such high christology tends to stress Jesus' divinity, low christology stresses his humanity. Jesus is not the one who brings us an alien grace from heaven; rather, he is the one who unveils domestic grace on earth. He does not so much hand down foreign truths as he uncovers ordinary truths. He does not so much reveal mystery from above as unmask it below in everyday life. This is the Jesus who not only is transfigured on Mount Tabor and hears the heavenly voice, but the Jesus who hugs kids, cries over a friend's death, and tells homely stories from everyday Palestinian life—and all the while unveiling the effable mystery and love that permeate them all.

The high christology obviously tends very much toward propositions, formulas, and creeds, and it was this posture that dominated the first ecumenical councils of the church. But low christology just as obviously tends very much toward stories as the synoptic gospels reveal. For we must remember that the gospels are a response to a very bewildered first generation of Christians who were suddenly bereft of the presence of one who held them together, healed their rifts, and moved their spirits. They were desperate for comfort, for some kind of contact with Jesus. So they did what we would do—and do do at the death of a parent or friend: they sat around the table and asked the original witnesses to tell them once more the stories and deeds of Jesus. And in the telling, as in all good stories, they sensed his presence again. The spirit of Jesus was rekindled. And this wasn't hard to do for the witnesses. There was much to tell and Jesus was in fact a fascinating person. So the stories began—and so did the faith. That's how the faith got started: in storytelling. And that's what was recorded (though not everything as John reminds us) in the gospels: stories of and about Jesus and the impact he made on people. The controversies of later centuries over christology and the constant philosophizing and theologizing soon overshadowed the pristine story form, however, and left us with a firm legacy of an intellectual and creedal approach to faith. But now in our day, there is a need to get back to the original situation, a need once more to return to the Rabbi of Nazareth and his imaginative stories. Back to the source, as they say, a source filled with Magi and vineyards and embarrassed bridal parties and wicked servants and calculating masters and thick headed disciples, and a personality so compelling that only metaphor, poetry, and story could do it justice.

Another factor in the emergence of storytelling has been the impact of modern science. Research as well as common sense tell us that we are not all "head," that in spite of prejudice to the contrary, we have been and are influenced mightily by an active imaginative life. We move daily in a world of images, myths, symbols, and dreams. These, it is maintained, are as much (and more?) vehicles of truth about ourselves and our world as any flat-minded rationalism bequeathed to us by the seventeenth-century Enlightenment. As a matter of fact, science itself is beginning to concede this. "Research in neuropsychiatry and the physiology of the brain reveals an extraordinary range in the power of human knowing, especially with reference to intuitive, metaphysical, and symbolic knowledge."[12] Lewis Thomas, who wrote the engaging *The Medusa and the Snail*, brings a sense of poetry and imagination to the "hard" science of biology; and he is not an exception. He went to the zoo one day and saw a group of otters and beavers in action. He was swept away from his position as scientist and pulled into the mystery of what he saw before him.

> I was transfixed. As I now recall it, there was only one sensation in my head, pure elation mixed with amazement at such perfection. Swept off my feet, I floated from one side to the other, swiveling my brain, staring astounded at the beavers, then at the otters. . . . I wanted no part of the science of beavers and otters. . . . I wished for no news about the physiology of their breathing, the coordination of their muscles, their vision, their endocrine systems, their digestive tracts. . . . All I asked for was the full hairy complexity, then in front of my eyes, of whole, intact beavers and otters in motion. . . : I came away from the zoo with something, a piece of news about myself . . . the behavior released in us, by such confrontations, is, essentially, a surprised affection. It is compulsory behavior and we can avoid it only by straining with the full power of our conscious minds, making up conscious excuses all the way. Left to ourselves, mechanistic and autonomic, we hanker for friends.[13]

A subatomic physicist writes:

> Probing inside the atom, scientists . . . could no longer rely on logic and common sense. Atomic physics provided the scientists with the first glimpses of the essential nature of things. Like the mystics, physicists are now dealing with a nonsensory experience of reality and, like the mystics, they had to face the paradoxical aspects of this experience.[14]

Finally, Sallie McFague summarizes well how science is forced to turn to story, imagery, and metaphor to describe its work:

> When we turn to the sciences, whether mathematics or the natural or social sciences, we also find metaphor to be central. Perhaps it is most surprising to those who suppose that metaphor belongs only in the arts and religion to discover it at the most basic level in mathematics: the numerical analogue. Seeing the similar number among otherwise disparate entities is a metaphorical act, as in six apples, six moons, six ideas, six generous acts. In the social sciences the ubiquity of metaphor is obvious: the human being has been seen as a child of God, as half-angel and half-beast, as a machine; the state has been viewed as an organism and a mechanism; the brain has been understood through the metaphor of the computer and vica versa. When one turns to physics, the evidence for the importance of metaphor in the form of

models is extensive. . . . Jacob Bronowski speaks for many philosophers of science when he insists that ideas in science, as in any other field, are derived from images. . . .[15]

The point in all these quotations is to demonstrate that even in so-called "pure science" high imagery abounds and indeed is so necessary that conversation and dialogue are impossible without it. It is the increasing awareness of much of the "poetic" and metaphorical language of science that has sharpened our own awareness of the poetic and storytelling qualities inherent in religion.

Psychology also has added its insight. It has shown us that the dream side of us, the wild side, the shadow side carries truth. Or, to use a kind of catchall word we have already seen, imagination carries truth. In fact, the French philosopher Paul Ricoeur sees the imagination as the one genuine means by which often contradictory elements can be held in tension at many levels. He sees the imagination, along with speculative knowledge, as a genuine and essential ingredient in all acts of creative knowledge. J.R.R. Tolkien distinguishes between two worlds, the primary world of the universe created by God and the secondary world created by the imagination of human beings. And these, he says, are no less real. "What really happens is that the story-maker proves a successful 'sub-creator.' "

There are whole systems in the East that hold that dreams, for example, are the one clue to reality, that the whole of reality is not to be confined to our waking hours alone. Our waking state may be just one level of consciousness in a multi-leveled dream world. Dream is a path to a heightened consciousness and many modern psychoanalysts hold that dream is the royal road to the unconscious, a voice of inner truth. Ann Faraday comments:

> The psychologist, Carl Gustav Jung, who centered most of his work on dream, told of a conversation he had with a chief of the Pueblo Indians called Ochwiah Biano. Jung asked the chief's opinion of the white man and was told that it was not a very high one. White people, said Ochwiah Biano, seem always upset, always looking for something, with the result that their faces are covered with wrinkles. He added that white men must be crazy because they think with their heads, and it is well known that only crazy people do that. Jung asked in surprise how the Indian thought, to which Ochwiah Biano replied that naturally he thought with his heart.

In our culture we not only train our children to think with their heads but we actively discourage them from listening to their hearts, even though we pay lip service to the power of feelings in human life. . . .

It is precisely because dreams help us get ourselves together that I have called them "thoughts of the heart. . . ." I have in my casebook count-less examples of dreams revealing a split between head and heart. . . . In every case the thoughts of the heart are pressing for recognition, and if we ignore them, we shall try to solve our problems in useless and destructive ways.[16]

Jung indeed saw human beings as having a spiritual nature as well as a biological one (the only one Freud saw) and that dreams express our living reality and essence. Dreams carry truth and they make sense, not logical sense but mythological, story sense.

In psychoanalysis people tell their dreams to uncover hidden truth. They also tell their stories, for their stories, to the trained analyst, tell him or her where they are and what they are repressing. Story revisits an old situation in a new way. Story, as we shall see later, helps the person to go back, not to change an unchangeable situation, but to reinterpret it creatively. As depth psychologist James Hillman says,

The stories are means of finding oneself in events that might not other-wise make psychological sense at all. . . . My practice shows me rather that the more attuned and experienced is the imaginative side of per-sonality, the less threatening the irrational, the less necessity for repres-sion, and therefore, the less actual pathology acted out in literal, daily events. Story-awareness provides a better way than clinical-awareness for coming to terms with one's own case history.[17]

So dreams, myths, symbols, imagination—all are related and all find their best expression in art, especially in the art of storytelling. The artist and the storyteller, therefore, become our guides in the pursuit of truth as do the philosophers and the theologians. This truism is another reason why we are looking at a theology of story. As Flannery O'Connor says, "A higher paradox confounds emotion as well as reason and there are long periods in the lives of us and of the saints when the truth as revealed by faith is hideous, emotionally disturbing, downright repulsive."[18] And that "higher paradox" that confounds both emotion and reason is dealt with in the story. And it is dealt with most forcefully, not by the theologians, but by those authors who are masters of the human paradox itself. This is why the mythologist Joseph Campbell writes:

> Dante, Aquinas, Augustine . . . were not bad scientists making misstatements about the weather, or neurotics reading dreams into the stars, but masters of the human spirit teaching a wisdom of death and life. And the thesaurus of the myth-motifs was their vocabulary. They brooded on the state of man, and through their broodings came to Wisdom; . . . motifs of folk tale and myth are derived from the reservoirs of dream and vision. On the dream level such images represent the total state of the individual dreaming psyche. . . . But clarified of personal distortions and profounded—by poets, prophets, visionaries—they become symbolic of the spiritual norm for Man the Microcosm."[19]

A final factor in storytelling's emergence is the impact of feminism. Maria Harris reminds us that women's imagination is now being granted its proper place in the religious education field, so long dominated by the experience of men. Along with men, women are adding their own perspectives and giving a proper balance to many fields. It is their voice, their writings, and their approach to life that is having its impact on theology as well. They are increasingly contributors to narrative theology. It is also significant that many storytellers in fact *are* women. Stephen Simmer, who teaches at LeMoyne College in Syracuse, New York, comments that most of the original people in history who told stories were women and that "many stories can be interpreted as a search for the feminine values that are missing in a patriarchal society." In her book *Gift From the Sea*, Anne Morrow Lindbergh expresses the idea beautifully:

> Moon shell, who named you? Some intuitive woman I like to think. I shall give you another name—island shell. I cannot live forever on my island. But I can take you back to my desk in Connecticut. You will sit there and fasten your single eye upon me. You will make me think, with your smooth circles winding inward to the tiny core, of the island I lived on for a few weeks. You will say to me "solitude." You will remind me that I must try to be alone for part of each year, even a week or a few days; and for part of each day, even for an hour or a few minutes in order to keep my core, my center, my island quality. You will remind me that unless I keep the island quality intact somewhere within me, I will have little to give . . . to my friends or the world at

large. You will remind me that woman must be still, as the axis of a wheel, in the midst of her activities; that she must be the pioneer in achieving this stillness, not only for her own salvation, but for the salvation of family life, of society, perhaps even of our civilization.[20]

In this connection we might remember that in the *Odyssey* Odysseus many times received help and insights from women and it is no accident that his whole journey is toward his feminine counterpart, Penelope. In symbolic terms, he is coming home to his own feminine side. To this extent he becomes a symbol, in turn, of a movement in the church today, for many centuries a male preserve, toward the feminine. This is seen not only in the revival of narrative story but also in the revival of various charismatic expressions. Carl Jung could have been writing of the church when he said:

> We might compare masculinity and femininity . . . to a particular store of substances of which, in the first half of life, unequal use is made. A man consumes his large supply of masculine substance and has left over only the smaller amount of feminine substance which he must now put to use.[21]

The revival of storytelling may well be the novel use of the feminine side by a church which has, at this point in history, exhausted its masculine side.

So it comes to this. Systematic theology engages the intellect; storytelling engages the heart and indeed the whole person. Systematic theology is a later reflection on the Christ story; the story is the first expression of Christ. Logic is one avenue of truth, however limited. Imagination as myth and story is another avenue, but one that involves, disturbs and challenges us and as such is to be preferred. The Romantic poets, in many ways the forerunners of narrative theology, tell us this. Thus, for example, read William Wordsworth:

> The world is too much with us; late and soon,
> Getting and spending, we lay waste our powers:
> Little we see in Nature that is ours;
> We have given our hearts away, a sordid boon!
> The Sea that bares her bosom to the moon;
> The winds that will be howling at all hours,
> And are up-gathered now like sleeping flowers;
> For this, for everything, we are out of tune;
> It moves us not. Great God, I'd rather be

A Pagan sucked in a creed outworn;
So might I, standing on this pleasant lea,
Have glimpses that would make me less forlorn;
Have sight of Proteus rising from the sea;
Or hear old Triton blow his wreathed horn.

Propositions are statements on a page; stories are events in a life. Doctrine is the material of texts; story is the stuff of life. "He was rejected" is a clear and firm statement of fact and there it rests. "He came unto his own and his own received him not" is a bit more catchy and poetic. But "there was no room for them in the inn" with its contextual richness of a cave, angels, Magi, shepherds, and an exotic star, is story. It will not let us forget, as time has demonstrated, the person written about: his life, rejection, and death. Theology is a secondhand reflection of such an event; story is the unspeakable event's first voice.

2

Characteristics
of Story
(Part I)

A gentile once came to Rabbi Shammai and said, "Convert me to Judaism on condition that you can teach me the whole Torah while I am standing on one foot." With a rod in his hand Rabbi Shammai angrily threw him out. Then the man went to Rabbi Hillel and repeated his request. "Convert me to Judaism on condition that you can teach me the whole Torah while I am standing on one foot." Rabbi Hillel converted him and taught him as follows, "What is hateful to you, do not do to your neighbor. . . . This is the whole Torah. All the rest is commentary."[1]

The reason we read this story all the way through is because it is a story, and stories are innately compelling and as such they tend to repeat themselves. Which is why, in a similar scene, another rabbi answered the question pretty much the same way. When his questioner accepted his answer but insisted on a further elaboration, what did he get? A story, of course (Luke 10:25-37). And he was not only compelled by the genius of the story to hear it all, but was trapped into providing its conclusion (although the word "Samaritan" stuck in his throat and he used a circumlocution when asked who was the neighbor in this case and he answered the one, I guess, who showed mercy).

Anyway, the story of the Good Samaritan contains all of the characteristics of a good story. In fact, we can discover thirteen characteristics of any good story. We will list them and, since this is a practical book, we will use many examples to illustrate them, as we will do throughout this book. These examples are not an "extra" to dress up the book but its essential content. So let us begin.

First Characteristic of Story: Stories provoke curiosity and compel repetition.

☐Writing on the power of the fable, Aesop tells this one: Demades, a famous Greek orator, was once addressing an assembly at Athens on a subject of great importance. However, it was in vain that he tried to catch the attention of his audience. They laughed among themselves, watched the nearby play of the children and in a hundred other ways showed their disinterest in the subject of the discourse. So Demades, after a short pause, spoke as follows: "Ceres one day journeyed in company with a swallow and an eel." At this there was a sudden attention and every ear strained to catch the words of the orator.☐

Such curiosity that stories provoke is not an idle one; it is compelling. We really want to know what it's about and how it will end. We will wade through a lot of dull pages and endure a lot of inane commercials to find out what happened. We'll sit on the edge of our seats to learn the ending—or to deliciously anticipate the ending—of a familiar and beloved tale. Stories are like that.

☐King Clorain was betrayed by an unfaithful wife. As a result, so distracted, hurt, and upset is he that he becomes harshly distrustful of all women. So he decides, being king, that every day he will marry a wife, but in the morning he will have her killed. And this he does. Finally, he marries a clever woman named Scheherazade. She is quite determined to keep her head on and that the cycle of death should be broken. So each evening as they retire she tells the king a fascinating story. But toward the end she grows so tired that she just can't finish the story and she falls asleep, leaving the king in high anxiety and quite beside himself until he can hear the rest of the story the next day. So, of course he puts off her death. But each evening she starts another fascinating story. And so it goes for 1001 nights. In this long process, be it noted, Scheherazade changes and so does the king. He works through his disgust with life and his hatred for women. And she? She falls in love with him. □

Good stories provoke curiosity—and other stories. That they compel repetition is proven by the venerable long history of the Arabian Nights tales. (We might note in passing here what we will discuss later: good stories bring healing, as this one did to the king.) A good story is like a secret: too good to be kept. For better or for worse, story must out. And should books be lacking, stories will still burst out and human beings, the "creatures who think in stories," will find a way to tell them. In Ray Bradbury's *Fahrenheit 451* (the degree of paper combustion) all libraries and books have been destroyed by the government so that it can more easily control the people. (Evil governments always know the power of story, which is why they suppress or promote them.) One night a friend reveals a secret to a man called Montag. The conversation goes like this:

□"Would you like, some day, Montag, to read Plato's *Republic*?"

"Of course!"

"I am Plato's *Republic*. Like to read *Marcus Aurelius*? Mr. Simmons is Marcus. . . . And this other fellow is Charles Darwin, and this one is Schopenhauer, and this one here at my elbow is Albert Schweitzer. . . .

Everyone laughed quietly. . . .

"It can't be," said Montag.

"It is," replied Granger, smiling. . . . "It wasn't planned, at first. Each man had a book he wanted to remember, and did. Then, over a period of twenty years or so, we met each other, travelling, and got the loose network together and set out a plan. . . . And when the war's over some day, some year, the people will be called in one by one, to recite what they know and we'll set it up in type."[2]□

To learn, recite, know, and share the story; that's its nature. Stories are sought, bought, caught, and taught, and that's their nature too.

We've all caught a story at one time or another. And we've been caught by them. That's the way they are.

Second Characteristic of Story: Stories unite us in a holistic way to nature, our common stuff of existence.

In American Indian lore the division between people and things is far less absolute than for us. In their myths all of reality springs from one source. All—men, beasts, or stars—figure as actors in a single ceremony. Their stories tell of a mythical age when there were only "people," some of whom were changed into "things" but, under special circumstances, they could at times revert to their people nature. But the pristine unity and connection remained.

☐Sr. Maria Jose Hobday, a Franciscan nun of Seneca Iroquois heritage, remembers her mother telling her as a little girl to "feel the earth. Your feet are trying to teach you about the land. Some day your toes will not be walking in this warm dirt, but your feet will remember the road, and this will make you happy."

Which one of us with our modern, sophisticated mentalities would tell this story? "My nephew was so angry! So mad at the world. I told him: 'Do like they used to do in the old days. You're mad, you think you're pretty tough? Well, go down to the beach in the high surf, you'll find out. You go fight the waves for a while, kick them and beat them and try to knock them down. Your Father, the ocean, will show you something. Now, when you've had enough, when you can't stand up any more, go lie on the beach, that's your Mother. Kick her and pound her and yell at her too. She'll forgive you. When you're done in just lie still and cry. She'll tell you something you need to know.'"[3]☐

The same author also quotes this one:

☐I was sitting with another older man by our fire. When we'd eaten, he held up a piece of wood that we'd gathered. "What's this?" he asked. "Piece of firewood," I answered. He looked sad, disgusted; he put down the stick, silent. I thought more, "It's wood, a piece of a tree." He brightened a shade, "That's a little better. What's a tree?"

Later that evening, turning in, he offered a rare piece of direct teaching: "When you can see each leaf as a separate thing, you can see the tree; when you can see the tree, you can see the spirit of the tree; when you can see the spirit of the tree, you can talk to it and maybe begin to learn something. Good night."[4]☐

As we have lost our stories, can it be that we have lost our relationship to nature? "Everywhere the White man has touched the earth, it is sore," said one Indian. Is there a connection between our story amnesia and our abuse of the environment? If there is, then story's power reunites us more holistically to nature.

Third Characteristic of Story: Stories are a bridge to one's culture, one's roots.

Every people, nation, and community have stories and myths that preserve and prolong the traditions that give them their identity. When a nation is in trouble, it often returns to its traditional stories to look for direction and healing, to regain a sense of what made it great in the past and what will nurture it into the future. So, for example, the English have their stories of King Arthur and of Alfred and Canute who held back the waves. They have their symbol, the determined bulldog, which reminds them of how they withstood evil predators from Napoleon to Hitler. We Americans have our Declaration of Independence, the Constitution, the Boston Tea Party, How the West Was Won, Paul Bunyon, and Johnny Appleseed, and all the rest who make up our national mythology.

Individuals, families, and communities also have their identifying stories that link them to who they are, to their culture. They tell the story over and over again of their spouse's death, what happened in our town twenty or thirty years ago that people will never forget. A region or a nation has its story concretized in shrine, statue, museum. A person without a story is a person with amnesia. A country without its story has ceased to exist. A humanity without its story has lost its soul. The motivation that led Italo Calvino to compile his marvelous *Italian Folk Tales* was this:

> For me, as I knew too well, it was a leap in the dark, a plunge into an unknown sea into which others before me, over the course of 150 years, had flung themselves, not out of any desire for the unusual, but because of a deep-rooted conviction that some essential, mysterious element, lying in the ocean depth, must be salvaged to ensure the survival of the race. . . .[5]

Alex Haley found his roots in those stories that formed a bridge to his culture in Africa. As a boy, he used to sit on the front porch of his grandmother's house in Tennessee and listen to her tell stories about his ancestors. These stories went all the way back to a certain Kin-tay who had been kidnapped and sold into slavery while he was chopping wood near Kambay Bolongo. Fifty years after he heard such stories, Haley went to Africa to try to learn something of his roots and of his ancestry. He talked with many of the villagers in the backcountry.

They told him of very old men called "griots" who were like gurus who on special occasions told the centuries-old histories of clans and families. In fact, there were certain lengendary griots who were known to narrate the facts of African history literally for as long as three days without ever repeating themselves. With this knowledge, Haley eventually found his own ancestral village. There he consulted the village griot who began the recitation of his village's story. When the griot came to the 1700s Haley was startled to hear him say that "Omorro Kinte begot Kunta. . . . Kunta went away from his village to chop wood . . . and he was never seen again." Haley couldn't believe his ears. Here in this backwoods African village a man who had lived all his life there was telling him the same story he had heard on his grandmother's porch in Tennessee! Stories had forged the bridge to his culture from continent to continent. Through a story were linked life, culture, and continuity. Truly it is a bridge to one's culture, one's roots.

Fourth Characteristic of Story: Stories bind us to all of humankind, to the universal, human family.

One of the saddest stories ever written, and the only one remembered or in print from many of his writings, is Edward Everett Hale's *The Man Without a Country*. Hale, grandnephew of Nathan Hale and nephew of Edward Everett, who delivered the main address at Gettysburg (the same day as Lincoln spoke there), told the story of a man who was banished from his country for treason, sentenced to spend the rest of his life upon ships at sea, never seeing the United States again, and never hearing its name spoken, never receiving a communication, and having all papers with any reference to or pictures of the country or its flag deleted. Although Hale meant the story as a patriotic theme for a country then very much divided (1863), we can take it as a paradigm of what it must mean to be cut off from all of humanity, sailing an empty ship alone on the planet.

And if there were other people out there, no story to forge a link with them, no common bond. But, if on the other hand, there were people out there and they met, the first thing they would do would be to tell their stories. Chances are that in the process they will discover how similar they are.

This similarity has long been a puzzlement to scholars, that is, why stories in extremely diverse times and places on the planet earth are so alike. The themes are the same and often the very same wording and phrasing are used. Separate and far-flung cultures come up with the same fundamental motifs and patterns. The prevailing theory to explain this phenomenon is given by Joseph Campbell: "By and large, it is now fairly agreed that the general continuity, and an occasional correspondence to the detail, can be referred to the psychological unity of the human species."[6]

There is a little book by Theodore Gastner, *The Oldest Stories in the World*, and they are literally that. They are possibly four thousand years old from peoples of the Near East and they carry familiar and perennial storylines of greed, trickery, foolishness, nobility, journey, conflict; all portray the human condition in all times and places. Which may prove the truth of Willa Cather's remark that there are really only two or three human stories that are told over and over again.

Even in our modern sophisticated times, stories that pretend to move beyond our planet still tap the perennial universal themes. One of the most popular movies of the early 80s was *E.T., the Extra Terrestrial*. It was enormously popular, the movie industry's largest money maker in history up to that point. The movie deals with a ten-year-old boy who finds an ugly, dwarfish outer-space child left behind by its parents. The psychologists point out that like all fairy tales the movie contains powerful myths. In story form it says that we need not be afraid of extraterrestrial beings who, after all, may be benign and even charming. Which means that the child can trust again. The movie also helps children to come to their moment of decision to let go of secure and comforting childhood for an adult life. After all, Elliot, the boy in the film who found the Extra Terrestrial, decides not to go aboard the spacecraft when it comes for it, where he could continue living his fantasy. He chooses instead to stay on earth and grow to adulthood. The movie also hits the old motif of the weaker (child) outwitting the stronger (adults) much like

Jack the Giantkiller or Dorothy and the wicked witch of Oz. The Extra Terrestrial is ugly like the Beast but with Beauty inside, just like the fairy tale. And clearly, in the movie love makes all things new again when Elliot's tears and love revive the dead E.T., just as the kiss of the princess releases the prince inside the frog.

It should not pass our notice that such universal human themes find their echo in the gospels where, for example, short tax gatherers and wanton women (Luke 19:1-10 and 7:37-30) discover rebirth and spiritual renewal in the love offered by Jesus. Stories indeed reflect our common humanity and bind us to one another in a common destiny, apparently even beyond time and space. And to this extent Harold Goddard's comment in his book *The Meaning of Shakespeare* is quite on the mark: "The destiny of the world is determined less by the battles that are lost and won than by the stories it loves and believes in."[7]

Fifth Characteristic of Story: Stories help us to remember.

Stories not only bridge us to our roots and our common humanity but they help us to remember. Remember what? Our past, our history, our glories, and our shame. People today still tell stories of the Jewish holocaust, of Vietnam, of Nagasaki, precisely so that we don't forget what we have done, can do, to each other. Israel's stories often told of infidelity. Alex Haley's stories remind us of the blot of slavery. Gandhi's story recalls the evils of racism and discrimination. Dee Brown and others recount our shameful treatment of the native Indians. As Henri Nouwen reminds us, these storytellers are out, not to plague our memories, but to help us remember, and in remembering to confess and in confessing to be made whole. As William R. White says:

> We are a forgetful people. We need storytellers. We need someone to lay the drama of God's love before us. We need to be reminded of the uncommon grace of God. We need to hear the stories of the almost-too-good-to-be-true promises of God, the story of good news in the midst of the world's bad news.[8]

☐An old pastor visiting a country jail came upon a despondent young man. "Leave me alone, pastor. I'm no good," the young man moaned. "Everything I have touched has been bruised. I have influenced others to turn to a life of crime. I have deeply wounded the only ones who care for me—my mother, my wife, and our young daughter. There is no hope for me."

The old man was silent for a moment before he spoke. "The hurt that you have inflicted on others may never be healed. What you have done is most serious. What you need now is to find a new compass, a new way to walk." He paused before he continued. "We must begin by teaching you some new stories."

"Stories!" the young man thundered. "I speak to you out of despair and you talk to me of idle tales? I live without hope and you speak to me of happy endings? If my life is to be spent behind bars, I may need new facts, but I certainly do not need fiction."

When the outburst had subsided, the pastor placed a caring hand on the young man's arm. "Humor an old man. Listen to one tale."

Once a very bad man died and went before the judgment throne. Before him stood Abraham, David, Peter, and Luke. A chilly silence hung heavy in the room as an unseen voice began to read the details of the man's life. There was nothing good that was recorded. When the voice concluded, Abraham spoke: "Men like you cannot enter the heavenly kingdom. You must leave."

"Father Abraham," the man cried, "I do not defend myself. I have no choice but to ask for mercy. Certainly you understand. Though you lied to save your own life, saying your wife was your sister, by the grace and mercy of God you became a blessing to all nations."

David interrupted, "Abraham has spoken correctly. You have committed evil and heinous crimes. You do not belong in the kingdom of light." The man faced the great king and cried, "Son of Jesse, it is true. I am a wicked man. Yet I dare ask you for forgiveness. You slept with Uriah's wife and later, to cover your sin, arranged his death. I ask only forgiveness as you have known it."

Peter was next to speak. "Unlike David, you have shown no love to God. By your acid tongue and your vile temper you have wounded the Son of God." "I should be silent," the man muttered. "The only way I have used the blessed name of Jesus is in anger. Still, Simon, son of John, I plead for grace. Though you walked by his side and listened to words from his own lips, you slept when he needed you in the garden, and you denied him three times in his night of greatest need."

Then Luke the evangelist spoke, "You must leave. You have not been found worthy of the kingdom of God."

The man's head bowed sadly for a moment before a spark lit in his face. "My life has been recorded correctly," the man began slowly. "I am guilty as charged. Yet I know there is a place for me in this blessed kingdom. Abraham, David, and Peter will plead my cause because they know of the weakness of man and the mercy of God. You, blessed physician, will open the gates to me because you have written of God's great love for the likes of me. Don't you recognize me? I am the lost sheep that the Good Shepherd carried home. I am your younger, prodigal brother."

And the gates opened and Luke embraced the sinner.

"You see," the old pastor concluded, "I want you to learn stories, not as an exercise in fiction, but in order to walk in mercy. Stories will help you find your way."[9]□

Sixth Characteristic of Story: Stories use a special language.

Storyteller Robert Bela Wilhelm points out that there are three kinds of language we use. One is our daily talk of declarative sentences and explanation. This is our daytime talk. But, then, there is the other side. There is our nighttime talk. This is our dreams we have alluded to already and will see more of later. This nighttime talk of our dreams is the language of the subconscious with its marvelous images and fantasies. These images express our deepest selves and, as some would say, the experience of the sacred that is embedded in that "psychological unity" that Joseph Campbell mentions.

Then there is storytelling. This language is a combination of the daytime and nighttime talk; it bridges and unites both. Storytelling is daytime talk because it makes sense. It is nighttime talk because it is rich in images that, like a dream, can happen in a story but not in everyday life. So the story combines the two, giving us a more holistic version of reality. Consequently, stories lead us more deeply into ourselves. They become ways by which we indirectly face what we might not face head on. Story then becomes more than an entertainment or a teaching device or even an art form, though it is all of these things. It is also a thread that binds our conscious and unconscious lives together and, in the richness that results, intimates the presence of mystery.

You can sense what I'm saying if you can recall a story or a movie that affected you very much. Here the story has gotten "inside of you"; it has a life of its own (even when you're done with it, it is not done with you) and it kind of rinses through you. You can't quite put into words what the effect is, but there is a resonance, perhaps even a free-floating disturbance. Coming out of the theater, let's say, you find it hard to discuss the picture with your best friend beyond some generalizations because you're both still caught up in the story's "aftertaste." Something in your unconscious has been tapped. You're in-between daytime and nighttime talk; you're in story time.

Take this excerpt from Willa Cather's book *Obscure Destinies*:

☐Sometimes in the morning, if her feet ached more than usual, Mrs. Harris felt a little low. (Nobody did anything about broken arches in those days, and the common endurance test of old age was to keep going after every step cost something.) She would hang up her towel with a sigh and go into the kitchen, feeling that it was hard to make a start. But the moment she heard the children running down the uncarpeted back stairs, she forgot to be low. Indeed, she ceased to be an individual, an old woman with aching feet; she became part of a group, became a relationship. She was drunk up into their freshness when they burst in upon her, telling her about their dreams, explaining their troubles with buttons and shoelaces and underwear shrunk too small. The tired, solitary old woman Grandmother had been at daybreak vanished. Suddenly the morning seemed as important to her as it did to the children, and the mornings ahead stretched out sunshiny, important.[10]☐

It is easy to appreciate, even in this excerpt, the symbols that resonate with us, especially in our society where there are so many lonely grandparents (and grandchildren); or even those who go to court to force a visit with grandchildren now the "property" of another marriage. It is easy to feel deeply her age and at the same time her rejuvenation, to catch the recurrent symbols of life, death, and rebirth in her grandchildren. We are pulled into her movements from darkness (her aching feet) to light (the grandchildren), her mood change in the face of loved ones, her loneliness dissolving into community, her self pulled lovingly into relationship. Even so small a passage has a "taste" to it, a special language that smoothly binds our conscious and unconscious and moves us easily into daytime-nighttime dialogue.

Seventh Characteristic of Story: Stories restore the original power of the word.

Well, at least partially, for I am not sure if that is possible anymore. Words have been devalued extensively. When spoken they are often used to deceive or solicit, as in commercials. When written, they tend to come out like computer printouts. Still, in spite of such persistent denaturing, words do have power, especially the spoken word. The ancients knew this. To know something's name was to have power over it. Which is why Adam could name the animals but Jacob could not name the angel who wrestled with him. In the Old Testament, the word was called *dabar*, meaning something of great power and potency. The word was not merely an uttered syllable but something of force and thrust and compulsion. Indeed, as Isaiah said, "The word of God goes forth and will not return until it accomplishes its end."

We can capture something of the power of words if we have ever heard a truly great actor or actress. Then words, as Leo Rosten says in *The Power of Words*, "sing. They hurt. They teach. They sanctify. They were man's first immeasurable feat of magic. . . ."

> Now think of words. Take *sky*
> And ask yourself just why —
> Like sun, moon, star, and cloud —
> It sounds so well out loud,
> And pleases so the sight
> When printed black on white.
> Take syllable and thimble:
> The sound of *them* is nimble.
> Take bucket, spring and dip
> Cold water to your lip.
> Take balsam, fir, and pine:
> Your woodland smell and mine.
> Take kindle, blaze, and flicker —
> What lights the hearth fire quicker?
> Three words we fear but form:
> Gale, twister, thunderstorm;
> Others that simply shake
> Are tremble, temblor, quake.
> But granite, stone, and rock:
> Too solid, they, to shock.

Put honey, bee and flower
With sunny, shade, and shower;
Put *wild* with bird and wing,
Put *bird* with song and sing.
Aren't paddle, trail, and camp
The cabin and the lamp?
Now look at words of rest —
Sleep, quiet, calm, and blest.

At words we learn in youth —
Grace, skill, ambition, truth;
At words of lifelong need —
Grit, courage, strength, and deed;
Deep-rooted words that say
Love, hope, dream, yearn, and pray;
Light-hearted words — girl, boy,
Live, laugh, play, share, enjoy.
October, April, June —
Come late and gone too soon.
Remember words are life:
Child, husband, mother, wife;
Remember, and I'm done:
Words taken one by one
Are poems as they stand —
Shore, beacon, harbor, land,
Brook, river, mountain, vale,
Crow, rabbit, otter, quail;
Faith, freedom, water, snow,
Wind, weather, floor, and floe.
Like light across the lawn
Are morning, seas, and dawn;
Words of the green earth growing —
Seed, soil, and farmer sowing.
Like wind upon the mouth
Sad, summer, rain, and south.
Amen. Put not asunder
Man's *first* word: wonder . . . wonder. . . .[11]

In William Luce's play about the life of Emily Dickinson, *The Belle of Amherst*, the poet is presented as one who really loves and reverences words. When, for example, she hears such words as "circumference" or "Massachusetts" or "gingerbread," she cries, "Now there's a word to lift your hat to!" Lifting one's hat in those days was a gesture of respect. Reverencing words lead the poet to write:

> A Word is dead
> When it is said,
> Some say.
> I say it just
> Begins to live
> That day.

In his autobiography, novelist Frederick Buechner tells of his early experiences with the power of words as he learned them from his old English teacher, a Mr. Martin, an Irishman with great zest for "the blarney and wizardry of words."

> I had always been a reader and lover of words for the tales they can tell and the knowledge they can impart and the worlds they can conjure up like the Scarecrow's Oz and Claudius' Rome; but this teacher, Mr. Martin, was the first to give me a feeling for what words are, and can do, in themselves. Through him I started to sense that words not only convey something, but *are* something; that words have color, depth, texture of their own, and the power to evoke vastly more than they mean; that words can be used not merely to make things clear, make things vivid, make things interesting and whatever else, but to make things happen inside the one who reads them or hears them. . . . it was a course less in literature than in language and the great power that language has to move and in some measure to transform the human heart.[12]

It is difficult for us to remember, I suppose, that the word was long spoken before it was written, long read aloud within community before it became a solitary pastime, long a source of nourishment and centering for a people before it became dissipated on the winds of babble. And perhaps it is even more difficult for us to remember that fundamentally most biblical stories have been lifted from the mouths of the ancient storytellers and put down on paper. In other words, this means that the biblical stories were not meant to be privately read but to be publicly told and publicly heard. The Bible is a written oral voice and when orally proclaimed easily regains something of its story power. For example, Protestant pastor William R. White gave testimony to the power of the oral word when he participated in a Mass celebrated by Catholic Bishop Kenneth Untener of

Saginaw, Michigan. He says that the bishop had memorized the gospel and so he told it rather than read it. The result was remarkable. A friend of his remarked that it was as if he heard the passage for the very first time. Another commented that he never realized how powerful the bare words of scripture were. This is not an odd or isolated experience. A few years ago the British actor Alec McGowan made a tour of England and America. He toured to critical acclaim. What did he do for his one-man show? He sat or stood center stage and recited the Gospel of St. Mark! Once more this gives powerful emphasis to the truism that the Bible is basically a proclaimed and spoken word, a book of told stories.

And the stories were nourishing. In the Middle Ages most of the monks, like the general population, could not read. Every morning, however, they would meet in chapel in front of a large Bible. In silence they would listen while a literate monk read a single passage out loud. He would step back after this short reading, bow, and retire in silence. He would get up and read again—the same passage. And this he did over and over again until the chapel was empty. The idea was that as each monk got something out of the reading to take with him during the day, he would leave. As the word invaded his life, he was ready for life. The word had power. Of course, even then, words

are only hints and guesses.
Hints followed by guesses; and the rest
Is prayer, observance, discipline, thought and action.
The hint half-guessed, the gift half-understood, is Incarnation. [13]

Still, good stories restore some of that power.

Eighth Characteristic of Story: Stories provide escape.

We must forget for the moment negative associations with the word "escape," such as picturing the TV addict who forever lives his or her life vicariously instead of authentically. Escapism is a good thing at times. It takes us from our immediacy and gives us a chance to regroup, reform, and reenter life. Every parent knows the calming power of a story to a tearful child, who, by story's end, has forgotten his hurt.

☐ It's like the incident of the little boy who ran into the house in near hysteria announcing that his pet turtle had rolled over and died.

He was inconsolable. His mother called her husband and when daddy came home, he gathered up the tearful boy in his arms as he sat in front of the dead turtle and told him that maybe they could have a funeral for the turtle. Yes, and not only that, but daddy would bury him in the little tin box they kept the candy in. By this time the boy had stopped crying and was listening intently. "Then," chimed in the mother, "we can have a party afterwards. Wouldn't that be nice?" By this time the boy was smiling. Encouraged, the father went on, "Yes, and we'll have balloons and some of your friends over, and everything." The boy was grinning from ear to ear. But then, suddenly, to the surprise of them all, the turtle rolled back on his legs and began slowly moving away. The boy looked startled and then exclaimed, "Oh, daddy—let's kill it!" □

What in general would we be escaping from? From loneliness for one thing, even though surrounded by loved ones who always have to some degree a love-hate relationship with us. Again Frederick Buechner relates in his autobiography an incident when he was six years old awaiting his favorite grandmother's visit. He decided to surprise her with a feast of cold string beans, causing the grandmother to make a caustic remark the boy overheard:

I do not remember what she said then exactly, but it was an aside spoken to my parents or whatever grownups happened to be around to the effect that she did not usually eat much at three o'clock in the afternoon or whatever it was, let alone cold string beans of another age, but that she would see what she could do for propriety's sake. Whatever it was, she said it dryly, wittily, the way she said everything, never dreaming for a moment that I would either hear or understand, but I did hear, and what I came to understand for the first time in my life, I suspect—why else should I remember it?—was that the people you love have two sides to them. One is the side they love you back with, and the other is the side that, even when they do not mean to, they can sting you like a wasp, the first telltale crack in the foundation of the one home which perhaps any child has when you come right down to it, and that is the people he loves.[14]

A story would help him escape from that common experience until he could reassess it. By identifying with people in his story and we in ours, we both can forge another bond for the time being, a new communion with a hero or heroine who will never deceive us and will never leave us.

Secondly, through story we escape from boredom and we escape from reality when "the world is too much with us." A good story can give us a break as well as pull us back to reality, renewed and determined. A "bad" story does not bring us back but leaves us there. It caters to that euphoria which, like a diver's, will do us in and give us emotional bends. A good story always energizes us back to the fullness of reality. Which is why our most popular and seductive story in the church, the Christmas story, is framed in red. Each day after Christmas we are hit with Stephen's prototype blood, the boiling of John, the screams of the Holy Innocents and the murderous fall of an archbishop in his cathedral. And I think the church does this because it instinctively knows that the Christmas story alone is euphoric and lulling, and might make us forget that the crib's wood and the cross's wood are conjoined. It's only through both that the "happy ever after" victory of Easter is possible.

Finally, we all need to escape from hurts of some kind. We need the subliminal affirmations of a story to help us. We need to know that we, like rejected Cinderella, will one day shine like a princess, that we are the apple of the prince's eye (and the Prince's eye as well); that we, physical or moral ugly ducklings, can become beauties; that we, certified betrayers ("I know not the man!"), can weep bitter tears of repentance and discover forgiveness; that a child can lead us:

> My little son, who look'd from thoughtful eyes
> And moved and spoke in quiet grown-up wise,
> Having my law the seventh time disobey'd,
> I struck him, and dismiss'd
> With hard words and unkiss'd,
> His mother, who was patient, being dead.
> Then, fearing lest his grief should hinder sleep,
> I visited his bed,
> But found him slumbering deep,
> With darken'd eyelids, and his lashes yet
> From his late sobbing wet.
> And I, with moan,
> Kissing away his tears, left others of my own;
> For on a table drawn beside his head
> He had put, within his reach,
> A box of counters and a red-veined stone,
> A piece of glass abraided from the beach

And six or seven shells
A bottle with bluebells
And two French copper coins, ranged there with careful art,
To comfort his sad heart.
So when that night I pray'd
To God, I wept, and said:
Ah, when we lie at last with tranced breath,
Not vexing Thee in death,
And Thou rememberest of what toys
We made our joys,
How weakly understood
Thy great commanded good,
Then, fatherly not less
Than I whom Thou has moulded from the clay,
Thou'lt leave Thy wrath, and say,
"I will be sorry for their childishness."[15]

Through stories we can be validated as persons.

Thus, our so-called escapism is in reality a temporary detour and we return refreshed, for most stories (at least children's stories) have happy endings—and that points to a redeemed world. This is, as J.R.R. Tolkien has written, because the story, and particularly the fairy story, denies universal defeat and so gives us a glimpse of ultimate joy. There is always a strange and wonderful grace at work in a story, and an "escape" to this retrieves the possibility of such grace for our own life's story. Which is to say that we come back from the story filled with the Good News. And to this extent every story is religious.

3

Characteristics of Story (Part II)

*I*n the first chapter we mentioned the power of imagination to proclaim truth and that this is being rediscovered today. In this regard, psychologists like Robert Ornstein (*The Psychology of Consciousness*) and Julian Jaynes (*The Origin of Consciousness and the Breakdown of the Bicameral Mind*) and doctors like David Galin have emphasized that not only is our brain divided into two sides, but that the right and left sides function differently. The left side of the brain, which controls the right side of the body, is the side of analysis and logic. The right side of the brain, which controls the left side of the body, is the side of imagination and feeling ("primary process thinking"). Galin points this out to remind us that in our society we are heavily pressured into left-brain living, to the great harm of our wholeness and well-being.

Ninth Characteristic of Story: Stories evoke in us right-brain imagination, tenderness, and therefore wholeness.

We are told that we must be "cool," reasonable, unemotional, in control, shrewd, analytical—qualities much prized, and increasingly so, in a computer society. We are already living in a consumer and industrial society that has little room for poetry and feeling, and so the harm from the loss of right-brain imagination is compounded. Einstein was right when he remarked that we are intellectual giants but moral pigmies. The result of this type of left-brain dominance is summed up (perhaps a little heavy-handedly) by Antoine De Saint-Exupéry in *The Little Prince*:

> "Grown-ups love figures," remarked the Little Prince. "When you tell them that you have made a new friend, they never ask you questions about essential matters. They never say to you, 'What does his voice sound like? What games does he love best? Does he collect butterflies?' Instead, they demand: 'How old is he? How many brothers has he? How much does he weigh? How much money does his father make?'
>
> "If you say to grown-ups, 'I saw a beautiful house made of rosy brick with geraniums in the window and doves on the roof,' they would not be able to get any idea of that house at all. You would have to tell them, 'I saw a house that cost $20,000;' then they would exclaim, 'Oh, what a pretty house that is!'"[1]

Even smiling at the 1943 figure of $20,000 for a house, we know the author's point. By the time we grow up we have been educated and programmed out of our imaginative lives. We learn to live only with our heads and not with our hearts as well, and so we have lost a profound source of truth about ourselves and our world. And we pass this prejudice on to our children, and the prejudice seeps into the fabric of our society even more deeply.

Notice, for example, our language. Someone who is right-brain—left-body controlled is highly suspect. Such people spawn a vocabulary of "sinister," which is the Latin word for "left." Our slang of poking fun is to say that someone has "two left feet" or is "way out in left field." Grudgingly we give people a "left-handed" compliment. We tell people at our dinner parties not to be "gauche," which is French for "left." For "don't lie!" we have an equivalent: "Don't be a storyteller!" And to those who are left-brain—right-body controlled, we save the praise, "You're all right!" and "That's all right by me" and "Right on!" Braininess, logic, and analysis are the roads to power in our society. Poetry, feeling, and tenderness are signs of weakness. And in spite of the ongoing disasters of failed human relationships in our country (say, for example, a fifty percent—world's highest—divorce rate), only a few weep for their children:

Reuven, the Master of the Universe, blessed me with a brilliant son. And he cursed me with all the problems of raising him. Ah, what it is to have a brilliant son! Not a smart son, Reuven, but a brilliant son, Daniel, a boy with a mind like a jewel. Ah, what a curse it is, what an anguish it is to have a Daniel whose mind is like a pearl, like a sun. Reuven, when my Daniel was four years old, I saw him reading a story, he swallowed it as one swallows food or water. There was no soul in my four-year old Daniel, there was only his mind. He was a mind in a body without a soul. It was a story in Yiddish book about a poor Jew and his struggle to get to Eretz Yisroel before he died. Ah, how that man suffered! And my Daniel *enjoyed* the story, he *enjoyed* the last terrible page, because when he finished it he realized for the first time what a memory he had. He looked at me proudly and told me back the story from memory, and I cried inside my heart. I went away and cried to the Master of the Universe, "What have you done to me? A mind like this I need for a son? A *heart* I need for a son, a *soul* I need for a son, *compassion* I want from my son, righteousness, mercy, strength to suffer and carry pain, *that* I want from my son, not a mind without a soul!"[2]

Psychoanalyst Bruno Bettleheim has written a book entitled *The Uses of Enchantment*. He deals in his practice with severely disturbed children, trying to restore some meaning to their lives. And while he rightly puts the impact of the parents in the first place of influence, he places after that the child's cultural heritage as a way of conveying meaning (our second characteristic of story) and says openly and bluntly that "it is literature that carries such information best." He says that children need some mechanism with which to come to terms with their feelings, to cope with the world. Since children cannot grasp abstract, ethical concepts, then stories, such as fairy tales, are the concrete ways of his wholeness. Bettleheim approvingly quotes the German poet Schiller who wrote, "Deeper meaning resides in the fairy tales told me in my childhood than in the truth that is taught by life."

He goes on to say that folk tales, fairy tales, religious stories, and the like, answer a child's most important questions on his own preconscious level. Stories to the child are most therapeutic, giving him in an imaginative way a means for coming to terms with life and with the things that threaten him. Stories are the carriers of deep insights, which the child cannot verbalize but which creep in, around, and under his skin, so to speak, and become a part of his sub-conscious imagery. Stories enable a child to cope with and make sense out of a bewildering world.

Bettleheim cites the example of a mother telling her son the story of "Jack the Giantkiller." When the child remarked at the end of the story that "There really aren't any such things as giants, are there, Mom?" the mother almost flubbed it. She was about to reply with left-brain common sense, "Of course not"—destroying in the process the whole value of the story for him—when he went on and said, "But there are such things as grown-ups and they're like giants!" Bettleheim's comment is, "At the ripe old age of five, he understood the encouraging message of the story: although adults can be ex-perienced as frightening giants, a little boy with cunning can get the better of them."[3]

He also relates the incident of another five-year-old who would make up a story to cope with his angry mother. At times she was so sweet and loving; other times she yelled at him and scolded him. How could he reconcile the two? He couldn't, so he invented a "Martian" mother who looked exactly like his mother but who was a witch. This way, in imagination, he could cope with mother in her two moods. By and by, he put the two together when he figured out that the Martian mother knew things that only the loving mother would know and vice versa. But it was his right-side brain that en-abled him to cope until he could reach a deeper level of under-standing.

Moreover, for children, the right stories are also redemptive and formative.

☐ Many centuries ago, a rich sultan in Baghdad gave a banquet in honor of the birth of his son. All the nobility who partook of the feast brought costly gifts, except a young sage who came empty-handed. He explained to the sultan, "Today the young prince will receive many precious gifts, jewels and rare coins. My gift is different. From the time he is old enough to listen until manhood, I will come to the palace every day and tell him stories of our Arabian heroes. When he becomes our ruler he will be just and honest."

The young sage kept his word. When the prince was at last made sultan, he became famous for his wisdom and honor. To this day, an inscription on a scroll in Baghdad reads, "It was because of the seed sown by the tales." ☐

But it's not just for children that stories awaken right-brain imagination, but for adults as well. Perhaps because adults *are* so left-brain trained, the story is more important than ever as a means to achieve balance. For stories can lead to repentance, laughter, peace, insight, healing, and true religion. ". . . really great Christianity," writes Karl Rahner, "and really great poetry have an inner kinship . . . great poetry exists where we radically face who we are."[4]

Here are a few examples of each quality, except healing, which we will deal with as our next characteristic.

One of the most famous stories leading to repentance is that of King David (2 Samuel, 11 and 12). You recall that David lusted after another man's wife, Bathsheba. He had her brought to him, had sex with her, and she became pregnant. To cover up his deed, he had the woman's husband, Uriah the Hittite, one of his mercenary soldiers, brought back from the front lines. But Uriah, a man of honor, would not sleep with his wife out of respect for his comrades at the front lines. All ruses failed to get him to do so. So, finally, David sent Uriah back with a message of his own doom. He was to give Joab, the commander, a letter telling him to put Uriah in the forefront of battle so that we would be sure to die. And this is what happened.

☐ The prophet Nathan appeared on the scene. He came, not to confront David directly for his wicked crime, but to tell him a story. And he told it craftily so that David could easily stir up his imagination and react. Nathan told him the story of a very rich farmer who owned hundreds and hundreds of sheep in contrast to a very poor farmer who had but one little lamb to his name. And this lamb was dear to the man and lived with him in his own house. Indeed it was "like a daughter to him." Well, one day the rich man had a sudden, very important visitor and so naturally he was bound to give him hospitality. But he was unwilling to take one of his own numerous sheep for a feast but rather simply went over and by force took the poor man's one lamb, who was less a pet than family member and killed and cooked it for his guest. David's imagination caught fire, his indignation rose. He was incensed and vowed destruction to the wretch who would do a thing like that. Who was the man? and he, David, would give vengeance. And Nathan shot back with his famous sentence, "You are the man!" And then he proceeded to unfold his story—his little parable, really—of exactly what David did to

Uriah. And David repented. And his story in turn has been a source of repentance for others. □

Stories can lead to laughter, which is a right-brain activity. In fact, some researchers today suspect that the body's "laugh central," as they call it, lies in the right hemisphere of the brain, and patients with damage in that area have a hard time laughing at jokes that send other people into convulsions. Paul McGhee, a psychologist from Texas Tech University says, "The right hemisphere is linked to emotion and, is, in general, holistic." He further remarks that when you dissect humor to see what makes it tick you are using your left, analytical hemisphere and this might explain why, when you analyze humor, you destroy it. Anyway, give your right-brain side a mild treat with these:

> There was an old man of Blackheath
> Who sat on his set of false teeth.
> Said he with a start,
> "Oh, Lord, bless my heart!
> I've bitten myself underneath!"

or

> There once was a barber of Kew
> Who went very mad at the zoo;
> He tried to enamel
> The face of a camel
> And gave the brown bear a shampoo.

Or this one from Edward Lear:

> There was an old man with a beard
> Who said, "It's just as I feared!
> Two owls and a hen,
> Four larks and a wren
> Have all built their nests in my beard!"[5]

Or you might want to try this one:

□The word had gone around in the little Eastern European town that one of its most respected citizens, Abraham the cobbler, had become an out-and-out atheist. Well, the whole town was shaken by the news. It was the sole topic of conversation all over. Nevertheless, all admitted that it was all hearsay. No one had spoken directly to Abraham about it. It was still only rumor, even though a shocking one.

On the following Sabbath, however, it became clear to everyone in town that for the first time in 30 years Abraham the cobbler did not sit in his customary seat in the synagogue. Could he be sick? No, for when the services were over, they found that Abraham the cobbler was walking quietly in the street, the very picture of health.

All stared, and finally Yussel the tailor, with a sudden burst of bravery, pushed forward and accused the cobbler. "Abraham," he cried, "there is a rumor that you have become an atheist. And you were not at the synagogue just now. Is this true? Are you indeed an atheist?" Abraham looked quietly at Yussel and turned away without a word.

Everyone looked after him in consternation, and by the next day it was clear that no work would be done in the town unless this matter was cleared up. So a delegation was appointed, with Yussel the tailor as its head, and it was understood that they were to face Abraham in his shop and insist on an answer once and for all.

In they went and Yussel said loudly, "Abraham, we must have an answer. You cannot leave matters as they are. Tell me, are you now an atheist?"

Abraham looked up from the shoe he was mending and said quietly "Yes, I am!"

Astonished at the quick and unequivocal answer, Yussel said, "Then why didn't you say so when I asked you yesterday?"

Abraham's eyes grew wide with horror, "You wanted me to say I was an atheist on the *Sabbath*?" □

Stories can provide left-brain insight through right-brain imagination. Here's a few short different approaches from Sr. M. Pamela Smith:

□ Nathanael (John 1:43-50)

I was only a man who daydreamed
and would have wished to forget a few things.
A plump fig, I sat there under the leaves
ripe for picking.
If only I had known he could mind read. . . .

The Leper (Luke 17:11-19)

If I could begin to tell you what it is like
to have watched yourself rot and ooze away for years,
you might begin to see how amazed, how wild

with glee, how crazed we were to be—suddenly!—clean.
You'd know why most rushed headlong, nonstop, to the priests.
You'd know what a few paused, turning this way, then that, lost,
foreign to their own hands and feet, dazed into helplessness.
When I raced back to fall on my knees, to pour
out my wonder upon him, and even to adore
this one who seemed a god in the flesh, he did not
seem to object to this fraction of gratefulness.
When he asked after the other nine, it was not as a man
who'd been disappointed at something—but more like
an old friend who seeks news of those he hasn't seen for a time.

A Neighbor from Nazareth (Mark 6:1-6)
Maybe the fact that he couldn't come through
with any stupendous signs back here
proves that he's not much of anyone.
But I'm still rather taken aback
by that Isaiah scroll moment.
And there is all that talk from Capernaum,
those rumors, really, across the whole countryside.
He was always a good boy.
I can't imagine him just going off
and saying such unheard of things and doing stunts.[6]□

Story does indeed provoke the imagination. In such a process a
whole other side of us is released. Through story we are a better
centered people. Through story we find healing, and that is story's
next characteristic.

Tenth Characteristic of Story: Stories promote healing.

□Martin Buber tells the story of his paralyzed grandfather who was
asked to tell a story about his great teacher, the famous and holy
Baal Shem Tov. The grandfather replied by telling how the Holy
Man used to jump up and down and dance when he was praying.
And while he was reciting the story, the grandfather stood up and the
story carried him away so much that he too had to jump and dance
to show how the Master had done it. From that moment he was
healed.□

This is not as far-fetched as it might seem. Modern psychology
uses storytelling to bring healing to people, especially the healing of

deep hurts and memories from the past. The tool here is precisely the imagination. This is the powerful force that aids us not only to go back and tell a long ago story but to relive it much like Buber's grandfather. And it is in the reliving that the person is often enabled to come to terms with whatever pain or hurt is buried there.

It is not difficult to go back at all to the past through the imagination. Any of us can recall easily the sights, sounds, and smells of the past. Just take a moment to close your eyes and think of your childhood kitchen. See where the stove was and the sink, where you sat at table. Smell the cooking or perhaps the tobacco of your father's pipe. Imagine the paint or wallpaper on your bedroom wall, your bed, the covers. All of us can retrieve this. We can distill a time frame and relive feelings both joyful and painful. And, if we wish, we can tell what we "see" in a story. We can replay the past. A simple "remember when . . ." around the table at holiday time can take us late into the night with tears of laughter rolling down our cheeks—just as they did in the original version, time, and place.

There are whole schools of Christian healing dedicated to the inner healing of people's hurtful memories. The dynamics are fundamentally those of engaging the imagination, and through the imagination inviting the person to relive his or her hurtful past, this time with Christ participating in it. The repressed parts are especially to be given over to his touch. Here are some direction questions from two Jesuit practitioners of inner healing of memories, Dennis and Matt Linn[7]: 1) Who are the persons, (family, friends, teachers) who loved me most? (I walk through the front door and through each room of the places where I lived until I find those who love me. Then I focus on one person and share with Christ, the Being of Light, how grateful I am). 2) What events (challenges, prayer times, successes) made me grow most? 3) What is the worst thing I ever did in my life? How were Jesus and the Father loving me even then? And so on with questions for the person traveling the imagination road to the inner self in search of healing.

In *Healing the Hidden Self*, Barbara Shlemon says, "Every inner healing prayer should begin by inviting Jesus Christ to walk with us into the past." She gives an example of a man who did this in one of her workshops, a man who was very skeptical about the whole thing, but who later gave this testimony, that is, told his story:

I felt Jesus leading me back in my life to the time before I was born and I became conscious of strong feelings of anger and resentment toward my mother, feelings I had never before recognized. As I asked Jesus to reveal the source of these emotions, I heard my mother's voice saying, "During my entire pregnancy with Danny I was hoping for a little girl." Suddenly I realized that my mother's attitude constituted a rejection from the very beginning of life. Small wonder I had problems relating to women and was confused about my sexuality. I asked the Lord to heal this wound and immediately began to sense waves of light washing over me. It seemed as if he was saying, "It's all right for you to be a man." I began to cry for the sheer joy of being able to accept myself for the first time in my life.[8]

The healing power of story and imagination is indeed powerful.

Here is a final, powerful story retold by Beldon Lane, showing us that story does indeed possess a redemptive and healing quality.

☐ On the day the Baal Shem Tov was dying, he assigned each of his disciples a task to carry on in his name, to do some of his work. When he finished with all of them, he had one more task. He called the last disciple and gave him this task: to go all over Europe to retell the stories he remembered from the Master. The disciple was very disappointed. This was hardly a prestigious job. But the Baal Shem Tov told him that he would not have to do this forever; he would receive a sign when he should stop and then he could live out the rest of his life in ease.

So off he went, and days and months turned into years and years of telling stories until he felt he had told them in every part of the world. Then he heard of a man in Italy, a nobleman in fact, who would pay a gold ducat for each new story told. So the disciple went to Italy to the nobleman's castle. But to his absolute horror he discovered that he had forgotten all the Baal Shem Tov stories! He couldn't remember a single story. He was mortified. But the nobleman was kind and urged him to stay a few days anyway, in the hope that he would eventually remember something.

But the next day and the next he remembered nothing. Finally, on the third day the disciple protested that he must go, out of sheer embarrassment. But as he was about to leave, oh, yes, suddenly he remembered one story, and this would prove that he indeed did know the great Baal Shem Tov, for he was the only one there when his master told this story. And this is the story he remembered.

Once the Baal Shem Tov told him to harness the horses, for they were about to take a trip to Turkey where at this time of the year the streets were decorated for the Christian's Easter festival. The disciple was upset, for it was well known that Jews were not safe during the Christian Holy Week and Easter. They were fair game for the Christians shouting God-Killer! And, in fact, it was the custom during the Easter festival to kill one Jew in reparation.

Still, they went. They went into the city and then into the Jewish quarter where the Jews were all huddled behind their shutters out of fear. They were secluded, waiting till the festival was over and they could go on out on the streets again in safety. So imagine how startled and surprised they were when the Baal Shem Tov stood up and opened all the windows of the house where they were staying. And furthermore he stood there in full view!

And looking through the window he saw the bishop leading the procession. He was arrayed like a prince with gold vestments, silver mitre, and a diamond studded staff. The Baal Shem Tov told his disciple, "Go tell the bishop I want to see him." Was he out of his mind? Did he want to die? But nothing could deter this order, so the disciple went out and went up to the bishop to tell him that the Baal Shem Tov wanted to see him. The bishop seemed frightened and agitated. But he went. He went and was secluded for three hours with the Baal Shem Tov. Then the Master came out and without saying anything else, told his disciples that they were ready to go back home.

As the disciple finished the story, he was about to apologize to the nobleman for the insignificance of the story when he suddenly noticed the enormous impact the story had on the nobleman. He had dissolved into tears and finally, when he could speak, he said, "Oh disciple, your story has just saved my soul! You see, I was there that day. I was that bishop. I had descended from a long line of distinguished rabbis but one day during a period of great persecution I had abandoned the faith and converted to Christianity. The Christians, of course, were so pleased that in time they even made me a bishop. And I had accepted everything, even went along with the killing of the Jews each year until that one year. The night before the festival I had a terrible dream of the Day of Judgment and the danger to my soul. So until you came the very next day with a message from the Baal Shem Tov, I knew that I had to go with you.

For three hours he and I talked. He told me that there still might be hope for my soul. He told me to sell my goods and retire on what was left and live a life of good deeds and holiness. There might still be hope. And his last words to me were these: 'When a man comes to you and tells you your own story, you will know that your sins are forgiven.'

"So I have been asking everyone I knew for stories from the Baal Shem Tov. And I recognized you immediately when you came and I was happy. But when I saw that all the stories had been taken from you, I recognized God's judgment. Yet now you have remembered one story, *my* story, and I know now that the Baal Shem Tov has interceded on my behalf and that God has forgiven me."

When a man comes to you and tells you your own story, you know that your sins are forgiven. And when you are forgiven, you are healed.[9]☐

Eleventh Characteristic of Story: Every story is our story.

If story links us all to our culture and roots and to all of humankind (second and third characteristics), it also links us to our deepest selves. We might miss this because, as we have seen, we are so left-brain orientated. This leads us to ask about a particular story (or stories in general for that matter), "Is it true?" We neglect to ask if it is true for us. When a child, for example, asks is it true about the Cinderella story he or she may really be asking, "Is it true that the Cinderella in me can become whole, happy, and accepted someday?" When an adult asks if Jesus really rose from the dead, that adult may ultimately be asking about his or her fear of death. "Is the Bible true?" may well mean, "Can I live in that world of faith?" In other words, all stories in one way or another are, or can be, our story. That's their fascination and power. Stories ultimately are about us. To paraphrase Pogo, "We have met the story and it is us."

So, Sleeping Beauty has been given eleven gifts before the curse sends her into a deep sleep, but she is redeemed by the final gift of life. We too are gifted, all of us, to some degree. Then we are tested (cursed) and finally redeemed. Hansel and Gretel go into the woods having been rejected by love (a woman who is a non-nurturing mother). There they confront evil in the person of the witch and her seductive gingerbread house. But they overcome. Can we? St. George sallies forth to slay the dragon. So do we—the dragon without and the dragon within. Hop O' My Thumb is sent away from home to get lost in the woods, but he leaves a trail of breadcrumbs to trace his way back—until the birds come one time and eat up his markers to home. Now he must continue on. The bread crumbs are his tie to home in case the going gets rough, his umbilical cord to safety and security. But sooner or later he must venture into adolescence, adulthood, the world. And so must we.

Jesus goes forth to confront evil but does not destroy it. On the contrary, it destroys him. But he overcomes it by the power of his love and death, which used to be the last word, but now becomes the next to the last word. The last word is his story and our last word is life. Peter protests loyalty but coughs up denial. Faithful follower Thomas doubts, close friend Judas betrays, hard-hearted Magdalen cries, extortionist Zaccheus, a small man (morally?), grows tall, dead Lazarus revives. Aren't these our stories too?

In the sixth month the angel Gabriel was sent from God to a city of Galilee named Nazareth to a virgin betrothed to a man named Joseph. . . . Now the serpent was more subtle than any other wild creature that the Lord God had made and he said to the woman. . . . Abraham, take your son, your only son, Issac, whom you love, and go to the land of Moriah and offer him there as a burnt offering. . . . Tell Pharoah, King of Egypt, to let the people of Israel go out of his land. . . . Now Joseph had a dream—Great story lines all! And they introduce not just the story of a particular people, but our stories as well.

This is why Joseph Campbell about a quarter of a century ago entitled his famous book *The Hero With a Thousand Faces*. By this he meant that there is really only one story and one hero, and he or she wears many faces, including our own. Furthermore, he even speaks of a "monomyth," that is, a single, archetypal motif within the story that every human being sounds: the motif of journey. Everyone is born. Everyone is born onto a path. Everyone, from the start, is on a journey. And a journey has two inseparable companions: conflict and new beginnings. Which is to say that every one of us meets some obstacle on our life's journey, and on a small or grand scale we struggle, hopefully overcome, and start anew. One hero, one journey, a thousand faces—including yours and mine. And insofar as this is true, then all stories are at bottom religious. Some cultures have been quite explicit about the journey motif. We see this quite sharply in those many Russian pilgrimage stories, not to mention the great classic, *The Way of the Pilgrim*. The pilgrim in these stories is Campbell's prototype hero on a prototype journey.

We may not know how to react to such stories. We probably will want to ask, "Is it true? Did it really happen that way?" We should be asking what it means and what it means for me, and if in this story there is anything of my story. In any case, listen to master novelist and collector of Italian folk tales Italo Calvino. After he finished his collection of stories, he wrote:

> Now my journey through folklore is over. . . . For two years I have lived in woodlands and enchanted castles, torn between contemplation and action, on the one hand hoping to catch a glimpse of the face of the beautiful creature of mystery who, each night, lies down beside her knight; on the other, having to choose between the cloak of invisibility or the magical foot, feather or claw that could metamorphose me into an animal. And during those two years the world about me gradually took on the attributes of fairyland, where everything that happened was a spell or a metamorphosis, where individuals, plucked from the chiaroscuro of a state of mind, were carried away by predestined loves or were bewitched; where sudden disappearances, monstrous transformations occurred, where right had to be discerned from wrong, where paths bristling with obstacles led to a happiness held by captive dragons. Also in the lives of peoples and nations, which until now had seemed to be at a standstill, anything seemed possible: snake pits opened up and were transformed into rivers of milk; kings who had been thought kindly turned out to be brutal parents; silent, bewitched kingdoms suddenly came back to life. I had the impression that the lost rules which govern the world of folklore were tumbling out of the magic box I had opened.

> Now that the book is finished, I know that this was not a hallucination, a sort of professional malady, but the confirmation of something I already suspected—folktales are real.[10]

Of course they're real. They're about us. Every story is our story.

Twelfth Characteristic of Story: Stories provide a basis for hope and morality.

When a people are in a hopeless situation, the only way out, so to speak, is to imagine other possibilities and alternatives. It is the imagination, therefore, that gives birth to hope, and it is the story that is imagination's vehicle. The Bible, for example, is full of stories of a people, betrayed and betraying, who are caught in moral and political death patterns. "Son of Man, can these bones live?" (Ezekiel 37:3) Can a people rise up again from political and moral ruin? Ezekiel's powerful imagery in the story of the Valley of the Dry Bones provides a basis, under Yahweh's mighty power, for optimism. It is just such an appeal to the people's imagination that gives them hope and a new foundation for moral action and life. Ezekiel's story is saved and savored as a standing reminder of God's unexpected and marvelous deeds of the past. It proclaims such possibilities in the future. This is why we can say that the stories of the Bible are really moral exhortations in the form of narrative.

In his stories, Jesus himself challenged his listeners to envision a different future. His parables were designed to provoke them into hope and into seeing a better way of living and acting. To this extent, the approach of the parables, as Dominic Crossan has suggested, is seen as a fundamental morality:

> Such a morality is concerned with the moral *dimensions* of the world around us: relationships between fathers and sons, or landlords and tenants; the problems of widows on fixed incomes; the struggles to show compassion when it means taking personal risks. These are stories of everyday life lived in the presence of God, not lists of do's and don't's. They show us what that presence means across a wide spectrum of situations in which we live with others and interact with them. They allow us to ponder our motives and actions within a context where God's perspective is part of the texture of the story itself. It is this perspective which opens up new possibilities for our imagination, shapes our moral vision, and sustains our hope.[11]

☐ About eighty years ago a man picked up the morning paper and, to his horror, read his own obituary! The newspaper had reported the death of the wrong man. Like most of us, he relished the idea of finding out what people would say about him after he died. He read past the bold caption which read, "Dynamite king dies," to the text itself. He read along until he was taken aback by the description of him as a "merchant of death." He was the inventor of dynamite and he had amassed a great fortune from the manufacture of weapons of destruction. But he was moved by this description. Did he really want to be known as a "merchant of death"? It was at that moment that a healing power greater than the destructive force of dynamite came over him. It was his hour of conversion. From that point on, he devoted his energy and money to works of peace and human betterment. Today, of course, he is best remembered, not as a "merchant of death," but as the founder of the Nobel Peace Prize—Alfred Nobel. □

This is a story of hope—"I can change"—and conversion and a new way of living and being. This story, like many stories, may provide a basis for hope and morality for others.

Thirteenth Characteristic of Story: Stories are the basis for ministry.

This comes from a brief but telling comment from John Shea. Ministry to others and for others really begins at the intersection between God and his people revealed in their stories and conversations. But if, on the contrary, ministry is seen as *serving* others, then disdain is not far behind. You serve and they do not respond. "No one turns out for anything," you complain. The people must be—are—indifferent and apathetic. How can one love such an uncooperative and unappreciative people? And all that you do for them! But if you leave this "serving" concept of people behind, and instead seek to enter into their conversations and stories, then you will be one with them. It will not be you and them, but we. We see this most dramatically in that well known story of Damien. We remember that frightening moment when he put his foot into the hot water after a futile day's evangelizing and felt nothing, the unmistakable sign of leprosy. That Sunday he got in the pulpit and did not begin with his customary "You lepers" but with "*We* lepers. . . ." From that point on, his unsuccessful ministry is electric, fruitful beyond his wildest dreams. He has now entered their conversation. *He* is their story and once more a word has been made flesh, however leperous, and dwelt among people.

Stories are not only the basis for ministry; they are also a fruitful guide to discerning when in ministry love must come before law.

□ Tanzan and Ekido were once travelling together down a muddy road. A heavy rain was still falling.

Coming around a bend, they met a lovely girl in a silk kimono and sash, unable to cross the intersection.

"Come on, girl," said Tanzan at once. Lifting her in his arms, he carried her over the mud.

Ekido did not speak again until that night when they reached a lodging temple. Then he could no longer restrain himself. "We monks don't go near females," he told Tanzan, "especially not young and lovely ones. It is dangerous. Why did you do that?"

"I left the girl there," said Tanzan. "Are you still carrying her?"[12]□

4

Paradoxes
of Story

*P*resbyterian educator Belden Lane has tapped the power of story, especially the genius of Jewish lore. Such lore, he has discovered, often centers around paradox: expecting one thing and being caught off guard with another. And that is precisely the point: to unsettle our common conventions and make us see reality anew. So here we list his six paradoxes and then go on to illustrate them with stories, most of them, not all, from the Jewish tradition.

First Paradox of Story: Spirituality is rooted in earthiness.

This is a paradox to trip up Christians. For us, real spirituality escapes the earthy; it is heavenly. A "spiritual" person is one who has emotionally moved beyond his or her body and distanced himself or herself from this planet. Think for the moment: whom do you consider a really spiritual man or woman? What is your image of that person? Is it not the image of the old prints that used to hang in churches, convents, and retreat houses: a saint with rolled up eyes? the recluse, thin and wan, who speaks in lovely phrases? The pale ascetic you can almost see through and in whose presence you lower your voice? Would you consider a 300-pound beer-drinking, back-slapping hulk of a man, who sometimes told off-colored stories a saint? Like Martin Luther, G. K. Chesterton, or Thomas Aquinas?

For us, spirituality is rooted in platonic other worldliness, not earthiness. But Judaism will have none of this. It is rather rooted in the sensual, the earthy, the Lord's creation (Isaiah 25:6-8):

> On the mountain, Yahweh Sabbaoth will prepare for all peoples a banquet of rich food, a banquet of fine wines, of food rich and juicy, of fine strained wines. On this mountain he will remove the mourning veil covering all people, and the shroud enwrapping all nations, and will destroy Death forever.

And Jeremiah adds his words (31:12-14):

> They will come and shout for joy on the heights of Zion,
> they will throng towards the good things of Yahweh:
> corn and oil and wine,
> sheep and oxen;
> their soul will be like a watered garden,
> they will sorrow no more.
> The virgin will then take pleasure in the dance,
> young men and old will be happy;
> I will change their morning into gladness,
> comfort them, give them joy after their troubles

Truly, as Matthew Fox reminds us, "Jewish thinking which is Biblical thinking and which was also Jesus' thinking takes it for granted that the sensual is a blessing and that there is no (spiritual) life without it. . . . To recover a sensual spirituality is to recover a Biblical one."[1]

If the Christian says, "The world is not my true home, I am only passing through," the Jew has the saying: "One is as good as the world." The Jew is tied into a creation-centered spirituality. We can see this, for example, in a quite unlikely place, Yiddish curses; for the way we curse is a mirror of the way we bless. Curses like: "May beets grow in your belly!" or "May all the teeth in your head fall out except one and in that one may you have a toothache."

We Christians would never dream of making earthly prayers like this to God: "If you think you can bring your people back into the fold by making them suffer, then I, Leib, son of Rachel, swear to you that you will not succeed. So why try? Save your children by giving them joy, by delivering them. By doing it that way, you have nothing to lose and everything to gain." Or this one from a victim of Hitler's persecution: "Lord, four thousand years ago, on the slopes of Mount Sinai, you chose the Jews as a people peculiar unto you, a holy people, a nation of priests, to bear the yoke of your holy Law and to serve as witness to all the world. Lord, I am deeply sensible of the honor, but Lord, enough is enough. Surely it is time you chose somebody else." Or: "Lord, save your people before it is too late. Otherwise there may be no one left to save."

How about this? "Do not think of man's sins, I beg of you. Think rather of his good deeds. They are fewer, I agree. But you must admit, they are more precious. Believe me, it isn't easy to be good in this world. And if I didn't see it with my own two eyes that man, in spite of all obstacles, is capable of kindness, I would not believe it. And so I ask of you, don't be harsh with your children. Rare as it may be, it is their kindness that should surprise you." Or, finally, "We shall give you our sins and in return you will grant us your pardon. By the way, you come out ahead. Without our sins, what would you do with your pardon?"

□ Once there was a man who had grown weary of life. Tired to death. So one day he decided to leave his own home town, his ancestral village, to search for the perfect Magical City where all would be different, new, full, and rewarding. So he left. On his journey he found himself in a forest. So he settled down for the night, took out his sack and had a bite to eat. Before he turned in for sleep he was careful to take off his shoes and point them to the new direction toward which he was going. However, unknown to him, while he slept a jokester came during the night and turned his shoes around. When the man awoke the next morning he carefully stepped into his shoes and continued on to the Magical City.

After a few days, he came to the Magical City. Not quite as large as he imagined it, however. In fact, it looked somewhat familiar. He found a familiar street, knocked at a familiar door, met a familiar family he found there and lived happily ever after. □

And this is as good a story as any to comment on the Jewish-Christian differences. We're always looking elsewhere for God, in the Magical City in the sky. The religious Jew finds him right where he's planted in the here and now, in earthiness.

□ Another story. Not symbolic, just earthy. Mrs. Moskowitz was having her house painted, and between the smell of the paint and the hassle she found life hard. It was the last straw when Mr. Moskowitz forgot himself and leaned against the wall and left a distinct hand mark on the fresh paint. The Mrs. made her feelings clearly known and the husband tried to calm her down. "What's the fuss?" he said, "The painter's returning tomorrow so he'll paint it over."

Nevertheless, Mrs. Moskowitz found it difficult to sleep all night. The thought of that hand mark bothered her. The next morning, then, the painter had barely stepped over the threshold when she was upon him saying, "Oh, I'm so glad you're here. All night long I've been thinking of you and waiting for you. Come with me. I want to show you where my husband put his hand."

The painter blanched and stepped back aghast, "Please," he said, "I'm an old man. A glass of tea, and maybe a cookie, is all I want!" □

A good guffaw here is a delight to God. Spirituality is found in earthiness.

Second Paradox of Story: The Absolute is known in the personal.

Our concept of God, in spite of the last story, persists that he is distant. He is "up there" somewhere. We even tend to call him by the philosopher's names: First Cause, Unknown Mover, and perhaps even The Force. We seek the Absolute in absolute remoteness. But this paradox says it isn't so, for the Absolute is known in the individual, never in the abstract. It is known in the personal and in the relational.

□ Two brothers worked together on a family farm. One was unmarried and the other married with children. They shared what they grew equally as they always did, produce and profit. But one day the single brother said to himself, "You know, it's not right that we should share the produce equally, and the profit too. After all, I'm all alone, just by myself and my needs are simple. But there is my poor brother with a wife and all those children." So in the middle of the night he took a sack of grain from his bin, crept over the field between their houses and dumped it into his brother's bin. Meanwhile, unknown to him, his brother had the same thought. He said to himself, "It is not right that we should share produce and profit equally. After all, I am married and I have my wife to look after me and my children for years to come. But my brother has no one, and no one to take care of his future." So he too, in the middle of the night, took to taking a sack of grain from his bin and sneaking across the field to deposit it in his brother's. And both were puzzled for years as to why their supply did not dwindle. Well, one night it just so happened that they both set out for each other's house at the same time. In the dark they bumped into each other carrying their sacks. Each was startled, but then it slowly dawned on them what was happening. They dropped their sacks and embraced one another. Suddenly the dark sky lit up and a voice from heaven spoke, "Here at last is the place where I will build my Temple. For where brothers meet in love, there my Presence shall dwell." □

That the Absolute God is known, not in the abstract, but in the personal is, of course, enshrined in the Lord's saying that as long as you did it to one of the least of my brethren or sisters you did it to me. It has also become the theme of countless stories, such as Oscar Wilde's *The Selfish Giant* or Van Dyke's classic, *The Other Wise Man*.

□In this latter story, you might recall, the Wise Man, Artaban, in his pursuit of finding the King of the Jews, misses his three friends who set out before him: Casper, Melchior, and Balthazar. He misses the Christ Child too because his adventures lead him into strange encounters with dying beggars, and frightened mothers to whom he gives two of his three jewels saved for the Child. He returns to Jerusalem after a fruitless search in Egypt and there for thirty-three years he still diligently searches for the child.

This year it is Passover time. Artaban, now an old man, notes an unusual commotion and he inquires as to its cause. People answer him, "We are going to the placed called Golgotha, just outside the walls of the city, to see two robbers and a man named Jesus of Nazareth hanged on a cross. The man calls himself the Son of God and Pilate has sent him to be crucified because he says that *he* is the King of the Jews." Artaban knows instinctively that this is the King he has been searching for. So he rushes to the scene. But on his way he meets a young girl being sold into slavery. She sees his royal robes and falls at his feet pleading with him to rescue her. His heart is moved and he gives away his last jewel for her ransom. Just then, darkness falls over the land and the earth shakes and great stones fall into the streets, one of them upon Artaban, crushing his head. As he lay dying in the arms of the girl he has just redeemed (ransomed), he cries out weakly, "Three and thirty years I looked for thee, Lord, but I have never seen thy face nor ministered to thee!" But then a voice comes from heaven, strong and kind, and says, "Inasmuch as you

did it to one of the least of my brethren or sisters, you did it to me."
Artaban's face grows calm and peaceful. His long journey is ended.
He had found his King!□

Notice the old refrains: a journey, obstacle, and ultimate grace
and redemption. Notice, too, where Artaban found his absolute
King: in the personal, in the people who crossed his journey's path.
Gerard Manley Hopkins says it this way:

As kingfishers catch fire, dragonflies draw flame;
As tumbled over rim in roundy wells
Stones ring; like each tucked string tells, each hung bell's
Bow swung finds tongue to fling out broad its name;
Each mortal thing does one thing and the same:
Deals out that being indoors each one dwells;
Selves—goes itself; *myself* it speaks and spells;
Crying *What I do is me; for that I came.*

I say more: the just man justices;
Keeps grace: that keeps all his goings graces:
Acts in God's eye what in God's eye he is—
Christ—for Christ plays in ten thousand places,
Lovely in limbs, and lovely in eyes not his
To the Father through the features of men's faces.

Third Paradox of Story: Freedom is discovered in obedience.

Again, this is a difficult concept especially for us North Americans.
We are brought up to be fiercely independent, never quite resolving
the deep tension between intimacy and freedom. Our ideal model is
the Marlboro Man. No ties, no strings, no commitments. Hang loose.
Be free. But in Jewish lore, freedom is found precisely in obedience.
Any other position is absurd. And perhaps the two words "absurd"
and "obedience" give us the clue as to what they mean. "Absurd"
comes from the Latin meaning "without sound"; that is, the words
say nothing, they are without sound or meaning to us. And this is our
attitude in reference to certain commands or demands. But the word
"obedience" comes from the Latin meaning "to listen thoroughly"
and suggests that if we only would, we might hear something more
than no sound. In other words, for the Jew, it is always a question of
freedom *to*, rather than, as for us, freedom *from*. To be under God's
law, to "listen thoroughly" to it, leads one to a stance that others

might consider "absurd" but only because they hear nothing of the divine voice. To be truly free is to be obedient to God's law. The 613 Jewish commandments of the Law are not seen as restrictions but as ways of being free to be God's people. Obedience is liberating.

Dama ben Nethina, although a pagan, is a hero to the Jew because he was obedient to the Law, in this case, to the law of honoring one's father and mother (and he was rewarded). Here's his story.

□Dama ben Nethina was head of the local city council. One day his mother got angry with him and hit him with her shoe in the presence of the whole council. The shoe dropped out of her hand. But Dama picked it up and returned it to his mother to save her the trouble of bending down.

Dama never sat upon the stone on which his father used to sit. When his father died, he revered that stone as an object of worship.

It happened one time that the jasper stone of the high priest's breastplate was lost. The jasper represented the tribe of Benjamin. Inquiries were made to locate someone who owned a jasper. It was learned that Dama ben Nethina was the owner of just such a precious stone. So the sages of Israel went to Dama and they reached an agreement with him that they would buy the jasper for one hundred denarii. But when Dama went to fetch the stone he discovered that his father was sleeping on the little chest in which the jasper was kept. And Dama refused to wake up his father on that account. The sages now offered him one thousand denarii, but Dama did not wake his father.

Later when his father did awake, Dama brought the stone to the sages. They wanted to pay him the latter price of one thousand denarii but he said to them, "How could I sell you the honor I owe my father?" Instead he sold them the jasper for the price on which they had first agreed, one hundred denarii.□ [2]

To make sure that we got the point that real freedom is discovered in obedience, there is a postscript to this story. It says that on that very night Dama's cow gave birth to a red calf. Once, when the Israelites were in need of a red heifer for the purification ritual, they bought that red heifer from Dama and paid him its weight in gold.

God rewards obedience. In obedience we hear God's voice and are made truly free.

Fourth Paradox of Story: Triumph grows out of suffering.

This paradox, at least, is not alien to Christians. Indeed it is the cornerstone of our faith as seen in the central Christian story of the death and resurrection of Jesus. It is firmly rooted in the gospel tradition. "If anyone would come after me, let him deny himself, take up his cross and follow me. For whoever would save his life will lose it, and whoever loses it for my sake will find it." (Matthew 16:24-26). It is precisely in suffering that God is known and is present. That is why even in exile the prophet Isaiah could speak of hope and proclaim that God's will shall still achieve its purpose. He will use the suffering of his people for the salvation of all. This conviction of ultimate triumph beyond current disaster lies behind the following stories. And it is this conviction that provides the basis for the peace and tranquility of the stories' characters in the face of personal trauma.

☐Rabbi Akieba took a trip to a strange land. He took an ass, a rooster, and a lamp. Since he was a Jew he was refused hospitality in the village inns, so he decided to sleep in the woods. He lit his lamp to study the Holy Books before going to sleep. But a fierce wind came up knocking over the lamp and breaking it. So he decided to turn in, saying, "All that God does, he does well." During the night some wild animals came along and drove away the rooster and thieves stole the ass. Rabbi Akieba woke up, saw the loss, but still proclaimed easily, "All that God does, he does well."

He then went back to the village where he was refused lodging only to learn that enemy soldiers had invaded it during the night and killed all the inhabitants. He also learned that these same enemy soldiers had traveled through the same part of the woods where he lay asleep. Had his lamp not blown out he would have been seen. Had not the rooster been chased it would have crowed, giving him away. Had not the ass been stolen he would have brayed. So once more he said, "All that God does, he does well!"☐

Finally, let me share a moving story from Father John Powell on the same theme:

☐Some years ago, I stood watching my university students file into the classroom for our first session in The Theology of Faith. That was the day I first saw Tommy. My eyes and my mind both blinked. He was combing his long hair, which hung all the way down to his shoulders. It was the first time I had ever seen a boy with hair that long. I guess it was just coming into fashion then. I know in my mind that it isn't what's on your head but in it that counts; but on that day, I was unprepared and my emotions flipped. I immediately filed Tommy under "S" for strange . . . very strange.

Tommy turned out to be the "atheist in residence" in my Theology of Faith course. He constantly objected to, smirked at, or whined about the possibility of an unconditionally loving Father-God. We lived with each other in relative peace for one semester, although I admit he was at times a pain in the back pew. When he came up at the end of the course to turn in his final exam, he asked in a slightly cynical tone: "Do you think I'll ever find God?" I decided on a little shock therapy. "No!" I said emphatically. "Oh," he responded, "I thought that was the product you were pushing." I let him get five steps from the classroom door and then called out: "Tommy! I don't think you'll ever find him, but I'm absolutely certain he will find you!" He shrugged a little and left my class and my life. I was a bit disappointed that he had missed my clever line.

Later, I heard that Tom had graduated, and I was duly grateful. Then a sad report. Tommy had terminal cancer. Before I could search him out, he came to see me. When he walked into my office, his body was badly wasted, and the long hair had all fallen out as a result of chemotherapy. But his eyes were bright and his voice was firm, for the first time, I think.

"Tommy, I've thought about you so often. I hear you are sick!" I blurted out.

"Oh yes, very sick. I have cancer in both lungs. It's a matter of weeks."

"Can you talk about it, Tom . . . ?"

"Sure. What would you like to know?"

"What's it like to be only 24 and dying?"

"Well, it could be worse."

"Like what?"

"Well, like being 50 and having no values or ideals, like being 50 and thinking that booze, seducing women, and making money are the real 'biggies' in life."

I began to look through my mental file cabinet under "S" where I had filed Tom as Strange. (It seems everybody I try to reject by classification God sends back into my life to educate me.)

"But what I really came to see you about," Tom said, "is

something you said to me on the last day of class. I asked you if you thought I would ever find God and you said, 'No!' which surprised me. Then you said, 'But he will find you.' I thought about that a lot, even though my search for God was not at all intense . . . at that time.

"But when the doctors removed a lump from my groin and told me it was malignant, I got serious about locating God. And when the malignancy spread to my vital organs, I really began banging bloody fists against the bronze doors of heaven. But God did not come out. In fact, nothing happened. Did you ever try anything for a long time with great effort and with no success? You get psychologically glutted, fed up with trying. And then you quit. Well, one day I woke up, and instead of throwing a few more futile appeals over that high brick wall to a God who may or may not be there, I just quit. I decided that I didn't really care . . . about God, about an afterlife, or anything like that.

"I decided to spend what time I had left doing something more profitable. I thought about you and your class, and I remembered something else you had said: 'The essential sadness is to go through life without loving. But it would be almost equally sad to go through life and leave this world without ever telling those you loved that you had loved them.' So I began with the hardest one, my dad.

"He was reading the newspaper when I approached him."

"Dad?"

"Yes, what?" he asked without lowering the newspaper.

"Dad, I would like to talk with you,"

"Well, talk."

"I mean . . . it's really important."

The newspaper came down *three slow inches*. "What is it?"

"Dad, I love you. I just wanted you to know that."

Tom smiled at me, and said with obvious satisfaction, as though he felt a warm and secret joy flowing inside of him: "The newspaper fluttered to the floor. Then my father did two things I could not remember him ever doing before. He cried, and he hugged me. And we talked all night, even though he had to go to work the next morning. It felt so good to be close to my father, to see his tears, to feel his hug, to hear him say that he loved me.

"It was easier with my mother and little brother. They cried with me too, and we hugged each other and started saying real nice things to each other. We shared the things we had been keeping secret for so many years. I was only sorry about one thing, that I had waited so long. Here I was, in the shadow of death, and I was just beginning to open up to all the people I had actually been close to.

"Then one day I turned around, and God was there. He didn't come to me when I pleaded with him. I guess I was like an animal trainer holding out a hoop, 'C'mon, jump through. C'mon, I'll give you three days . . . three weeks.' Apparently, God does things in his own way and at his own hour.

"But the important thing is that he was there. He found me. You were right. He found me even after I stopped looking for him."

"Tommy," I practically gasped, "I think you are saying something very important and much more universal than you realize. To me, at least, you are saying that the surest way to find God is not to make him a private possession, a problem-solver, or an instant consolation in time of need, but rather by opening yourself to his love.

"Tom, could I ask you a favor? Would you come into my present Theology of Faith course and tell them what you have just told me? If I told them the same thing, it wouldn't be half as effective as if you were to tell them."

"Oooh . . . I was ready for you, but I don't know if I'm ready for your class."

"Tom, think about it. If and when you are ready, give me a call."

In a few days Tommy called, said he was ready for the class, that he wanted to do that for God and for me. So we scheduled a date. The day came, but he never made it.[3]□

Truly, he who loses his life for my sake will find it. Triumph grows out of suffering.

Fifth Paradox of Story: Security is found in uncertainty.

For us, security is having all things in place, the future predicted with certainty and assurance, and being well provided for. But in religion one is called to let go of false securities (idols), and to take a journey to discover real security on a higher level. This is the paradox. So Aram left both his city and his name for the uncertainties of the Promised Land. Moses left the tense security of Egypt, where at least they were fed, for the wild uncertainty of the wild Sinai desert. Francis left the security of his father's house, his name, and even his own clothes in the village square of Assisi to go naked and exposed to the uncertainties of the Portiuncula. Ignatius left the security of his castle to dwell in a cave and there discover God.

And so it goes. For all seekers after truth, it is only in leaving the security and certainties of home and going into exile as it were, into the desert, to a world of uncertainty, that real security will be found. This was behind those changing of names, for example, from Aram to Abraham, and Simon to Peter. It is behind those old customs of those entering religious life changing their names and taking new ones. They are being invited to uncertainty. They are being asked not to lose their identities, but to find out who they truly are. Just as Tom Wolfe could go back to Ashville, North Carolina only after he left it.

☐ There was a poor rabbi who lived in the city of Krakow. He lived on the street of the Lost Angel, in the last hovel on that street with his wife and his four children. Since he was extremely poor, he dreamed every night of riches. But one night the dream was exceptionally vivid. He dreamed that underneath a bridge in the city of Warsaw there was a treasure. When he awoke in the morning, he excitedly told his wife and his children about his dream. He then packed food and clothes and set off on the long journey to find that bridge. He traveled many long days and long nights and finally arrived at Warsaw. It was just as the dream had pictured it—except for one thing. There was a guard on the bridge, a sentinel who paced back and forth. And so the poor rabbi, tired from his journey, fell asleep in the bushes. When he awoke, he rattled the bushes with his arm and the guard spied him.

"You there, come here!" He was a simple man and he did not run. He sheepishly came forward. The guard said, "What are you doing here?" The simple man who would not run was also a simple man who would not lie. He said, "I have dreamed that underneath this bridge there is a treasure and I have traveled many long miles to find that treasure and be rich." The guard said, "That is strange! Just last night I too had a dream. I dreamed that in the city of Krakow, on the street of the Lost Angel, in that last hovel on that street, where lives a rabbi and his wife and four children, there is buried behind the fireplace a treasure. But, it's just a dream. It can never be true. Now, you, you get out of here before I run you in. Never let me see you again!"

So the rabbi raced away and took the long journey back home. He went to his house on the street of the Lost Angel, went into his parlor, moved away the fireplace, dug underneath and found the treasure and lived happily ever after. □

One listener commented about this story, "While the treasure was at home all along, the knowledge of it was in Warsaw." Which is to say, we are not able to get in touch with our inner treasure directly but only if we venture *away* from home, "going to Warsaw" in order to be brought back to ourselves. Security is found in uncertainty.

And the tradition of this paradox has room to laugh at itself as well:

□The great rabbi was dying and, as we all know, deathbed wisdom is the best. So his students lined up, single file, to receive his last words. The most brilliant student was at bedside, the second most brilliant student behind him, and so on, till the line ended at a pleasant enough fellow who was a good room and a half away. The most brilliant student leaned over to the slowly slipping rabbi and asked, "Rabbi, what is the meaning of life?"

The rabbi groaned, "Life is like a cup of tea." The most brilliant student turned to the second most brilliant student. "The rabbi said, 'Life is like a cup of tea.'" And the word was whispered from student to student till it arrived at the pleasant enough fellow who was biting his nails a room and a half away. "What does the rabbi mean, 'Life is like a cup of tea'?" he asked. And the word was passed back up the line till the most brilliant student leaned once again over the slowly slipping rabbi. "Rabbi, what do you mean, 'Life is like a cup of tea'?" The rabbi shrugged, "All right, then, so maybe life is *not* like a cup of tea!" □

Sixth Paradox of Story: Prayer is offered through study.

Most of us tend to make a distinction between the scholar and the saint, to separate the intellectual and the spiritual life. As Tertullian of the third century remarked with disdain, "What does Athens have to do with Jerusalem?" Our equivalent today would be, "What does the Monastery have to do with Harvard?" The spiritual life and the academic life do not mix. And so we have kept them apart. We have fostered a strain of anti-intellectualism in spite of a sterling tradition of many systems of thought in our church. The result is that some intellectuals have a positive horror of the emotional and the pious in religion, and ordinary people have a suspicion of the theologian who does not pray. And both sides conclude that there is no connection between prayer and study. But in Judaism the scholar and the saint are one. Mind and heart are both pleasing to God. The academic and the spiritual can never be separated, which is why there is the Jewish saying that "No table is blessed if there is not a scholar to eat at it." For them an ignorant man cannot be pious. And that is why Teyve in *Fiddler on the Roof* really wants to be a rich man, so he can spend seven hours a day discussing the Holy Books with the Wise Men!

□One day the Rabbi Hersh had displeased God and was transported with his faithful scribe to a distant, uncharted island where they were promptly taken prisoners by a band of pirates. Never had the master been so stunned and so resigned.

"Master" the scribe pleaded, "do something, *say* something!"

"I can't," Rabbi Hersh said; "my powers are gone."

"What about your secret knowledge, your divine gifts. What happened to them?"

"Gone, forgotten," said the master, "disappeared, vanished. All my knowledge has been taken away; I remember nothing."

But when he saw his scribe's despair, he was moved to pity. "But," he said, "don't give up. We still have one chance. You are here and that is good. For you can save us. There must be *one* thing I taught you that you can remember. Anything—a parable, a prayer —anything will do."

Unfortunately, the scribe too had forgotten everything. Like his master, he was a man without a memory.

"You really remember nothing?" the master asked again, "nothing at all?"

"Nothing, master, nothing at all . . . except. . . ."

"Except what?"

"Except the first letters of the alphabet."

"Then what are you waiting for, man?" shouted the master excitedly. "Start reciting. Start reciting! Right now!"

Obedient as always, the scribe proceeded to recite slowly, painfully, the first of the sacred letters which together contain all the mysteries of the universe. "Aleph, beth, gimel, daleth. . . ."

And the master, impatiently, repeated after him, "Aleph, beth, gimel, daleth. . . ."

Then they started all over again, from the beginning, and their voices became stronger and clearer: aleph, beth, gimel, daleth . . . until the rabbi became so excited, so entranced, that he forgot who and where he was. And when the rabbi was in such ecstasy, nothing could resist him; that is well known.

Oblivious to the world, he transcended the laws of time and geography. He broke the chains and revoked the punishment, and master and scribe found themselves back home, unharmed, richer, wiser, and more nostalgic than ever before. □

Learning had saved them.

Such are the six paradoxes of story: catching us off guard, sneaking by our defenses, and opening us up to unexpected mystery. We adults who tend to disdain story somewhat and who extol only logic and "good sense" are currently being invited into narrative theology. We are being solicited to learn of God as the Bible wants us to, by way of the heart and the imagination. We are being asked to learn a language again that resonates with rich metaphor and image. Too long we have been trapped in the perfect square of a stylized laboratory where all things are subject to our measurements. We are being called back to the enticing and foreboding mansion of our Father's house where, becoming like little children (a stated condition), we are more vulnerable, more subjected to his cunning love. Like this:

□It once happened that a certain woman in Sidon lived with her husband for ten years without giving birth to a child. Following the law that in those days governed such matters, they went to Rabbi Simeon ben Yohai to arrange for a divorce.

The rabbi said to them: "By your life! Just as you had a festive banquet when you got married, so you should not separate now without first having a festive banquet."

They followed the rabbi's advice and prepared a great banquet. During the banquet the woman gave her husband more to drink than usual. When he was in high spirits, he said to his wife: "Little daughter, you may take with you out of my house whatever you like best; and then return to the house of your father."

What did she do?

After he had fallen sound asleep, she ordered her manservants and her maidservants to take him and the bed upon which he was sleeping to her father's house. About midnight the man awoke. When his intoxication had worn off, he looked around in astonishment. "Little daughter," he said, "Where am I?" "You are," she replied, "in my father's house." "But what business do I have in your father's house?" She replied, "Don't you remember your telling me last night that I may take with me whatever I like best when I return to my father's house? Nothing in the whole world do I like better than you!"

They then went again to Rabbi Simeon ben Yohai. The Rabbi prayed for her and the woman became pregnant.[4]☐

There is nothing in the whole world that God likes better than us. He is calling us back to our childhood (not childish) openness to mystery and love. Stories carry us back to the richness of our Father's house.

5

Christian Story Land Revisited

I t has been obvious so far that in our illustrations we have largely been tapping our Jewish heritage. This is for two reasons. One, that this *is* our heritage and we should be reminded of it. Remember that we have rightfully called the Bible a whole anthology of stories, which indeed it is. Secondly, Jewish tradition has not only kept up its storytelling propensities, but continually repeats the old ones, passes them on, adds to their depth, and so becomes a model for us. But does all this mean that we Christians have no story tradition of our own? Yes and no. We have no story tradition in the popularly perceived sense. Remember that we Catholic Christians are famous for our creeds, formulas, laws, and catechisms—not our stories. In the popular mind, these are what we stand for and what we pass on. We are thought to be a head-centered religion, full of doctrine, propositions, and creedal statements. That's our "image." And so, from this perspective, we have no or little story tradition.

But if we step back a little and think a moment, the answer is yes, we *do* have a marvelous (if hidden) story tradition as Christians. We just don't advert to it, but it's there, and there with power. The Christmas stories of Matthew and Luke, for example, are perennially awesome and compelling. Our story-liturgies of Holy Week and the liturgical year are rhythmic experiences of force and persuasion.

81

They give credence to William James's remark that "In the religious sphere, in particular, belief that formulas are true can never wholly take the place of personal experience." Yet, somehow, as we have indicated, these enduring story traditions are seen as separated from the mainstream of our religion, oddities to dress up the doctrine. But, of course, the truth is that these so-called oddities are the whole substance of the faith and the so-called doctrines are the dressing. We *do* have a substantive tradition of storytelling. In the past centuries it has fallen on hard times, but now it is being revived. Here, then, in this chapter is a brief review of some of Christianty's high points in story.[1]

In the Beginning

It is obvious that Christianity was founded on story from the beginning. We have noted this already. First, Christianity believed in the Bible, which means that it believed in and practiced a tradition of story reading and telling. Jesus himself was a true rabbi. Like his contemporaries, he told stories as a way of teaching. The first generations of Christians were nourished on these Jesus stories. They wanted to know them and wanted to pass them on. For many decades they orally told these stories around the Mediterranean basin until some of them, not all, were finally written down by the four gospel writers, those Good News proclaimers whose names we do not really know even though tradition has assigned to them the names of Matthew, Mark, Luke, and John. And what they recorded was a master who told "right-brain" stories designed to provoke both response and involvement. Only later, we recall, did theologizing come in, inevitably and rightfully. Only later did people systematically reflect on these stories, put them in some order, and draw theological conclusions from them. But we do well to remember that our religion is founded on the stories of Israel and of Jesus the Nazarene.

The Age of Martyrdom

After the Jesus stories, the stories of the first martyrs entered the tradition. There are those ancient names, for example, in our first Eucharist Prayer: Perpetua, Felicity, mistress and servant, both pregnant, who went to their deaths for Christ. There are Peter of the upside-down cross and Andrew of the X-shaped one. There are

John tossed in boiling oil, James beheaded. And there are Linus, Cletus, Clement, Sixtus, Cornelius, Cyprian, Lawrence, Chrysogonus, John, Paul, Cosmas, Damian and all the rest of these strange Greek and Latin names of persons who underwent various tortures and execution for the sake of the gospel. Their stories were told and retold, even to the point of legend, to encourage a struggling church. Their deeds, their miracles, their bravery, their deathbed songs were cherished stories. Such stories were whispered among many a small Christian community under siege. And where facts were meager, imagination supplied. Even a Joseph of Arimathea eventually got his story and, in the Coptic Church, story elevated the pernicious Pontius Pilate to sainthood!

Stories, by nature, grow. For example, a legend of Joseph of Arimathea says that he went to England to share the Good News, bringing with him the chalice used at the Last Supper, the Holy Grail. In the course of time, to protect this sacred cup from theft, he and his friends buried it at the bottom of a little mountain called Glastonbury Tor. It was winter when they did this. And to mark the spot, Joseph stuck his tall walking stick into the ground. And, lo! the walking stick, in the middle of winter, grew roots and leaves and flowers and turned into a hawthorn tree all in the same afternoon! And, instead of flowering every summer like hawthorns always do, this one flowers every winter. Anyway, as the centuries passed, as you may know, people forgot just what it was that the tree marked. And from this forgetfulness we get a whole new set of stories, the marvelous search for the Holy Grail by the Knights of the Round Table. But, literally, that *is* another story.

The Desert Fathers

A third stage in Christianity's storytelling tradition is the Sayings of the Desert Fathers. These sayings came from the beginnings of Christian monasticism of the fourth and fifth centuries. The great center here was Egypt, which by 400 was a land of hermits and monks, much like Ireland would become the land of saints and scholars. The Sayings of the Desert Fathers, very much like the old rabbinical stories, are a combination of folk wisdom, parable, anecdote, and the like. They eventually passed into the world of the Middle Ages and finally into pre-Revolutionary Russia, which, of all the nations, has cherished the stories, especially those told by the time-honored pilgrim.

The spiritual father, the Abba, is the hero here. Really knowing God from his own desert experience, he is the one who could most truly intercede for his sons. He discerned what was truly real in these words, and people hung upon his words as words of life. The common approach of pilgrims or his disciples to the Desert Father was the stereotyped request, "Speak a word, Father, that we might live." And we must note well that the word sought and the word spoken was not some kind of theological explanation of doctrine, not some kind of Socratic argument or the equivalent of modern counseling. Rather, the word here was conceived of as a word of relationship, a word that would give life to a pilgrim or disciple if it were received. These Desert Fathers were not spiritual directors as we understand the term. They simply were fathers who begot children in the Lord by their wisdom, experience, and holiness.

Their words, sparse and to the point, were totally uncompromising when it came to seeking holiness. And, in this regard, the Fathers were shrewd enough to distinguish the sincere from the merely curious. The shallow, the hangers-on, the celebrity seekers were given a bowl of soup and sent away. The genuine seekers, the true disciples, could stay all night and listen to and reflect on the word of the Desert Fathers. The Fathers, in their wit, referred to the former as "visitors from Babylon" and the latter as "visitors from Jerusalem"—good symbolic names!

The Fathers appeared eccentric at times but there was a deep purpose in what they did. If they went without sleep, it was because they were watching for the Lord. If they did not speak often, it was because they were listening to God. If they fasted, it was because they were fed by God's word. It was God that mattered to them and their asceticism was only a means to that end. Anyway, it was their sayings, passed around, collected, meditated on, that kept the Christian story tradition flourishing. Here are four of them: two on being balanced, a third on discipleship, and the fourth on the primacy of love.

☐ John the Dwarf announced to his brother monk one day that he was going off deeper into the desert by himself to live as an angel. After several days the monk heard a knock on his door. "Who is it?" he asked. A voice, weakened by hunger, replied, "John!" The monk inside responded (with some satisfaction, I suspect), "John it can't be, for John is now an angel and has no need of food or shelter." But, after a pause, he took the humbled John in and set him to work again in a more balanced life. ☐

☐Once the great St. Anthony was relaxing with his disciples outside his hut when a hunter came by. The hunter was surprised and mildly shocked and rebuked Anthony for taking it easy. It was not *his* idea of what a monk should be doing. But Anthony said, "Bend your bow and shoot an arrow." And the hunter did so. "Bend it again and shoot another," said Anthony. And the hunter did, again and again. The hunter finally said, "Abba Anthony, if I keep my bow always stretched, it will break." "So it is with the monk," replied Anthony. "If we push ourselves beyond measure we will break; it is right from time to time to relax our efforts." ☐

This story has a close kinship with Jesus' telling of the young would-be disciple who wanted to first go home and bury his father. "Let the dead bury their dead; you come and follow me." In other words, it is a story of a call to wholehearted discipleship.

☐Some monks were proposing to go to the city of Thebaid to look for some flax, and they agreed that as long as they were in the area they would look in on the famous Abba Arsenius. So a messenger came one day to the Abba and announced, "Some brothers who have come all the way from Alexandria wish to see you." The old Abba shrewdly asked why they came and learned that they were here mainly to look for flax at Thebaid. So he told the messenger, "They will certainly not see the face of Arsenius for they have not come primarily on my account but because of their work. Make them rest and send them away in peace and tell them that the old man cannot receive them."[2] ☐

This tale, by the way, is cousin to the story of the disciple who came to an Abba seeking God. The Abba then took the young man down to the river and held him under the water to the point where the young man sprang up gasping for breath. He demanded to know why the Abba did that and the Abba replied, "When you desire God with the same intensity you desire air, you will find him!"

Our final story, a charming one, is about the famous Abba Abraham:

☐Abba Abraham was a holy man and great ascetic. He had eaten nothing but herbs and roots for fifty years. He lived simply and very austerely in total self-discipline. Well, his brother died and left a niece, and there was no one to care for her. So Abba Abraham took her in and nourished and cherished her. She grew up to be beautiful both in body and in spirit. She followed Abraham, prayed with him, and was filled with grace. One day a wandering monk came to hear a word from Abba Abraham and was smitten by the beauty of his niece. While taking advantage of the hospitality offered by Abba Abraham, who was out visiting other monks, he was overcome by lust and raped the poor girl.

She was so mortified and ashamed that she stayed away from Abba Abraham and in fact fled to the city where, feeling so violated and disgraced, she became a prostitute. In vain did Abba Abraham look for his niece, until he heard one day that she was plying her trade at a certain tavern. Abba Abraham disguised himself as a military man with all the regalia, went to the tavern and ordered bottles of wine and rich meat. He ate to his heart's content, downed it all to the amazement of the onlookers. After he finished his dinner, he asked the keeper for the "wench" named Mary: "I have come a long way for the love of Mary." She was brought to him and she did not recognize this hard eating and drinking soldier. He grabbed her and she said coquettishly, "What do you want?" And he looked into her eyes and said, "I have come a long way for the love of Mary"—and she recognized her uncle and she wept bitterly and returned home with him. □

She became known as St. Mary the Harlot. But Abba Abraham — not in fifty years did he eat meat—did that night "for love of Mary!"

The Middle Ages

Here we find in the lives and legends of the saints, a kind of crowning glory of Christian storytelling. Such lives were often fascinating stories of conversion, conflict, and heroism, replete with miracle and wonder. Legends abounded, but we should not be put off by that. We should remember the power of myth, for legends are not without validity. Their power lies in the symbol of what they are saying. Listen, for example, to Joan Windham, a writer of charming lives of the saints for children:

Most of the things I have written about really did happen to the Saints, but some of the things I have written about are just Stories that people tell about them, and these Stories are called Legends. All the Legends *could* have happened if God wanted it that way, and that, I think, is how most of them got started. If the Saint was a Gardening kind of a man, there are Gardening Legends about him. If he was a man who lived in a Starving place then there are Legends about plenty of Food arriving very surprisingly. . . . And so, in this way, we find out what kind of person the Saint *was*, as well as what kind of things he *did*, by reading Legends about him.[3]

And she adds in another preface:

I'll tell you something . . . There is a legend about me. In my garden is a pond and once I dropped a trowel into it and I nearly fell in when I was fishing it out. A very little boy thought I had fallen in and every time he sees the pond he says, "Aunt Joan fell in there!" And the other people hear him, and although it was some time ago now, a good many people describe exactly what they think happened and how wet I was and how there were water lilies round my neck and all kinds of other stories! But they all believe that I really did fall into the pond. I didn't but it is just the sort of thing that I might have done![4]

What we are saying and what this excerpt says is that even legends about the saints have some symbolic truth to them and legends therefore are not to be disdained. It seems to me that one of the grave mistakes of Vatican II renewal was to leave the redesigning to "left-brain" intellectuals. It was and remains a loss that those in charge did not call in the "right-brain" prophets, pastors, and poets as a balance. *They* would have loudly proclaimed what symbolist Mary Douglas tells us all the time, that the symbolic power of things is important. The strict lenten fasting of old, for example, was far more valuable for what it meant than any use or abuse of it. The deleting of some of the saints as "unhistorical" or unreal overlooked the power of, say, a Christopher who carried Christ over the waters (the old symbol of chaos) to speak to us of overcoming our daily chaos. As a real person, Christopher may be unreal. As a legend, he says something to us.

Anyway, here is a delightful sampling that Joan Windham has written for children. "Sts. Gregory and Raphael" is a simple re-counting of an old story that forms part of the storytelling tradition of Christianity:

☐Once upon a time there was an Abbot called Gregory. He was clever at books and writings and things, and all the Monks that he was head of liked him. A long time after this story happened Gregory was the Pope and he was the one who sent St. Augustine to England to tell us about being Christians.

One day after breakfast, Gregory was writing in his Cell (a Cell is a Monk's bedroom), when somebody knocked at the door.

Rat! Tat! Tat!

"Come in!" said Gregory, busily writing. After a minute, when he had finished the word he was writing, he turned round, and there was a Sailor! Now, a Sailor is Rather Unusual to find in a Monastery. He was quite an ordinary-looking Sailor with wide trousers and a square collar and a Round Hat with H.M.S. Raphael written on it.

Gregory was very Surprised, but he was very polite, too, so he said:

"Good morning, what can I do for you today?"

"Oh, Father," said the Sailor, "I fell out of my ship and got Washed Ashore and my purse is in my Hammock and a Thousand Miles away, and the Captain he is sleeping there below and he never even noticed that I wasn't there!"

"I'm very sorry indeed to hear that, my poor sailor," said Gregory kindly, "and what are you proposing to do about money, now that you have no purse?"

"Well, Father," said the Sailor, "I thought perhaps you might give me a penny or so; I have always heard that you were such a Kind man."

"And so I will," said Gregory. "Just ring that Gong, will you, and someone will come."

"Yes, Father," said the Sailor, and he picked up the Gong Stick and hit the Big Black Gong, Bom! Bom! Bom!

In a minute he heard a Clappety noise coming down the stone passage. Clippety Clap! Clippety Clappety! He was wondering what it would be when round the Corner came running the Youngest Monk of All, and, as he ran, his sandals went Clippety Clap! Clippety Clappety! because they were both unfastened!

"Before we proceed, Brother," said Abbot Gregory (Monks often call each other Brother because they are all Sons of God, so they must be brothers); "before we proceed, Brother, why do your sandals have to be that way?"

"I'm very sorry, Father, indeed, Father," said the Youngest Monk of All, who was Out of Breath with Running, "but I was just drying my feet. They got Rather Wet while I was feeding the Chickens, when the Gong went, and I hadn't time to do up my Sandals because the Buckles are Rather Difficult. I must ask your Pardon."

"Granted," said Gregory kindly, "and now will you go and find a Penny out of my purse in the Study, please, Brother, and give it to this Unfortunate Sailor?"

"Yes, Father," said the Youngest Monk of All.

"Thank you, Father," said the Sailor, and they went away.

After Lunch Gregory was writing in his Cell (you know what a Cell is now), when somebody knocked at the door.

Rat! Tat! Tat!

"Come in!" said Gregory, busily writing. After a minute, when he had thought how to spell "Antediluvian," he turned round and there was the Sailor again!

Gregory was Very Surprised, but he was very polite, too, so he said:

"Good afternoon,what can I do for you this time?"

"Oh, Father," said the Sailor, "I've lost the Penny!"

"I'm very sorry indeed to hear that, my poor sailor," said Gregory kindly, "and what are you proposing to do, now that you have lost your Penny?"

"Well, Father," said the Sailor, "I thought perhaps you might give me another one. I always heard that you were such a Generous man."

"And so I will," said Gregory, "Just ring that Gong, will you, and someone will come."

"Yes, Father," said the Sailor, and he picked up the Gong Stick and hit the Big Black Gong, Bom! Bom! Bom! Bom!

After a minute he heard a Clappety noise coming along the stone passage, Clippety Clap! Clippety Clappety! and round the Corner came running the Youngest Monk of All, and, as he ran, his Sandals went Clippety Clap! Clippety Clappety! because they were both unfastened.

"Before we proceed, Brother," said Gregory (because they were both Sons of God); "before we proceed, why do your Sandals have to be that way?"

"I'm very Sorry, Father, indeed, Father," said the Youngest Monk of All, who was Out of Breath with Running, "But it was the Ducks, this time. I must ask your Pardon."

"Granted," said Gregory kindly. "But now, Brother, go and find a Penny out of my purse in the Study and give it to this Unfortunate Sailor."

"Yes, Father," said the Youngest Monk of All.

"Thank you, Father," said the Sailor, and they went away.

After Tea Gregory was writing in his Cell (do you remember what a Cell is?) when somebody knocked at the door.

Rat! Tat! Tat!

"Come in!" said Gregory, busily writing. After a minute, when he had Blotted his page, he turned round and there was the Sailor again.

Gregory was Very Surprised, but he was very polite, too.

"Good evening. What can I do for you now?"

"Oh, Father," said the Sailor, wiping his eyes with a Blue Pocket Handkerchief to match his Sailor's Suit, "I've lost the Penny again!"

"I'm very sorry indeed to hear that, my poor sailor," said Gregory kindly, "and what are you proposing to do for money, now that you have lost your Penny again!"

"Well, Father," said the Sailor, "I thought perhaps you might give me another one. I always heard that you were such a Forbearing man."

"And so I will," said Gregory, "just ring that Gong, will you, and someone will come."

"Yes, Father," said the Sailor, and he picked up the Gong Stick and hit the Big Black Gong, Bom! Bom! Bom! Bom! Bom!

After a minute he heard a Clappety noise coming down the stone passage, Clippety Clap! Clippety Clappety! and round the corner came running the Youngest Monk of All, and, as he ran, his sandals went Clippety Clap! Clippety Clappety! because they were both unfastened.

"Before we proceed, Brother," said Gregory (because of both being Sons of God); "before we proceed, why do your Sandals have to be that way?"

"I'm very sorry, Father, indeed, Father," said the Youngest Monk of All, who was Out of Breath with Running, "It's those Turkeys. Their field is wet. I must ask your Pardon."

"Granted," said Gregory kindly. "and now, Brother, go and find a Penny out of my purse in the Study and give it to this unfortunate Sailor."

"Yes, Father," said the Youngest Monk of All.

"Thank you, Father," said the Sailor, and they went away. But in a few Minutes they came back, again; and the Youngest Monk of All said:

"There isn't any more money, Father. There is only the Silver Dish that your Mother sends you your Porridge in."

Well, give that to the unfortunate Sailor, then," said Gregory, "perhaps he won't lose it so easily because it is bigger than a Penny."

"Yes, Father," said the Youngest Monk of All.

"Thank you, Father," said the Sailor, and they went away.

After Supper Gregory was writing in his Cell (what is a Cell?), when there came a knock at the door.

Rat! Tat! Tat!

"Come in!" said Gregory, busily writing. After a minute, when he found the stamps, he turned round and there was . . . who? No! not the sailor! Surely you have had enough of him by this time? No, there was a Very Beautiful Angel!

Gregory was very Surprised, but he was very polite, too, so he knelt down and said:

"Good evening! May I do something for you?"

"Good evening, you have already done something for me three times today," said the Very Beautiful Angel. "I am the Archangel Raphael, and I was pretending to be a sailor so as to see how Kind and Generous and Forbearing you were! And you were! Very! And God says that you can have your two Pennies and your Silver Porridge Dish back again, if you like, and that he is very pleased with you."

"Good," said Gregory. "Wasn't it lucky that I was Forbearing and everything just when you happened to come?"

"Yes," said the Archangel Raphael, "it was, rather."

Now, of course, there are two Special Days belonging to this Story. One belongs to St. Gregory whose Story that is, and his Day is on September 3rd. And the other Day belongs to St. Raphael-who-was-pretending-to-be-a-Sailor, and that is on September 29th.[5]

This kind of story persisted all through the Middle Ages. Perhaps these stories were an unconscious antidote to the abstract realism of scholastic philosophy and theology. If they were, then we should expect that Aquinas' philosophical genius had its counterpart in Dante's story genius. And I presume that it is not without meaning that Virgil, the symbol of reason, leads Dante to hell, but that Beatrice, the feminine, the dream, leads him from purgatory to heaven. And in those late Middle Ages, replete with violent contracts when, as Huizinga observes, "life bore the mixed smell of blood and roses," an exuberant story art flourished in the sculptures and stained glass of the great cathedrals and in the theater that had its origins there.

And animal stories. The late medieval peoples loved them: wild, grotesque, cunning animals. The animals were often symbols to all kinds of unconscious thoughts and the purveyors of insight and scriptural wisdom. For example, it was said that when a lioness gives birth, her cubs are born dead. They lie there dead for three days until the Father comes and breathes into their faces and makes them alive. Did you know that when the lion detects hunters, he uses his tail to sweep away his tracks? And that Jesus, the Lion of Judah, is not easily recognized but must be sought after only by faith? And do you know today's most famous lion of them all? Not the MGM trademark, but Aslan, C. S. Lewis' God-figure in his *Narnia Chronicles*:

Wrong will be right, when Aslan comes in sight,
At the sound of his roar, sorrows will be no more,
When he bares his teeth, winter meets its death
And when he shakes his mane, we shall have spring again.[6]

Here's a story of a saint *and* a lion:
□St. Jerome, that crotchety scholar of the fifth century, who fought with everyone and translated the Bible into Latin, lived in a cloister at Bethlehem with other monks. One day a wounded lion appeared, causing havoc and panic among all—except Jerome. The lion had a thorn in his paw and was in pain. Jerome took it out and the lion was grateful and became tame.

The problem was, what does one do with a tame lion? Some monks suggested that the lion keep watch over the donkey when he went to the woods to gather wood, although others said a lot of good that would do, for the lion sooner or later would pounce on the helpless donkey and eat him up. But this is what was decided and it worked out well. The lion kept the donkey safe from wild animals and protected him.

One day the lion fell asleep and some robbers came along, spied the donkey, and stole him. When the lion woke up and realized what had happened, he blamed himself and trotted guiltily back home. Some of the monks said, "Aha, we knew it. He ate the donkey!" But Jerome said, "No, we don't know for sure. Let's not be hasty to judge."

One day, while the lion was resting outside near a road, he saw a caravan—and who was leading it but the donkey! He was over-joyed. He ran to meet his old friend, scaring the hell out of the robbers. They fled to the nearest protection, which was the monks' cloister. They fell down at the feet of Jerome, begged his forgiveness if only they would be spared. They promised that whenever they came back that way they would provide for the monks.

The lion came in, lay down, stretched out, wagged his tail as if asking for forgiveness for a crime he never committed.

To this day, St. Jerome is pictured with a lion crouched at his feet. □

This is the very same Jerome who was a great lover of the pagan classics and, try as he might, could not keep his hands off of them. There is a story that says that Jerome was transported "in the spirit" (as Jerome tells it himself) before his eternal Judge. "Asked who and what I was, I replied, 'I am a Christian.' But he who pre-sided said, 'Thou liest; thou art a follower of Cicero and not of Christ. For where thy treasure is, there will thy heart also be.'" This sobering revelation did not, however, prevent Jerome from peeking into Cicero now and then.

The Post-Middle Ages to Modern Times

There is not much to say here. The rude laughter of the everyday peasant folk, the stories of Erasmus of the sixteenth century, the earthy *Table Talks* of Luther, and the insistence on the use of imag-ination by Ignatius of Loyola, all contemporaries, were in the line of the old storytelling tradition, but one that was clearly declining. Later on, to be sure, there were More's *Utopia*, Robert Foxe's *Book of Martyrs*, and Bunyon's *Pilgrim's Progress*. Kierkegaard told shocking tales to awaken the complacent Christian, but still storytelling, allegory, myth, legend—all fell on hard times. This was due to the steady impact of the so-called Enlightenment, which was supposed to usher in the perfect Age of Reason, industrialization, and rationalism. It was a time for the mind, for science, for logic, for progress. Inevitably, stories were put under the scrutiny of "scientific" examination and found wanting. Those who promoted the age of reason could not suppress stories entirely, so they did the next best thing: they relegated them to the children whose yet unscientific minds could tolerate them.

But there were some significant reactions to all this in the 1920s and 1930s. In fact, two movements kept alive the Christian story tradition and even furthered it. One group sought to promote the Christian value system through intrigue and entertainment. This group came up with the detective novel. The big names here are Dorothy Sayres and two Catholic converts: Msgr. Ronald Knox, and G. K. Chesterton who gave the world the beloved Father Brown detective stories.

The second movement involved a group that traced its roots back to a Presbyterian clergyman, George MacDonald who, in the mid-1800s, wrote delightful fantasy stories. He claimed, "I do not write for children, but for the childlike, whether of five, or fifty, or seventy-five." That is, he wrapped the Christian revelation in rich imagination for all who would seek the truth. It was of MacDonald that modern Christian storyteller, Madeleine L'Engle, said, "Surely, George MacDonald is the grandfather of us all—all of us who struggle to come to terms with truth through fantasy."

This second group was known as "The Inklings." They used to meet in an Oxford Pub to read and discuss one another's works. It was they who turned to fantasy and science fiction as a vehicle for the gospel. The famed trio included, first of all, Charles Williams (*All Hallows Eve, War in Heaven*), whom *Time* magazine has called "one of the most gifted and influential Christian writers England has produced this century." Rosemary Haughton describes Williams as one "in a class by himself. Where they [the other two Inklings] saw things head on, with beautiful and uncompromising clarity, Williams saw them all round and stereoscopic vision of unparalleled intensity. . . . He could not be popular, but those who catch fire from him are never the same again."[7]

Then there is C. S. Lewis (*Chronicles of Narnia* and so many other extraordinary works) who openly acknowledged his inspiration from MacDonald's writing: "It must be more than thirty years ago that I bought . . . [MacDonald's] *Phantasies*. A few hours later I knew I had crossed a great frontier. . . . What it actually did to me was to convert, even to baptize my imagination."[8]

Finally, there is J. R. R. Tolkien, author of *The Hobbit* series. These people have kept the Christian storytelling alive and more than alive. They have infused it with new vigor and no in-the-making narrative theology will be able to ignore them.

Still, they haven't quite succeeded in rescuing the story from the domain of children, but there are distinct signs that in our day some progress is being made.

> I think children need less convincing of the importance of story than do adults. To be adult has come to mean to be adulterated with rationalist explanations, and to shun such childishness as we find in fairy stories. I have tried to show in my work how adult and child have come to be set against each other: childhood tends to mean wonder, imagination, creative spontaneity, while adulthood, the loss of these perspectives. So the first task, as I see it, is restorying the adult—the teacher, and the parent and the grandparent—in order to restore the imagination, the primary place of consciousness in each of us, regardless of age.[9]

It's time to close this chapter with two short but very relevant stories that summarize what the past chapters have been about. They are a convenient transition to the next part of the gospel story. And I will include a brief commentary on each. The first is from that dark and strange writer, Franz Kafka, called "An Imperial Message."

☐The Emperor, so a parable runs, has sent a message to you, the humble subject, the insignificant shadow cowering in the remotest distance before the imperial sun; the Emperor from his deathbed has sent a message to you alone. He has commanded the messenger to kneel down by the bed, and has whispered the message to him; so much store did he lay on it that he ordered the messenger to whisper it back into his ear again. Then by a nod of the head he has confirmed that it is right. Yes, before the assembled spectators of his death—all the obstructing walls have been broken down, and on the spacious and loftily mounting open staircases stand in a ring the great princes of the Empire—before all these he has delivered his message. The messenger immediately sets out on his journey; a powerful, an indefatigable man; now pushing with his right arm, now with his left, he cleaves a way for himself through the throng; if he encounters any resistance he points to his breast, where the symbol of the sun glitters; his way is made easier for him than it would be for any other man. But the multitudes are so vast; their numbers have no end. If he could reach the open fields how fast he would fly, and soon doubtless you would hear the welcome hammering of his fists on your door. But instead how vainly does he wear out his strength; still he is only making his way through the chambers of the innermost palace; never will he get to the end of them; and if he succeeded in that, nothing would be gained; he must next fight his way down the stair; the courts would still have to be crossed; and after the courts the second outer palace; and once more, stairs and courts; and once more another palace; and so on for thousands of years; and if at last he should burst through the outermost gate—but never, never can that happen—the imperial capital would lie before him, the center of the world, crammed to bursting with its own sediment. Nobody could fight his way through here, even with a message from a dead man. But you sit at your window when evening falls and dream it to yourself.[10]□

A strange parable. Listen to Howard Schwartz's insight into it.

. . . it may be read as an allegory of the process any dreamer goes through in receiving messages from his unconscious mind. The king gives the message to the faithful messenger before his death, but because of the delay between the sending and the receiving, the messenger is delivering a message from a dead man. The dead king, then, may be viewed as a symbol of the past, which preserves itself in memory and the unconscious mind, and sends messages into the future through dreams, works of art, etc. The fact that the messenger never appears with the message, although the man who dreams it to himself is certain he is on the way, signifies the fact that we can never fully comprehend the meaning of such unconscious messages, never fully receive them, i.e., we can never pin down their symbolism to a precise interpretation. It has long been understood that any true symbol can never be fully comprehended, that the circle of its meaning continues to expand.[11]

And that, as we have been saying, is the power of the story. It reaches us in pre- and sub-conscious ways. It vibrates our dreams, fires the imagination, and resonates us into possibility and life's ultimate meaning. Every good story is an "imperial message."

The second story is from John R. Aurelio's delightful tale, "The Search"; and its message is clear for all those who would tell and listen to stories.

□ Once upon a time there was a great castle by the seashore. It was not like all the other castles you've heard or read about. It had many, many rooms the way all castles should, but they were not filled with furniture as you would expect. Instead all the rooms were filled with books. There were books everywhere—geography books, history books, science books, books on architecture, books on mathematics, books on politics and government, books on every subject you could imagine and some on subjects you never even thought about. There were books piled on tables and chairs, in the closets and hallways, and in some rooms they were stacked from the floor to the ceiling.

It was the castle of Count Corky who, people said, was the wisest man in the whole world. Indeed he was, for he had read every book in the castle. His fame and wisdom had spread far and wide over the earth. People came from everywhere to learn from this great wise man. Mighty kings and rulers came to him with their problems and he solved them all. Teachers and learned men came to him to discuss complex theories and left marveling at his wisdom. Even simple people came, for no difficulty was too great or too small for him to deal with. And when he was not busy solving the problems of the world, he read.

One day Count Corky left his books for a while to take a leisurely stroll along the seashore. He was deep in thought about matters too difficult for us to understand when he came upon the most unusual and amusing sight. There before him was a little fat boy. He had dug a hole in the sand and with a bucket in his hand was scooping water from the sea and pouring it into the hole. Again and again he filled his little bucket with water and poured it into the hole. Each time that he returned to the sea, the water in the hole would sink into the sand and disappear, leaving an empty hole once again. It was a funny sight to see the boy return patiently each time only to have the water quickly disappear—funny, that is, to anyone except Count Corky. To him it was just another problem to be solved. He wisely decided that what the boy was trying to do was impossible. He was much too busy and practical to watch this continue.

"What are you doing?" he asked the boy.

"Filling the hole," he answered without stopping.

"You can't do that," Count Corky proclaimed. "It's impossible."

"No, it's not," the boy replied, continuing his efforts.

"This is foolishness. You cannot fill that hole with water. The sand won't hold it. It will sink away and return to the ocean."

"If I wanted to," the boy said, "I can put the entire ocean into this hole."

"Nonsense," the count retorted, rather annoyed.

"I'll show you," said the boy. He then took his little shovel and walked to the edge of the sea. He began to dig a channel in the sand all the way to the hole. The water from the sea poured into the hole. "There! You see?" he asked. "The hole is now a part of the sea."

"Incredible!" exclaimed the count. "Incredible. How can such a young boy have such great wisdom?"

Before the count could continue, the boy interrupted him with the most amazing statement. "I'm not such a young boy. I'm over eight hundred years old."

"Impossible! That cannot be. No one lives that long."

"It's true, I tell you, and where I come from people live to be two and three thousand years old and older.

Wisdom had taught the count to think before he spoke. The boy must be telling the truth or else how could he possibly have out-smarted him. No one had ever done that—no one ever, and most especially not a child. He must know more about this boy.

"Where do you come from?" he asked.

"The Great Land," the boy said casually.

"Where is the Great Land and how do I get there?"

"Ask the book," he replied, pointing behind the count. The count turned to see where the child pointed. There, upon a rock, was a large black book. He walked over and picked it up. It was a truly peculiar book. It had only one page and that was blank. He turned back to question the boy but he was gone. He had disappeared.

"Now what?" thought the count. "Was it a dream?" It couldn't be, because he was holding a real book between his hands. Was it a hoax? That couldn't be either because the child was much too wise to be a normal child. If the child was real and what he said was true, then more than anything he wanted to visit that Great Land. Imagine what wisdom and knowledge he could learn from those who were older than the boy. He must go there. But how? "Ask the book," the boy had said. It seemed foolish to ask a book. One reads a book; one doesn't speak to it. This entire episode was foolish to him, but it had happened. He was certain of that. There was no other recourse left to him but to ask the book. He held it before him, his hands trembling.

"Where is the Great Land and how do I get there?" Slowly he opened the cover. The page that was blank before now had writing on it. Clearly and boldly it said, You must laugh. "What foolishness is this?" the count said out loud to himself. "Laugh? Who has time to laugh?"

Indeed, if the truth were told, it had been many, many years since Count Corky had laughed—not since he was a child. But then he had discovered books, and learning had become more important than playing and laughing. Yes, if the truth were told, he didn't remember how to laugh or know what was funny anymore. But the book said that to go to the Great Land he must laugh. More than anything now he wanted to go there. So he wisely decided that he must once again learn how to laugh.

He left the seashore and his castle for the first time in years and set about to learn how to laugh. He remembered that his books had taught him that children often laugh, so he wandered into the nearest village in search of children. Sure enough, he found children laughing and playing in the village square. He sat down quietly and watched them.

He noticed carefully that when they laughed, their eyes narrowed as if they were squinting, their cheeks puffed up and their lips curved upward. This was all very scientific to him. All of these things happened as they belched out a sound, Ha! No, it was many Ha's put together. The noise was Ha! Ha! Ha!

For several hours Count Corky observed the children before he tried it himself. He went off to where no one would see him, especially the children. He squinted his eyes, crinkled his nose, curled up his lips, puffed up his cheeks, and said "Ha!" The noise startled him. He looked around to see if anyone had heard him. This was embarrassing, he thought, but he did it again. Ha! The sound wasn't full enough. Ha! He repeated over and over again until it sounded right. When it sounded right he realized that he had forgotten about his eyes and nose and lips. He must get it all together. So he practiced and practiced until at last he had all the right gestures and just the right sound. It was a perfect imitation—not real laughter but as close as you could come without being real.

The count hurried back to the seashore and picked up the book. "I can laugh now," he said seriously. "Watch. Ha! Ha! Ha! Ha!" He had learned well, which was no surprise. After all, he was the wisest man in the world. "Now," he said to the book, "where is the Great Land and how do I get there?"

He opened the book and on the only page it now said, You must cry.

"Stuff and nonsense," the Count exclaimed. He said this because he did not know how to cry. It had been so long since he had last cried that he could not even remember what to do. But the thought of the wise boy and the Great Land made him willing to try.

Once again the Count ventured into the village. He certainly knew what the dictionary said about crying. The difficulty was that he had to do it. This meant that he would have to observe people very carefully again.

Count Corky was very intelligent so he was a quick learner. He saw that when people cried their eyes became narrow, squinting in the same way as when they laughed. Only now tears flowed. This was rather difficult for him to manufacture but in time with much practice he was able to do so. Having his lips curve downward, the opposite from laughing, was no problem at all. He could even get his whole body to move up and down, as happens when you have the hiccups. It was a perfect imitation. Not the real thing, but as close as you could come.

He hurried back to the seashore. "I can cry now," he said, holding the book before him. At once he began to sob, with many tears, like someone who was really crying.

"There! Now—where is the Great Land and how do I get there?" He opened the book. It said, You must sing.

"Enough!" he shouted. "How much more of this must I endure? Is there no end to these ridiculous requirements?" But the words on the page were quite clear. He must sing. If he wished to go to the Great Land and learn of its treasures and wisdom, he must sing. He returned to the village.

He had to admit that singing was easier to learn than the other two. Singing was mathematical, with rules and scales. He could not learn the sound from books, so he went to a music teacher.

It did seem foolish to learn—Do, Re, Mi, Fa, Sol, La, Ti, Do— but once he learned the scale, he mastered it quickly. He had a perfect ear for pitch and tone. Singing, however, was another thing. He could sing well, almost flawlessly, but there was no real feeling in it. It was a good imitation, as close as you could come to the real thing. He hurried back to the seashore.

Holding the book before him, proud of his accomplishments, he shouted "I can laugh. Ha! Ha! Ha! I can cry Boo Hoo! Boo Hoo! And I can even sing. Do, Re, Mi, Fa, Sol, La, Ti, Do. Now where is the Great Land and how do I get there?" This time when he opened the book it said, "Take hold of me and jump!" The statement startled him. At once his keen mind began to question it. Jump? Jump where? Only the ocean was before him. Could it mean that the Great Land was at the other end of the great ocean? What else could it mean? After all his efforts of learning how to laugh and cry and sing, the answer was that simple. If only the book had told him that at the beginning he could have saved a lot of time and wasted effort. But no matter. Now he knew the answer and that was what was important. The Great Land was beyond the Sea. At last he could go there. He had only to take hold of the book and jump.

This last thought brought him back to his senses. Jump? Jump where? Into the ocean? Nonsense! He would drown. The ocean was far too large to attempt to jump over. No matter. Now that he knew where it was, he would use his own intelligence to decide how to get there. The first and most obvious solution was to swim. He put the book down and hurried to his castle.

He at once read all his books on swimming and quickly taught himself how to do it. He then waded out into the sea as far as he could go and began to swim. He swam for hours, but when the sea grew turbulent, he knew that he could not make it, so he returned to shore.

He decided then that he must make a boat and sail across to the Great Land. So he read and learned and made himself a fine boat. He set sail across the ocean, but before long a violent storm arose and forced him back to shore.

There was only one other way, he thought. He must fly across. Again he read his books and then built himself an airplane. He felt confident that this time he would succeed. But the ocean was far bigger than he expected, and he had barely enough fuel to get him back safely to shore.

He was exhausted and angry. There was no way he could

devise to get across the ocean to the Great Land. He picked up the book once again to make sure of its reply. It was still there, "Take hold of me and jump." He had tried everything else but what the book said. His wisdom had failed him. If he wanted to go there he must do what the book commanded.

Count Corky stood at the edge of the sea with the book clenched in his arms. Reason told him that to jump would mean that he would drown. But he also knew that he could never be satisfied again unless he learned the secret of the little boy's wisdom. He closed his eyes for fear of what was about to happen. Then he took a deep breath, held it—and jumped.

He waited to hear himself, feel himself splash into the sea, but it didn't happen. He waited but it didn't happen. He had the peculiar feeling that he was floating. He knew that it was impossible for him to float but the feeling was unmistakable. He was floating. He wanted to open his eyes but he was afraid that if he did, he might plummet down into the sea. He kept his eyes closed tightly while he continued to float.

It was a wonderful feeling, he thought—unlike anything he had ever experienced in his whole life. It was impossible and yet it was happening. No book, no scholar, no wisdom could ever explain how he could float through the air, but that's what he was doing. He held desperately to the book while he floated and floated.

At long last he felt himself come back to earth. He could feel it firmly beneath his feet again. He knew that when he opened his eyes, he would be in the Great Land. This was what he wanted and had worked for more than anything else in his whole life. He wanted to enjoy his first glimpse of it and remember it always. He slowly opened one eye, then the other. He looked ahead and then around him in utter amazement. He was standing in exactly the same spot where he had started from. He turned around again and again disbelieving. He was in the same place. He had gone nowhere. It was all for nothing.

For the first time in many years he was confused—confused and disappointed. There was no Great Land; therefore there could have been no little child. It must have been his overworked mind playing tricks on him. "Strange!" he thought. "What a strange experience!" Lost in deep contemplation, he turned away from the seashore and walked back toward his castle.

The happy sounds of playing children broke into his reverie. There was a group of them chasing a butterfly down the beach. Jumping, laughing, swinging their arms wildly in pursuit of their elusive prey, the children approached the Count. At first he paid no attention. His mind was far too disciplined to allow himself to be distracted. But very strangely his concentration began to falter. He was intrigued by their antics. The more he watched them, the more absorbed he became in their activity—until, at last, unable to remain aloof any longer, as if he had lost complete control of his senses, the Count joined the children gambolling merrily after the butterfly.

Quite suddenly he began to laugh. It was a strange sound coming from him. It was different too from his learned laugh. This one seemed to come from deep down inside him. He shyly put his hand up to his mouth trying to conceal it, but it would not be suppressed. Another laugh burst forth through his lips, then another, and another. The very sound of himself laughing made him laugh all the more. He could no longer contain himself. Soon he lost all control. He doubled over in uncontrollable hysteria, hands on his knees gasping for breath. The feeling was wonderful, exhilarating.

The butterfly, still pursued by the children, made an abrupt change in direction and began flying back toward the Count. The children in front turned quickly to follow after it but were bumped by those coming from behind. They fell to the sand, startled and hurt. Some of them began to cry. Count Corky saw them in distress and came over to comfort them. Then another strange thing happened. Seeing the children so hurt and so upset, and watching the tears streaming down their sad faces, he found himself moved to great compassion. Again a sense of strangeness came over him. His eyes began to fill, then overflow as real tears trickled down his cheeks—then more, and more. He was crying. For the first time in his life he was crying.

To some people, I suppose, it would look strange to see a grown man sitting on the sand with children and crying. But it's not so strange to children.

The Count knew that he must do something to change the situation. "What can we do?" he thought. Then, in an instant he jumped to his feet and shouted, "I know. Let's sing." Before the children could make up their minds about if they would rather sit and cry, the Count pulled them to their feet and got them all standing in a circle holding hands. "London Bridge is falling down," he sang. "Falling down." The children automatically started circling. "Falling down." They began to move faster and faster as the nursery rhyme picked up speed. "London Bridge is falling down." Now they were all singing—singing and circling and falling happily to the ground. Count Corky was like a child among children, singing, laughing and playing as he had never done in his entire life.

Then it struck him. There in the midst of the playing children, it at last occurred to him. He jumped into air at the discovery, shouting, "I know now. I know." Running down the beach to where the book lay, he picked it up and held it before him. "Where is the Great Land?" he repeated as he had so many times before. "And how do I get there?"

He opened the book. This time he was neither anxious, nor disturbed, nor even curious. He had the expression of one who knew.

"I knew it! I knew it!" he screamed happily. "I knew it!" he laughed jumping up and down. "I knew it!" he shouted as he tossed the book high into the air and danced off merrily back to his castle.

The book lay open on the sand. On the page it read: "You are there."[12]

The simplest and shortest commentary on this story is a line from the gospel: "Unless you become like little children you cannot enter the Kingdom of God." To be affected by this story you must surrender yourself to it on its terms, like a child. There is a leap of faith required here. We, the "left-brain" Count Corky, must learn the magic of letting go to our "right-brain" imaginative selves, that tender, feminine side of ourselves that will more readily lead us to truth beyond truth.

Maybe the best attitude in all of this is summed up by C. S. Lewis' Mr. and Mrs. Beaver who hope for the appearance of Aslan the Lion.

Susan asks, "Is he—quite safe? I shall feel nervous about meeting a lion."

"That you will, dearie, and no mistake," said Mrs. Beaver, "If there's anyone who can appear before Aslan without their knees knocking, they're either braver than most or else just silly."

"Then he isn't safe?" said Lucy.

"Safe?" said Mr. Beaver ". . . 'Course he isn't safe. But he's good."[13]

Stories aren't safe. But they're good.

6

Scripture As Story

*R*obert Alter opens his excellent book, *The Art of Biblical Narrative*, with these words:

> What role does literary art play in the shaping of biblical narrative? A crucial one, I shall argue, finely modulated from moment to moment, determining in most cases the minute choices of words and reported details, the pace of narration, the small movements of dialogue, and a whole network of ramified interconnections in the text.[1]

If this is so, if the biblical narratives are truly artful and a work of craft, then we should suspect that not only are we dealing with stories when we pick up the Bible, but that the stories themselves conceal more than they reveal. Further, we should be prepared to apply the same skills in unlocking this concealment, as we have so far in the previous secular stories we have seen. So let us proceed immediately to an example. Fortunately, we have at hand not only the ever-appealing Christmas story but also the artistry of novelist Frederick Buechner to disclose the story's meaning. Here is a long, contemporary, and poetic quotation from him, a fine summary of all that we have so far meant to say on storytelling:

> We live in a skeptical age where the assumption that most of us go by, consciously or otherwise, is that nothing is entirely real that cannot

somehow be verified by science. It seems to me at best a dubious assumption, but it is part of the air that we breathe, so let us be as skeptical as our age about this story of Christmas. Let us assume that if we had been there that night when he was born we would have seen nothing untoward at all. Let us assume that the darkness would have looked very much like any darkness. Maybe there were a few stars, the same old stars, or the moon. For a long time the only sound perhaps was the rough, rapid breathing of the woman in labor. If the tradition of the manger is accurate, there was the smell of hay, the great moist eyes of the cattle. The father was there, possibly a shepherd or two attracted by the light, if there was any light. There was a last cry of pain from the mother as the child was born, and then the cry of the child. In the distance maybe the lonely barking of a dog. The mother stares up at the rafters from where she is lying, too exhausted even to think of the child. Someone has taken him from her to wrap him up against the cold and darkness of the world. Maybe a mouse burrows deeper into the straw.

Maybe that is all we would have seen if we had been there because maybe that or something like that was all that really happened. In the letters of St. Paul, which are the earliest New Testament writings, there is no suggestion that the birth of Jesus was accompanied by any miracle, and in the gospel of Mark, which is probably the earliest of the four, the birth plays no part. So a great many biblical scholars would agree with the skeptics that the great nativity stories of Luke and Matthew are simply the legendary accretions, the poetry, of a later generation, and that were we to have been present, we would have seen a birth no more or less marvelous than any other birth.

But if that is the case, what do we do with the legends of the wise men and the star, the shepherds and the angels and the great hymn of joy that the angels sang? Do we dismiss them as fairy tales, the subject for pageants to sentimentalize over once a year come Christmas, the lovely dream that never came true? Only if we are fools do we do that, although there are many in our age who have done it and there are moments of darkness when each one of us is tempted to do it. A lovely dream. That is all.

Who knows what the facts of Jesus' birth actually were? As for myself, the longer I live, the more inclined I am to believe in miracle, the more I suspect that if we had been there at the birth, we might well have seen and heard things that would be hard to reconcile with modern science. But of course that is not the point, because the Gospel writers are not really interested primarily in the facts of the birth but in the significance, the meaning for them of that birth just as the people who love us are not really interested primarily in the facts of our births but in what it meant to them when we were born and how for them the world was never the same again, how their whole lives were charged with new significance.

Whether there were ten million angels there or just the woman herself and her husband, when that child was born the whole course of history was changed. That is a fact as hard and blunt as any fact. Art, music, literature, our culture itself, our political institutions, our whole understanding of ourselves and our world—it is impossible to conceive how differently world history would have developed if that child had not been born. And in terms of faith, much more must be said because, for faith, the birth of the child into the darkness of the world made possible not just a new way of understanding life but a new way of living life.

Ever since the child was born, there have been people who have gotten drunk on him no less than a man can get drunk on hard liquor. Or if that metaphor seems crude, all the way down the twenty centuries since that child was born, there have been countless different kinds of people who in countless different kinds of ways have been filled with his spirit, who have been grasped by him, caught up into his life, who have found themselves in deep and private ways healed and transformed by their relationships with him so much so that they simply have no choice but to go on proclaiming what the writers of the Gospels first proclaimed: that he was indeed the long-expected one, the Christ, Wonderful Counselor, Mighty God, Everlasting Father, Prince of Peace—all these curious and forbidding terms that Christians keep on using in their attempt to express in language one thing and one thing only. That in this child, in the man he grew up to be, there is the power of God to bring light into our darkness, to make us whole, to give a new kind of life to anybody who turns toward him in faith, even to such as you and me.

This is what Matthew and Luke are trying to say in their stories about how he was born, and this is the truth that no language seemed too miraculous to them to convey. This is the only truth that matters, and the wise men, the shepherds, the star, are important only as ways of pointing to this truth.[2]

Here beautifully told, is all that we have been saying in the first five chapters, only applied to Sacred Scripture. The evangelists, for example, were not journalists working for the local newspaper. They were out-and-out propagandists trying to convey the experience and meaning of Jesus Christ. Mark, for instance, likely the first of the evangelists, boldly opens his gospel with the words, "The beginning of the gospel of Jesus Christ, the Son of God." How does one explain the "Son of God"? What can this possibly mean? In response, Mark and the others had no choice really but to turn to that language that speaks truth beyond truth: myth, poetry, and story. After all, ordinary reality is always larger than our capacity to word it accurately. Even so-called objective reporting implicates more meaning than can be said. How much more, then, when speaking about the mysteries of life?

Paul Hofmann, a long-time correspondent for the *New York Times* on Roman affairs, has written a book of his collected wisdom and insights on the foibles and fancies of that Eternal City. In one chapter, he tells of the state dinner held at the headquarters of the fabulous Knights of Malta in a sixteenth-century palace on the Via Condotti. All the costumed grand dignitaries are there awaiting the evening's guest of honor: Father Pedro Arrupe, superior general of the Jesuits. He is late. When he does arrive, this slightly-built ascetic is wearing a gray civilian suit, an old, ill-fitting jacket, a white shirt with a badly pressed collar and a dark necktie.

> The knights are flabbergasted. What message does the superior general of the powerful Society of Jesus mean to convey by showing up without black cassock . . . ? Does Father Aruppe by his modest, not to say threadbare, secular attire intend to hint that he doesn't think much of the knights' aristocratic and archaic pretensions . . . ? The almost ostentatious plainness of the Jesuit chief's appearance when he paid an official visit to the grand master will be endlessly discussed in embassies, curial offices, and convents throughout the city.[3]

Indeed! Everyone realizes that more was meant than what was on the surface. There was more than meets the eye, as we say. Intent, symbol, interpretation are all at work; not to mention the eventual myth-story that will emerge from this incident. So it is with the scriptures. There is an art here coaxing intent, symbol, and interpretation. And there is no doubt about art's form: it is story. The scripture, dealing as it insists with God and mystery, *must* take the form of story with story's natural expressions of epic, legend, poetry, myth, metaphor, and all the other ways that it intends to supply, not information, but meaning, inspiration, and commitment. Therefore, John Westerhoff is right when he observes:

> The Scripture contains the sacred myths of the Christian community. They ought not to be reduced to rational discourse. The Bible is poetry plus, not science minus. . . . For too long we have attempted to understand reality solely through reason and have forgotten the importance of symbolic narrative, metaphor, and sacred story. Christianity is a historical, but also a metaphorical, religion.[4]

Let's go back to the Christmas saga. Frederick Buechner made it plain that the literal, surface story line was not nearly as important as its implicit revelation. The Christmas story is a fabulous account of what this Child meant and means to all of humankind. He is one who has made a fantastic difference and only the language of poetry could convey that. Scripture scholar Raymond Brown says the same thing in his thorough study of Matthew and Luke's infancy narratives in *The Birth of the Messiah:*

> It is the central contention of this volume that the infancy narratives are worthy vehicles of the Gospel message; indeed, each is the essential Gospel story in miniature. The appreciation for them among ordinary Christians may in part reflect sentimentality, as well as the fact that they are stories well told. But on a much deeper level it reflects a true instinct recognizing in the infancy narratives the essence of the Good News, namely that God has made Himself present to us in the life of His Messiah who walked this earth, so truly present that the birth of the Messiah was the birth of God's Son. I maintain that genuine biblical criticism, for all the historical problems that it raises, sets this claim in clear perspective.[5]

Notice that Brown speaks of the Christmas story's "much deeper level" and that it contains "the essence of the Good News." That's the way the whole Bible is: stories concealing much deeper levels, colorful narration wrapped around the essence of mystery. The Bible is a book rich in metaphor and imagination and appeals to head and heart. And, in fact, the language of the New Testament itself is so multileveled "because it conveys the truth precisely in and by its evocation of feeling . . . it is first order language, the language of imagination. . . . This is why the text must be read not just with the critical intelligence but with the whole mind and heart, that is, with the imagination in full operation."[6]

All this means too that we must be prepared for a wide diversity of story forms and acknowledge that no one form will contain all the possibilities of revelation. God's story will explode in a wild variety of ways. In this regard, it might be helpful to think of scripture in terms of the arts. That is, in your mind's eye, take the printed words off the biblical page and put them into the plastic arts, say, sculpture and painting. And what do you get? You get Michelangelo's *Pieta* and Mestrovic's *Virgin and Child*, the same biblical people in different interpretations. Or, as we might say, two stories of the same event. You get a crucifixion scene by Dali that is dazzlingly different from the one by Valesquez. There's El Greco's powerful painting of a sobbing Peter and the awesome Rembrandt of the two Emmaus disciples at the moment their eyes were opened and they recognized the Lord. How different, yet how compelling and how truthful, they all are in all of their diversity. But this has always been so, as anyone knows who is familiar with the splendors of illuminated manuscripts, stained glass windows, and the incredible sculptures—those three-dimensional Bible stories—of the medieval cathedrals.

The point I am trying to convey, then, is threefold: that scripture is story; that story, like all art forms, is a free expression of something deeper; and, finally, that story, like all art forms, is highly pluralistic. As in art, there are many diverse, imaginative weaves in story's fabric. In announcing the mystery there must be metaphor, parable, poetry, legend, and all the rest. And more than one way to tell it. Which is why we really do not have a doctrine, say, of creation. We have stories of creation.

This is why, then, we really cannot even speak of strict history in the Bible if we mean an "objective" account of what really happened. History, too, becomes an art form. History too becomes legitimate material for the biblical storyteller's craft. And, therefore, we must go further, perhaps to the scandal of the reader, and say that if there is any objective history (whatever that is) in the Bible at all, it must be "storified" history in the same way that Shakespeare's history is "storified" history. So:

> There is indeed a Julius Caeser, but Shakespeare's play is not bound by the historical record. Rather historical data are selected and adapted to bring out Shakespeare's conception of human destiny. Similarly, historical data may be used in Exodus but are taken up and refash-

ioned in the light of the author's conception of Israel's origin and destiny. In the same way, the gospels give us a portrait of Jesus but few details in that portrait can be established as factual. If then historical material is not predominant, with fictional elements in a minor role, but rather the opposite is the case, it would seem that the paradigm should not be "history" but "story." In short, when we read a biblical text, our initial assumption should not be that it is historical but rather that it is a fiction which may or may not incorporate historical elements.[7]

If this is too much to absorb at this point, go back and read Frederick Buechner's commentary on the Christmas story. You will see once more that we are dealing with, not a newspaper, but a book; not a treatise, but a story; not an accounting, but a meaning: a meaning wrapped around real events but interpreted to show forth the writer's grand scheme to divine intervention and compassion. Robert Alter, whom we mentioned, adds his voice:

> As odd as it may sound at first, I would contend that prose fiction is the best general rubric for describing biblical narrative. Or, to be more precise . . . we can speak of the Bible as *historicized* prose fiction. . . . Let me hasten to say that in giving such weight to fictionality, I do not mean to discount the historical impulse that informs the Hebrew Bible. The God of Israel, as so often has been observed, is above all the God of history: the working out of His purposes in history is a process that compels the attention of the Hebrew imagination, which is thus led to the most vital interest in the concrete and differential character of historical events. The point is that fiction was the principal means which the biblical authors had at their disposal for realizing history.[8]

At this point some examples may be helpful. Take the story of Adam and Eve. Their story in Genesis begins with the uncultivated land. Adam is made, not from nothing, but from pre-existing materials, the dust of the earth. Then there are two trees mentioned in the garden Adam inhabited, the tree of life and the tree of knowledge of good and evil. And right here we understand that we are not dealing with any kind of trees known to botany. Right here we get the first unmistakable clue that we are not in the realm of history but in the realm of story. And a few lines later we come upon a talking serpent, clearly too the stuff of story land.

Eventually, as we know, Adam and his newly-formed helpmate, Eve, eat the fruit and there is disaster. They attempt to hide from God who comes for his daily walk in the garden. They are found and curses ensue, curses describing accurately the common form of life as known in ancient Israel. The curses are not scientifically correct; snakes, for example, do not eat dust. . . . But the curses *do* tell us of the common anxieties of life. Man does work by the sweat of his brow. Women do have pains in childbirth. In a word, we have here a story, not a history. We have a story trying to explain why life is so hard. And we further sense that we're dealing with a story here when we recognize that Adam and Eve are not proper names at all, but simply the generic terms for man and woman. And the "death" penalty spoken of is obviously not physical death—after all, the Bible says that Adam lived to be 930!—but the moral death of expulsion from the pristine happiness of the Garden, from all that is ideal.

The story of Adam and Eve is one of high imagination and power. Adam and Eve—Everyman and Everywoman—are persons with whom we can identify. And like any good story, its elements can be multileveled and we can discover many meanings in them. We still do work by the sweat of our brows. This remains a world where we are forever lured by temptation. We know shame. We seek to hide. We all have experience of limit (represented by God's command). The Adam and Eve story does reflect life as it is, and this accounts for its perennial popularity. Their story illumines our story.

We might say the same thing about the Exodus story written at the time of the Jewish return from the fifth-century exile. The Exodus easily becomes a paradigm, a living figure of speech, a motif for any peoples journeying to freedom under harsh and repressive conditions. We still use the terms in song and film and in common speech. The Exodus has become not so much a history as a way of articulating a specific area of human experience. And to this extent, the Exodus theme grows and reshapes and deepens and eventually becomes a vital point of reference contributing to the ongoing unfolding of revelation.

This last point is worth noting. The Exodus and all the other themes are not the last word or the whole of revelation. They are parts of the whole and agents of wholeness. The biblical themes fall into tension with one another to contribute to a larger fullness. I say this because each biblical theme, each story is, in isolation, incomplete. And to this extent it can even be contradictory. For instance, it is clear that the books of Job (14:13-22) and Sirach (Ecclesiasticus) deny an afterlife that later biblical books believe in. When these two books were inserted into the Hebrew canon—and remember, until that point they were joined to others such as Daniel, Isaiah, II Maccabees and Wisdom, which *do* speak of an afterlife — we have two opposites joined. Then the whole bundle was taken into the official Christian canon, which certainly professes belief in an afterlife. When this process occurs, then the older, incomplete stories such as Job and Sirach, become stepping stones to a larger truth. Which is why, by the way, it is always proper and correct to speak of the overall biblical meaning of the whole Bible rather than an isolated meaning of a particular section or individual book.[9]

Let us move to the New Testament for two more examples. We want to see how the scholars (exegetes) get beneath the obvious story line, how they get through to the writer's creative imagination, to the story's deeper meanings. "Three days later there was a wedding feast at Cana of Galilee" (John 2:1-12). So begins a beloved and familiar story where, at his mother's request, Jesus does his first "sign." He turns the water in six stone jars into wine—anywhere from 120 to 180 gallons of it. On the surface we have an episode of compassion, one that rescues an embarrassed bride and groom from a social disgrace. But there is obviously more to it than that. It is a story of much deeper meanings, and those who know the writer's mind and his fondness for symbols are justified to look for something deeper here. This is why a popular middle-of-the-road Protesant scholar, William Barclay, remarks, "We must always remember that beneath John's simple stories there is a deeper meaning which is open only to those who have eyes to see. In all his gospel John never writes any unnecessary or insignificant detail. Everything means something and everything points beyond."[10] And Catholic scholar George McRae reminds us too that we must read this story of the wedding at Cana "on a symbolic level and not merely on a story level."[11]

There are, for instance, six Jewish water jars. In the ancient biblical symbol system, seven is the number of perfection and fullness. Obviously, then, six is less; six is imperfect. So John is saying, story-fashion, that the Jewish law, which requires the jars, is inadequate. It needs Jesus to bring it to fulfillment. And when Jesus does do this, we wind up with almost 180 gallons of wine, a symbol of the overflowing graces of the new messanic era that Jesus inaugurates. Then, too, the fact that the story is situated within a wedding feast recalls that a wedding is a biblical symbol of God's union with his people, now manifest in Jesus' presence. "You have kept the good wine until now!" is less a commentary on its quality than a commentary on the joy that at last the Messiah has come. Even the opening words, "three days later," refer to the death and resurrection of Jesus that ushers in the new messanic times. So this is really the way the sacred writer intended his story: a vehicle, imaginatively done, to reveal a truth beyond the truth, a meaning beyond the obvious.

Take, briefly, another gospel story, the story of Jesus dismissing the crowd he had just fed with the loaves and fishes. He goes off to pray alone and later walks across the water toward the boat struggling against head winds. Peter, reassured that it is no ghost he sees, gets out of the boat to meet Jesus halfway; but he falters only to be rescued by a reproving Jesus, "O man of little faith, why did you doubt?" Again, from what the scholars know of Matthew's interest, namely, his high stress on the church, they sense that there is a story beneath the story here.

For instance, the apostles are in a boat, clearly a symbol of the church. The church is threatened by the turbulence of discord and dissension because Jesus is gone (back to the Father) and they are alone and leaderless. But, Matthew would say, the church is not alone at all. When it is in its worst straits, the Lord is there to save it. Just have faith. Don't be like Peter (often a representative figure of all the brethren) and doubt the power of the risen Lord.

Nor should it go unnoticed that the waters themselves are the ancient symbol for chaos and the very abode of the evil serpent or dragon. (Note that the old biblical sea monsters, the Leviathan or Rahab, dwell in the waters; this is reflected in our own times in the Loch Ness Monster in Scotland and "Nessie" in Lake Champlain: the Evil One inhabits the waters.) For Jesus to walk on the waters is to say that he has overcome the Wicked One; he is victor, have no fear. No wonder all those in the boat (that is, the church) fall down in adoration.

And so it goes. Stories have a point beyond the mere surface line. Stories, even the biblical stories, are mythological and inherently imaginative in that they point to much more than meets the eye; they are out to elicit a response from both head and heart.

When we allow the Scriptures to speak through their images and symbolic language, we take their evocative value into account. This means that we have to recognize that the Scriptures can have a multiplicity of meanings. Ideas can be defined, but not images. Sensitivity to images requires that we abandon efforts to control what people think. This does not mean that we have to give up our creed, but it does mean that we must give the creed life and flesh. To say concreteness is to say diversity. Each one can then contribute from the richness of his or her imagination to a truly ecclesial incarnation of biblical images.[12]

So, the Bible is a storybook, relating to us in a lively and accessible idiom. None of us has to be a theologian to appreciate the story of the Good Samaritan and no one, however degreed, has a claim on all of its meaning. Stories like the Good Samaritan do not give us facts nor do they really give us proofs for anything. Instead, they do what they are meant to do: provide us with images and ways of thinking about life's imponderables with God as the reference point. The biblical stories illumine the areas of human experience and show us possibilities. Indeed, the biblical stories go further and invite us to live out those possibilities. This is the area of grace. This is why the sacred stories reveal to us the face of God. As John Shea says:

> They are stories meant to disclose aspects of our relationship to God and through that relationship our commitments to each other. The stories of scripture were remembered and today remain memorable because they are similar enough to our own lives for us to see ourselves, yet different enough from our lives for us to see new possibilities. They tell us what we want to know and more. They come close to home and yet are an invitation to a journey. Robert McAfee Brown has said, "A story . . . must reach me on some level to which I can respond, but it must also 'stretch' me, pull me beyond where I am now." The traditional stories, both historical and fictional, reflect concerns and conflicts present in our lives and suggest ways of dealing with them.[13]

Somewhere along the line, that face of God took on specific human contours in the face of the Man from Nazareth. In fact, as a convenient transition to the next chapter, we might say that Jesus himself is all that God wants to say in his story; that Jesus himself is God's Story-Word in the flesh:

□God, as everyone knows, created the heavens and the earth and everything in them. And, as we are now aware, he created them through the use of words, for words, of course, are power. "Let it be done" God proclaimed, and it was done. And everything he made was good.

Well, God was especially proud and loving of the man and woman he made because he had breathed into them a part of himself, his spirit.

But, not surprisingly, the devil was jealous and angry. So one day when God was enjoying the man and woman, the devil casually happened to walk by. He sauntered up to God and asked him what he liked so much about these creatures. And when God opened his mouth to speak, the devil craftily put a bond upon his tongue so that he could not speak! God could not talk! And since God's creative power was in his words, the devil had bound that power.

The devil laughed at God and quite had his way with the man and the woman. Well, as some eons went by, the devil came back to mock God—he couldn't resist, such is his nature. Well, he came back to mock God. He scoffed at the silent deity and taunted this helpless God. God responded to all this by holding up one finger.

"One?" asked the devil. "Are you trying to tell me that you want to say just one word? Is that it?"

Yes, God nodded, pleading with his soft eyes and urgent hands.

The confident devil thought to himself, "I don't suppose that even God could do very much harm with one word. OK." So the devil removed the bond from God's tongue.

And God spoke his one word, in a whisper. He spoke it for the man and the woman and it brought them great joy. It was a word that gathered up all the love, forgiveness, and creativity God had been storing in his heart during the time of his silence.

The word he spoke was Jesus!□

7

Parables
That Uncover

"All this Jesus said to the crowds in parables." So wrote St. Matthew. In fact, he went on to make his point even more emphatic by adding, "Indeed, he said nothing to them without a parable" (13:34). It is true. Virtually nothing Jesus said is recorded in lecture form. Rather the record shows him teaching and preaching in parable-story form. At this stage of our investigation, we can see why he did this, why he preferred parables, the ancient teaching tradition of his people. Parable-stories had power. They were disturbingly paradoxical and challenging.

Such writers as Dominic Crossan and David Tracy have shown that the very language of the Gospel parables has been designed to establish tension, to cut through existing structures of perception with the sharp knife of paradox. There is tension built into, for example, the juxtaposition of the words "good" and "Samaritan," or "first" and "last," which, even before we hear the stories, catch us by surprise and set us to wondering. Both in their substance and in their language the parables are paradoxical, shattering, exploding, and disclosing narratives. Every child, and the child in every one of us, is ready to plead, "Tell me a story." For the role of stories is to explain life, and the good stories, in their very substance and in the structure of their language, become revelation. In the shattering, disturbing, confusing, and

117

challenging parables of the Gospel we are confronted with "one possible mode of being in the world: to live with explicit faith, with complete trust, with unqualified love." The story asks us to consider the possibility that we can live a life of fundamental trust, confidence, and total commitment to the goodness which has exploded out of the story and is seeking to take possession of us.[1]

But there were other reasons that Jesus told stories. For one thing, he was acutely aware of people. He knew that they were widely diverse in their perceptions and understanding as could be. He knew that no one easy tidbit from his lips would answer everyone's needs. He knew that people were at various stages on their life's journey. The story, as it turns out, with its multileveled meanings and messages was just the right vehicle of communication for a universal religion. For another thing, Jesus respected each person's integrity and free will. He chose the story-parable because it, more than any other form, gives each person room to work on what was said. The use of the parable is automatically an invitation to the listener's involvement and response. Of course, any man or woman may listen and willfully not understand—Matthew nods to that (13:13-15)—but that's the risk. But, on the other hand, the listener may be caught. He or she may ruminate and respond to his or her grace within the story. Parables are like that: with their concrete details of everyday life, their back-door message and sensitive images, they are seductive ways of involving the listener.

The parables *were* catchy. It takes no wild imagination to guess that they were dear to the first Christians who cherished them and made sure that they would not be lost. In fact, later generations of Christians paid Jesus' parables and the stories about Jesus the ultimate compliment: not only did they remember and preserve many stories and happenings, but they even modified them for their contemporary audiences, lest something be lost through obsolescence. If we are slightly taken aback at this, just recall that for us, modification is a fact of life. We accommodate ourselves to our hearers almost automatically. We often suppress irrelevant details that are foreign or confusing so that our main point is not lost in a lot of explaining. Jokes, for example, are notoriously modified to fit the listeners in, say, Alaska or Africa. The joke is the same and so is the punch line, but for both those diverse audiences there's going to be many a change in translation. Try this:

☐Smith, seated in a movie house, could not help being aware that the man sitting right in front of him had his arm around the neck of a rather large dog which sat in the seat next to him. The dog clearly was taking in the picture with understanding. He snarled at the villain, yelped happily at the funny remarks, and so on. Smith leaned forward and tapped the man in front of him on the shoulder. He whispered, "Pardon me, sir, but I can't get over your dog's behavior." The man turned and whispered back, "Frankly, it surprises me too. He hated the book."☐

How would you tell this to a village in Asia that never heard either of movies or a movie house? Or a part of the world that had never seen a dog? You'd probably substitute a cat or whatever. The story's too good (I think, anyway) not to tell even if you have to change the details somewhat. And this is what we expect, and get, in the gospel versions. In Mark, for instance, a rather primitive gospel and written for the Palestinian audience, the paralyzed man is lowered through a roof of common thatches. When this story was transported to Greece, for example, or for city people, Luke changed a detail: the man was lowered through the roof tiles (not thatches) they were familiar with.

Or consider this parable used in two ways by Luke and Matthew. In Luke's version, Jesus tells a story to the Pharisees who were forever criticizing him for hobnobbing with "those outside the law." The story is the one of the farmer who leaves his ninety-nine sheep to search for the lost one, and when he finds it there is a celebration. And Jesus swiftly draws the parallel: so, too, "there will be more joy in heaven over one sinner who repents than over the ninety-nine who have no need of repentance." The point Jesus is making in this version of the story is not lost on the Pharisees. Jesus' story is one of self-defense. He is responding to Pharisaical criticism for consorting with sinners by saying in effect,"But don't you see? My Father delights in forgiveness. That's what God is all about and so that's what I must be about."

Now we turn to Matthew. He has this story in hand, but he has a different agenda. He's going to use this story, not to chastize the Pharisees, but to chastize the faithful, the disciples of the church of Christ! So at the end of his version, Jesus remarks that so it is, that it is not God's will "that one of these little ones should perish." For Matthew, ever the churchman, the story means that pastors and followers of Christ must be diligent in searching out fallen away members.

So it is with many of the parables and the stories about Jesus. They get different twists depending on the point the evangelist wishes to make. But that's the nature of a good story. It's too good not to tell and it's too good not to remodel so that others will get its full impact.

Pointing out that the evangelists have special agendas they are addressing brings us to consider: What about Jesus himself? Yes, he told stories, but was there one central theme that colored them all? What did he have in mind? Was there a main point with variations? What led him on? If his apostle Paul would write someday that "the love of Christ urges me on!", what about the Master?

What urged him on is answered in his own words and it is essential, if we are to understand his stories, that we keep his answer in mind. "My food is to do the will of the one who sent me" (John 5:30). That's the central hinge of Jesus' life, his relationship to the Father. Jesus was the quintessential Jew of the First Commandment. There is no God but God. Therefore, we are all his creatures, children of the same Abba. Creaturehood is in the marrow of our bones, a common paternity is our irreversible condition and fraternity our abiding posture. This was Jesus' core, and it is understood that it should be our core too and that we should operate from it. But it is not so; we have become disoriented somewhere along the way. We may still nod to God our Father, but we all too easily displace him with the idol of ourselves. We may give lip service to a common paternity, but we are beset with rivalry. Fraternity should be our posture, but jealousy is our action. So Jesus comes along with his parables. They are parables that unsettle, shock, invite, and challenge. They are parables on one theme: parables of the kingdom—a kingdom of inclusion.

> The kingdom was for sinners, tax-collectors, lepers, prostitutes, and club-foots. It was a kingdom for the messy and the miserable. Through his shocking and provocative parables, Jesus subverted all ordinary expectations about how God works in the world. Instead of being the Chase Manhattan Bank, the kingdom was like a poor old woman who lost a dime and swept her house all day until she found it. Instead of being a dramatic "close encounter of the third kind" the kingdom was as hidden and humble as a bit of yeast in a batch of dough.[2]

The kingdom became for Jesus a kind of logo, a theme that challenged our divisiveness and exclusions. His stories of the kingdom call us to decision, to return to our core posture as children of God and brother and sister to one another. This is so, for at the heart of the notion of kingdom is the concept of relationship.

> The parables of the New Testament are united by a number of characteristics, of which one of the most outstanding is their concern with relationships of various kinds. What is important in the parables is not *who* the characters are (a static notion) but *what they do* (a dynamic one). The plot is always the heart of a parable, what a character or several characters decide in matters having to do with their *relationships with each other*. Whether one thinks of the parable of the Prodigal Son, the Good Samaritan, the Unjust Steward, or the Great Supper, it is relationships and decisions about them that are critical.[3]

Keeping this in mind will help us as we investigate six random types of stories Jesus told and what they are meant to say to us.[4]

First Type of Jesus Story: Uncovers our competitiveness and envy, and invites us to brotherhood and sisterhood instead.

Take Matthew's gospel. We have that irritating and perplexing parable about the last-hired servants getting the same pay as those all-day, hot-sunned servants. Our sense of fairness is outraged, no matter how many preachers try to explain this parable away. But this we should know: this outrageous parable—and it is that—carries with it an invitation to search out the basis of our outrage. We must not be content with the surface injustice of the story—that's one level—but must look for something deeper. And it is this: we have established our sense of worth and importance by constituting ourselves, in our relationship to others, as being on top, superior. We have a vested interest, therefore, in the subtle inferiority of others. Which is to say, when you come right down to it, that generosity is the *last* thing we want because it equalizes everything. What good is that? It takes away our privilege, our earned reward, our basis for being better. Where do we stand if everyone is the same, everyone treated equally by the vineyard owner? Therefore our anger and annoyance are not over the patent unfairness; our anger and annoyance turn out to be symptoms uncovering our fundamental competitiveness and envy. We are *not* children of the same Father who lets it rain on the just and unjust alike. We want to be more than others in every way, and the owner's generosity has just wiped that out. No wonder we're disgusted. No wonder this is not our favorite parable.

We get the same exposure of our envy and competitiveness in the story of the cure of the man with the withered arm (Matthew 12:9-14). One might think that the Pharisee's indignation is based solely on the grounds that this cure took place on the Sabbath. But there is more to it underneath. What is underneath is their, and our, disappointment that the man was cured at all. As long as we have two good arms and he has one bad one we can feel superior, some pity perhaps, but deep down superior. We perceive this in a reverse pattern when we admit how really hard it is for us to genuinely rejoice at another's good fortune. Once more, such realities show us that we are not grounded in brotherhood and sisterhood under Abba, but in competition and jealousy.

Such are some of the stories that Jesus told that uncover something deeper in ourselves. But we must remember: the stories are not meant only to indict. They are meant to invite.

Second Type of Jesus Story: Uncovers our wrong centering, and invites us to a right centering.

We are beings full of desires. We desire people and we desire things. But it doesn't stop there. We want the reverse. We want to be desired. Surely to be "desirable," as countless perfume and skin cream commercials persuade us, is to have reached a pinnacle of acclaim. And if the perfume or the skin cream don't work, we turn to other strategies. We might, for example, seek money. The unspoken (and maybe unconscious) implication is that people *must* love us, desire us, if we have all that wealth. "Say, do you know how much I make?" we whisper after the fourth drink at the cocktail party. Or we seek goodness (yes, even that) on the premise that people must love us if we are so good. Or we might pursue fame because, as the whole world knows, everybody loves a celebrity.

But there is a backlash to all this. If money makes us lovable, then we must keep others poor. If goodness makes us lovable, then we have a vested interest in others' evil. It is well known, for example, that the "offended" and long-suffering spouse of an alcoholic would often resent the other's sobriety (not consciously, of course, but subconsciously). Were the partner completely converted, how would the other feel superior? Who would want to lose all those people who feel sorry for themselves? If fame makes us lovable, we must keep others out of the limelight. If talent makes us lovable, then we must rejoice at others' lack of it. If beauty makes us lovable, then we must be pleased at others' ugliness. And all this, of course, is wrong centering. All this keeps us in a perpetual state of watchfulness and perhaps even envy and depression.

There is, as you suspect, a classical biblical story about this. It is the story of the Prodigal Son (Luke 15:11-32). It is really the father who is prodigal with his generous, open-handed forgiveness. The one really out of joint is the older brother. He is quite unhappy with his younger brother's return to home and to favor. With such equalization, where is his claim to superiority and virtue? He has a vested interest in his brother's sinfulness. So unhappy is he over his brother's equality that he cannot even call him brother. And *that* becomes the real point of the story. He refers to his brother with the oblique phrase "that son of yours" (verse 30)—and there's the problem. As long as he cannot call him his brother, he is centered wrongly. Until he loses his need to be better, he cannot know brotherhood itself.

Here is another gospel story, gloriously retold by John Shea, the story of Peter and the large catch of fish (Luke 5:1-11).

☐ It is well known by everyone who cares to know that the Lord Jesus and St. Peter used to repair to the local tavern after a hard day of ministry to knock back a few brews.

On a certain rainy night after St. Peter had had a few beers, he turned to the Lord Jesus and grinned, "We're doing real good."

"We?" said the lord Jesus.

Peter was silent. "All right, you're doing real good," he finally said.

"Me?" said the Lord Jesus.

Peter was silent a second time. "All right. *God's* doing real good," he reluctantly admitted.

The Lord Jesus laughed and hit the table with glee.

It was the laugh that got St. Peter. He pushed his face toward Jesus and blurted out, "Look! I was somebody before you came along. You didn't make me. I know now everybody says, 'There goes the Lord Jesus and his sidekick St. Peter. Jesus cures the sick and Peter helps them up.'

"But it wasn't always that way. People knew me in my own right. They would say, 'There goes Peter, the greatest fisherman in all of Galilee.' I was respected and looked up to."

"I heard that you were a very good fisherman, Peter," said the Lord Jesus.

"Damn right I was! And tomorrow I am going to prove it. We are going to go fishing, you and me, and you'll see how the other fishermen respect me and look to my lead."

"I would love to go fishing, Peter. I have never been fishing," said the Lord Jesus, who was always looking for new adventures.

So the next morning at dawn the Lord Jesus and St. Peter were down at the shore readying the boat. And it was just as St. Peter had said. When the other fishermen saw St. Peter, they sidled over.

"Going out, Peter?" they asked.

"Yes," answered Peter, not looking up from the nets.

"Mind if we follow along?"

"Why not," shrugged Peter. And he looked at the Lord Jesus and said, "See!"

St. Peter's boat led the way with the Lord Jesus hanging on tightly in the prow. Now St. Peter was a scientist of a fisherman. He tasted the water, scanned the sky, peered down into the lake, and gave the word in a whisper, "Over there."

"Why isn't anyone talking?" asked the Lord Jesus.

"Shhhh!" Peter shook his head.

The boats formed a wide circle around the area that Peter had pointed to. "Let the nets down," Peter's voice crept over the surface of the water.

"Why don't they just toss them in?" asked the Lord Jesus, who had hopes of learning about fishing.

A second "shhhh!" came from St. Peter.

As the fishermen were letting their nets slowly into the sea, the Lord Jesus took his messianic finger and tapped the side of the boat. And all the fish in the sea of Galilee dove to the bottom.

As they pulled in the nets, the muscles of their arms did not tighten under the weight of the fish. The nets rose quickly, the arms of the men slack. All they caught was water. The fishermen rowed over to St. Peter.

"The greatest fisherman in all of Galilee, my grandmother's bald head! You brought us here for nothing. We have wasted the best hours of the day and have not one fish to show for it. Stick to preaching, Peter." And they rowed toward shore, shouting over their shoulders at Peter.

The Lord Jesus said nothing.

St. Peter checked the nets. He tasted the sea a second time. He scanned the sky a second time. He looked at the Lord Jesus a second time and said, "Over there!" No sooner had he said this that the Lord Jesus was at the oars rowing mightily. And all day long under the searing sun the Lord Jesus and St. Peter rowed from place to place on the sea of Galilee. And all day long under the searing sun the Lord Jesus and St. Peter let down their nets. And all day long under the searing sun the Lord Jesus and St. Peter hauled in their nets. And all day long under the searing sun the Lord Jesus and St. Peter caught nothing. Evening fell and an exhausted St. Peter raised the sail to make for shore. The weary Lord Jesus held on tightly in the prow.

It was then as the boat glided toward shore that all the fish in the sea of Galilee came to the surface. They leapt on one side of the boat and they leapt on the other side of the boat. They leapt behind the boat and they leapt in front of the boat. They formed a cordon around the boat, escorting it toward shore in full fanfare.

And then in a mass suicide of fish, they leapt into the boat, landing in the lap of the laughing Lord Jesus, smacking the astonished St. Peter in the face. When the boat arrived at shore, it was brimming, creaking, sinking under the weight of fish.

The other fishermen were waiting. They gathered around St. Peter and slapped him on the back. "Peter, you old rascal," they said, "you knew where the fish were all the time but you never let on. You put us on. You surely are the greatest fisherman in all of Galilee."

But Peter was uncharacteristically silent. He only said, "Give the fish to everyone. Tonight no home in this village will go without food." After that, he said nothing.

As for Jesus, he went to the mountains, alone. □

John Shea's commentary is pointed:

Peter needs to claim credit for doing the good things that are happening in their ministry. "We're really doing good." Jesus has no need to claim credit. He establishes himself not out of his own power but out of the power of Abba Father. Peter is at first unable or unwilling to admit such centeredness. As a result, he is forced into his competitive statement that he is the greatest fisherman in all of Galilee and he is forced to establish himself over against his brothers and sisters and so know he is somebody because he is better than the rest.

The Lord Jesus goes with him and will row wherever Peter directs even though they catch nothing. Which means that God will not abandon us in our failures. He and Peter bear together the emptiness of the day.

It is only when Peter lets go that a change is made. This is symbolized by his putting up the sail and letting the breeze take over. This is the ancient symbol of the Holy Spirit—the breeze, the breath of God which will breathe where it will.

If Peter had caught the fish himself he would have hoarded them, as he said, for a better sale on the market and made money for himself. But since the fish were such a gift, then St. Peter must give them back as a gift. "Tonight no home in the village will go without food." The question is: will we use our strengths to divide or bind? Will we use our talents to establish ourselves over and against others or as a contribution toward the common good for we are all brothers and sisters of Abba Father?

The Lord Jesus and St. Peter go fishing and we are caught in the net.[5]

Third Type of Jesus Story: Uncovers our need to hoard and to exclude, and invites us to share and include.

The stories of Jesus in this category are basically ones of the right and wrong use of power. The right use of power is service and inclusiveness, while the wrong use of power is lording it over others and exclusiveness. The instance here is Peter's confession (Matthew 16:13-23). His proclamation that Jesus is the Messiah earns Peter both praise and position. He is now "Rock," leader of the church. But a few lines later his protestation at Jesus' going up to Jerusalem to suffer earns him rebuke and imposition. He is now "Satan," no real leader at all. What is at stake here is that Peter, with his new title and power, wants to use that power to exclude himself from ordinary life ("going up to Jerusalem to suffer"). He is much like, say, an unscrupulous congressman who might use his position to get his son excluded from military service. For this abuse of power Jesus reprimands Peter. His rebuke tells Peter and us that power is not to be used to exempt from life and its demands, but must be used to embrace life and its demands.

Then there is that other incident in Matthew 18:21 where Peter asks how many times he must forgive an errant brother. The question is not really dealing with forgiveness as such. It has to do with limitation and exclusion. Peter is asking at what point he can cut his brother off. Therefore Jesus' reply is not meant to say that we must forgive endlessly as much as to say that it is never God's way to exclude at any point. God's way is to share and include.

We see the same dynamic in the incident of Mark 9:38 where the disciples find out that someone not of their little group is casting out devils in Jesus' name. Their reaction? "Stop him!" Jesus' reaction? "Let him be. He who is not against us is for us." The disciples were speaking of exclusion, of hoarding power. After all, they were the official devil caster-outers around here! Jesus speaks of sharing and including. So it goes with the disciples and with us. Jesus told such stories to catch us up short, to uncover more than we like to have uncovered about ourselves. But remember, too, his stories also are always invitations.

□Once upon a time there was an old man from the lovely island of Crete. He loved his land with a deep and beautiful intensity, so much so that when he perceived that he was about to die he had his sons bring him outside and lay him on his beloved earth. As he was about to expire he reached down by his side and clutched some earth into his hands. He died a happy man.

He now appeared before heaven's gates. God, as an old white-bearded man, came out to greet him. "Welcome," he said. "You've been a good man. Please, come into the joys of heaven." But as the old man started to enter the pearly gates, God said, "Please. You must let the soil go." "Never!" said the old man stepping back. "Never!" And so God departed sadly, leaving the old man outside the gates. A few eons went by. God came out again, this time as a friend, an old drinking crony. They had a few drinks, told some stories, and then God said, "All right, now it's time to enter heaven, friend. Let's go." And they started for the pearly gates. And once more God requested that the old man let go of this soil and once more he refused.

More eons rolled by. God came out once more, this time as a

delightful and playful granddaughter. "Oh, granddaddy," he said, "you're so wonderful and we all miss you. Please come inside with me." The old man nodded and she helped him up for by this time he had grown indeed very old and arthritic. In fact, so arthritic was he that he had to prop up the right hand holding Crete's soil with his left hand. They moved toward the pearly gates and at this point his strength quite gave out. His gnarled fingers would no longer stay clenched in a fist with the result that the soil sifted out between them until his hand was empty. He then entered heaven. The first thing he saw was his beloved island. □

Other
Jesus Stories
That Uncover

W e continue with three more categories of stories that Jesus told or was involved in. These stories challenge us to see ourselves as we really are and change us.

Fourth Type of Jesus Story: Uncovers our assumptions, and challenges us to turn them around.

All of us go around with certain unexamined assumptions about ourselves, our world, and God. Jesus comes along with his version of the Socratic dictum that the unexamined life is not worth living. He makes us reconsider these assumptions by turning the table on our expectations. Here, for example, are four staccato assumptions counterpointed by gospel stories:

First Assumption: Natives are trustworthy; foreigners are suspect. We might have accepted this—until Jesus told a story about a native priest and a native Levite who passed by a man lying half dead in a ditch and a foreigner who did not pass by but helped him. Which proved neighbor, lover, saint? Or, a variation: the Lord cured ten people of leprosy. Nine were natives, one was a foreigner. Guess who came back to give thanks?

129

Second Assumption: God works on the merit system. This means that you must earn your graces, work hard at it. God will give you a commensurate reward. Work little and you'll get little. Then there's that parable again of the last-hour people getting a pay equal to the first-hour ones. This overturns our assumptions and makes us furious. Then Jesus adds insult to injury by asking, "Are you jealous because I am generous?" Yes, by damn, we are! Others shouldn't have things handed to them while we break our backs. God should work on a straight commission system.

Third Assumption: Correct liturgy wins approval; sloppy liturgy does not. Jesus comes along and tells the story of a man who was liturgically correct. He stood in the proper place, began his prayers with thanksgiving, and offered the gifts of his virtues to the Lord. His form was impeccable. The other man in church that day did everything wrong. He stood far back like Catholics in the last pew, had no gifts to offer, and just mumbled mercy, mercy, mercy. And *his* prayer was heard!

Fourth Assumption: Life is all about security. This means that we must be sensible and provide for our future. And that certainty is good as far as it goes and if that providing is holistic. But, recites Jesus, once upon a time there was a man with overflowing barns who said, "Now I can take it easy. I can eat, drink, and be merry because I've got it made. I will never be hungry again!" He wasn't. That night he died.

If you want a modern story to think about on the same themes, here's Martin Bell's "Arnold":

□Once there was a bird with fur. He had a long yellow beak and pleasant green eyes. Everyone who knew him called him Arnold. But his real name was Bill.

Bill would never fly when he wanted to go somewhere. He was more than satisfied to shuffle along the ground at a leisurely pace. And sooner or later he always got where he was going.

When a group of his friends saw Bill shuffling quietly to or fro they would say, "Hello, Arnold!" And Bill would say, "Hello." And then after he was gone the whole group would spend a lot of time talking about all of the reasons why Arnold should fly instead of shuffle.

It made Bill happy whenever friends said hello to him. And he rather liked the name Arnold, even though it wasn't his name. Interestingly enough, Bill didn't know that his friends thought he should fly, because no one ever told him what they said when he wasn't there.

Now and then Bill was mistaken for a kitten. This was due in part to his appearance, of course. But it was also because he could, and did, purr whenever he wanted to.

Perhaps you have never seen a bird with fur that shuffles and purrs. Certainly, the same is true about many others. So please don't be discouraged. But do stay alert. Heads up and all that could avoid many a passing-by-unnoticed.

Anyway, Arnold, as he was called, enjoyed life immensely. And although he had only one possession, it was enough. I wonder if you can guess what he had? Would it surprise you to learn that Bill owned a wrist watch? Well, he did. On one furry wing Bill wore a tiny Timex wrist watch.

The watch didn't work. And so Bill never really knew what time it was. Still, he was always hopeful that someone might notice it there on his wing and ask, "What's the time?" Bill chuckled softly when he thought about his reply. Naturally, he would make up a time. And then without so much as blinking a green eye he would say, "It's 3:45." Or perhaps, "Ten fifteen by my watch." He could decide on whatever time he wanted. Such fun to own a watch that didn't work.

Glenda the bobcat liked "Arnold." Ordinarily birds weren't safe when she was around. Not at all. But, as luck would have it, Glenda was terribly nearsighted. And she actually did think that Bill was a tiny bobcat. (You may be certain he had never indicated otherwise.) Whenever Glenda found Bill shuffling, she always carried him back to her lair by the fur on his neck. Then Bill would purr for a long while until Glenda went looking for food. When the coast was clear, so to speak, he shuffled on about his own business—until she found him again, and the process was repeated.

During the various interludes between being found by Glenda and waiting for someone to ask about the time, Bill spent many a happy hour pretending to wind his watch. I say "pretending" because it is nearly impossible to wind anything with a wing. It wasn't that Bill didn't try. He just never succeeded.

Finally, the day came when one of his friends approached him on behalf of the entire group who had been insisting that he should fly.

"Arnold," he asked cautiously, "why don't you ever fly?" It was Charles, the groundhog.

"Because flying is for the birds, Charles," replied Bill, shuffling around a bit as if to emphasize the point.

"But you are a bird, Arnold," the groundhog insisted. "And you really ought to fly. You're making everybody uncomfortable."

Bill was silent. He looked perplexed and lost in thought. Then, after a moment or two, he brightened up and said, "No, I don't think so, Charles. I don't want to fly. I'm sorry it makes you uncomfortable. Truly I am. However, flying is out of the question."

"But, Arnold," said the exasperated groundhog, "what shall I tell the others? You're embarrassing all of us."

"Tell them anything you want to, Charles. Just get the point across. No flying. I'm sorry." Bill glanced at his watch. "Why, however did it get to be so late? It's 8:37—past your suppertime, Charles. Time for me to be on my way, too." Bill seemed genuinely surprised and chagrined by the lateness of the hour. "Thank you for stopping, though. I know it took a great deal of courage to be spokesman for the entire group. Goodnight, Charles. Can you believe the time? Wherever did the evening go?"

After the confused groundhog had scurried off in order to make it home for supper, Bill sat down in the warm afternoon sun. He decided to make up a shuffling song to sing while moving about.

Shuffle, shuffle to and fro
I'll get where I'm going.
Never even have to know
Which way the wind is blowing.

I suppose that I could fly,
There's really nothing to it.
Still, I've always wondered why
A bird would want to do it.

There, that was a fine song. Bill smiled as he thought about Charles running home for supper. Then he placed both wings behind his neck and lay back in the grass for a short nap.

Shuffle, shuffle to and fro
I'll get where I'm going.
Never even have to know
Which way . . . the . . . wind. . . .

Soon, Bill was asleep. The afternoon sun warmed his fur and he dreamed an appropriate dream.

After a while he heard a voice beside him saying "Hello, Arnold." Slowly, Bill opened one eye. It was nearly dark. Evidently, he'd slept a good bit longer than he planned. "Hello, Arnold." Bill turned in the direction of the greeting. It was a firefly acquaintance.

"Hello, Alice. Nice evening and all," he said pleasantly.

"Arnold, will you tell me what's going on? Whatever did you say to upset Charles so? Why won't you fly like you're supposed to? And what are you doing lying here in the grass? Alice seemed puzzled and concerned.

"Why, of course, I'll tell you, Alice," said Bill, dusting himself off and resuming an upright position. His green eyes reflected the firefly's glittering. He blinked at Alice once or twice and then began.

"For the most part, I'm convinced that we forest animals—birds, groundhogs, even fireflies—take ourselves too seriously. Each of us seems to believe that he or she has a certain set part to act out in some great big cosmic play. Incidentally, I don't think that's true, Alice. But, God knows, it might be. All I'm saying is that either way, it's funny. If there really is a script, the whole idea tickles me. And if there isn't any script at all, but we keep insisting on acting out a part that hasn't even been assigned to us, then that's hilarious."

Alice looked distressed. "I don't think it's funny, Arnold. Everyone knows there is a script. And it's very important that you act the way you are supposed to. Your part has been assigned."

Bill shuffled some. "Perhaps," he said.

Alice waited for a minute or two and then she added, "Arnold, are you OK?"

"Oh, yes. Fine, fine. I was just thinking that I am more of a mind to believe the play isn't composed until after the actors themselves have created the script by what they say and do. I'm sure we take ourselves much too seriously, Alice." Bill pretended to wind his watch.

"Is that a wrist watch, Arnold?"

"Why, yes it is," Bill replied without looking up. "Yes, indeed. It is—a wrist watch. And a favorite possession of mine, too."

"What's the time?" Alice asked.

Without so much as blinking a green eye, Bill said, "It's nearly midnight. Eleven fifty-four to be exact."

"Gracious, Arnold! Are you sure? It doesn't seem that late."

"Am I sure? Oh, yes, certainly—11:54 exactly. It's always later than we think, you know." Bill looked up and blinked thoughtfully.

"Goodnight, Arnold," mumbled the bewildered firefly.

"Goodnight, Alice. And thanks for stopping."

That night Bill slept out under the stars. He awoke feeling refreshed and even more delighted with his world than ever. For a while he pretended to wind his watch.

Shuffle, shuffle. To and fro. A bird with fur. A long yellow beak and pleasant green eyes. "I'm sure we take ourselves much too seriously," he mumbled while making an attempt to stand on his head. Then, upside-down, Bill saw Glenda the bobcat headed earnestly in his direction, and he immediately toppled over in silent laughter. "There can be no mistake about it," he thought. We do take ourselves much too seriously."[1]□

Fifth Type of Jesus Story: Uncovers our timidity, and invites us to risk all for the sake of God's Kingdom.

Here we have those pithy sayings of Jesus that tell us about the man who found a treasure in the field and sold all he had to purchase the field. Then there is the merchant who discovered the pearl of great price and also sold all he had and bought it. These and other stories of the same nature, these stories of total response and action to what is really valuable, uncover our hesitancy, our half-heartedness. They uncover our holding back, our trying to have it both ways as we serve God and Mammon equally, not willing to offend either. Shakespeare replays this theme thus:

> Cromwell, I did not think to shed a tear
> In all my miseries; but thou hast forced me
> Out of honest truth, to play the woman.
> Let's dry our eyes; and thus far hear me, Cromwell;
> And, when I am forgotten, as I shall be,
> And sleep in dull cold marble, where no mention
> Of me more must be heard of, say, I taught thee,
> Say, Wolsey, that once trod the ways of glory,
> And sounded all the depths and shoals of honour,
> Found thee a way, out of his wreck, to rise in;
> A sure and safe one, though thy master miss'd it. . . .
> O Cromwell, Cromwell!

Had I but served my God with half the zeal
I served my king, he would not in mine age
Have left me naked to mine enemies.[2]

Furthermore, our timidity can even lead us into inaction altogether, preferring frightened security to the risk of living. The parable that Jesus told of the talents in Matthew 25:14-30 is a powerful indictment of this attitude. Here it is, retold.

☐There was once a village chief with three sons. Each of them had a special talent. The oldest had the talent of raising olive trees and would trade the oil for tools and cloth. The second was a shepherd and when the sheep were ill he had a great talent for making them well again. The third was a dancer and when there was a streak of bad luck in the family or when everyone was bored during the hard winters and tired of work, this was the son who would cheer them up and dance.

One day the Father had to go away on a long journey and so he called his sons together and said, "My sons, the villagers are depending on you. Each of you has a special talent for helping people and so, while I am gone, see to it that you use your talents as wisely and well as possible so that, when I return, I will find our village even more happy and prosperous than it is now." He embraced his sons and departed.

For a while things went well. Then the cold winter winds began to blow and the blizzards and snows came. First, the buds on the olive trees shrank and cracked, and it was a long time before the trees could recover. Then the village, because of the especially long winter, ran out of firewood. So the people began to cut down the trees but in the process they were denuding and destroying the village.

Then, too, the snow and ice made it impossible for the traders to come up the river or over the mountain pass. The result was that the villagers said, "So, let us kill the sheep and eat them so we do not starve to death." The second son refused for a time, but finally had to give in to the hungry villagers. His remark was, "What good would it be to spare the sheep only to have the villagers perish?"

In this way, the villagers got just enough wood for their fires and food for their tables but the bitter winter had broken their spirits and they began to think that things were really worse than they were and they even began to lose all hope. So much so, that family by family they deserted the village in search of a more hospitable environment.

As spring began to loosen the icy grip of winter, the village chief, the father of the three sons, returned only to find smoke rising from his own chimney. "What have you done?" he asked when he reached his house and spoke to his sons. "What has happened to the villagers?"

"Oh, father, forgive me," said the oldest son. "The people were freezing and begged me to cut down the olive trees and so I did. I gave away my talent. I am no longer fit to be an orchard keeper." "Don't be angry Father," said the second son. "The sheep would have frozen to death anyway and the people were starving and I had to send my flock to the slaughter."

But the father understood and said, "Don't be ashamed, my sons, you did the best you could and you acted rightly and humanely. You used your talents wisely in trying to save the people. But, tell me, what has become of them? Where are they?"

The two brothers looked with fixed eyes on the third son who said, "Welcome home, father. Yes, it has been a hard time. There was so little to eat and so little firewood. I thought that it would be insensitive and improper to dance during such suffering and, besides, I needed to conserve my strength so that I could dance for you when you came home."

"Then, dance, my son," said the father, "for my village is empty and so is my heart. Fill it with joy and courage once again. Yes, please dance!" But as the third son went to get up, he made a face of pain and fell down. His legs were so stiff and sore from sitting that they were no longer fit for dancing. The Father was so sad that he could not even be angry. He simply said to the third son:

"Ours was a strong village. It could have survived the want of fuel and food but it could never survive without hope. And because you failed to use your talent wisely and well, our people gave up what little hope they had left. So now? Now the village is deserted and you are crippled. Your punishment has already fallen upon you."

And with these words he embraced his two sons and wept. □

Sixth Type of Jesus Story: Uncovers our self-centered despair and distrust, and invites us to hope.

That we live in an "age of anxiety" is not to be denied. Young children, when polled, fully expect a nuclear war in their lifetimes. There are the continuing problems of political instability, unemployment, hunger, homelessness, broken marriages, crime, and all the rest that we have learned to live with. Jesus, the realist, who had his own worries, did not deny such realities but, on the other hand, he invites us to trust in Abba Father, who feeds the birds of the air, clothes the lilies of the fields, and counts the hairs on our heads. This is the Abba into whose hands he commended his own dark moments on Calvary, the one who reduced death, formerly the last word, to a penultimate one. In a word, Jesus invites us to hope, and the whole great Easter experience, the foundation of our faith, is a celebration of our victory.

A few years ago I began an Easter homily like this:

□ The story is going around about the sudden awakening in the year 2000 of a man who had been in a coma since 1980. When he came to, the man immediately called his stockbroker. "What are my investments now? he demanded. The broker replied, "Your Exxon stock is worth five million dollars and your IBM stock is worth four million." "I'm rich! I'm rich!" shouted the man joyously, only to be interrupted by the telephone operator who said, "Your three minutes are up. Deposit one million dollars, please!"

Then there was the man dressed as Napoleon who went to see a psychiatrist at the urging of his wife. "What's your problem?" asked the doctor. "I have no problem," replied the man. "I'm one of the most famous people in the world. I have a great army behind me, I have all the money I'll ever need, and I live in great luxury."

"Then why are you here?"

"It's because of my wife," said the man. "She thinks she's Mrs. Levine."

Mrs. Finkelstein was bursting with pride. "Did you hear about my son Louie?" she asked Mrs. Goldberg. "No. What's with your son Louie?" "He's going to a psychiatrist. Twice each week he's going to a psychiatrist." "Is that good?" "Of course it's good. Fifty dollars an hour he pays, fifty dollars! And all he talks about is me."

Finally, this one about Archbishop Fulton J. Sheen. He often gave a lecture entitled "On the Nature of the Universe." After he had delivered it in a small town, an elderly woman confronted him, saying, "That was a brilliant lecture, Bishop, but you are all wrong. The universe is *not* as you described it. The earth for example, is not a little ball moving around the sun. Our world is just a crust of earth on the back of a huge turtle." Very gently the Archbishop replied, "That is an interesting theory, Madam, but tell me: what is the turtle standing on?" The woman replied, "I see that you are a very intelligent man, Bishop, and that is an intelligent question, but I've got the answer. The turtle is standing on the back of a much larger turtle." Archbishop Sheen patiently asked, "And what is the *second* turtle standing on?" To which the woman replied, "It's no use, Bishop, it's turtles all the way down!"☐

What was I doing, telling jokes on Easter Sunday? I was borrowing from the ancient Russian Orthodox tradition, when the day after Easter was devoted to sitting around the table all day telling jokes. Even in church they told them. And why? Well, this was the way, they felt, that they were imitating that cosmic joke that God pulled on Satan in the resurrection. Satan thought he had won, and was smug in his victory, smiling to himself, having had the last word. So he thought. Then God raised up Jesus from the dead, and life and salvation became the last words. And the whole world laughed at the devil's discomfort. This attitude passed into the medieval concept of *hilaritas*, which did not mean mindless giggling, but that even at the moment of disaster one may wink because he or she knows there is a God. It's like Zorba and his boss dancing on the shores of the Aegean after their ore mine had collapsed and they had lost everything.

All these are variations on the theme of hope sounded in the stories and life of the suffering Messiah, and they invite us to hope. Renewal, surprise, fresh starts, new beginnings are always possible.

☐There was a famous monastery which had fallen on very hard times. Formerly its many buildings were filled with young monks and its big church resounded with the singing of the chant, but now it was deserted. People no longer came there to be nourished by prayer. A handful of old monks shuffled through the cloisters and praised their God with heavy hearts.

On the edge of the monastery woods, an old rabbi had built a little hut. He would come there from time to time to fast and pray. No one ever spoke with him, but whenever he appeared, the word would be passed from monk to monk: "The rabbi walks in the woods." And, for as long as he was there, the monks would feel sustained by his prayerful presence.

One day the abbot decided to visit the rabbi and to open his heart to him. So, after the morning Eucharist, he set out through the woods. As he approached the hut, the abbot saw the rabbi standing in the doorway, his arms outstretched in welcome. It was as though he had been waiting there for some time. The two embraced like long-lost brothers. Then they stepped back and just stood there, smiling at one another with smiles their faces could hardly contain.

After a while the rabbi motioned the abbot to enter. In the middle of the room was a wooden table with the Scriptures open on it. They sat there for a moment, in the presence of the Book. Then the rabbi began to cry. The abbot could not contain himself. He covered his face with his hands and began to cry too. For the first time in his life, he cried his heart out. The two men sat there like lost children, filling the hut with their sobs and wetting the wood of the table with their tears.

After the tears had ceased to flow and all was quiet again, the rabbi lifted his head. "You and your brothers are serving God with heavy hearts," he said. "You have come to ask a teaching of me. I will give you a teaching, but you can only repeat it once. After that, no one must ever say it aloud again."

The rabbi looked straight at the abbot and said, "The Messiah is among you." For a while, all was silent. Then the rabbi said, "Now you must go."

The abbot left without a word and without ever looking back.

The next morning, the abbot called his monks together in the chapter room. He told them he had received a teaching from "the rabbi who walks in the woods" and that this teaching was never again to be spoken aloud. Then he looked at each of his brothers and said, "The rabbi said that one of us is the Messiah."

The monks were startled by this saying. "What could it mean?" they asked themselves. "Is Brother John the Messiah? Or Father Matthew? Or Brother Thomas? Am I the Messiah? What could this mean?"

They were all deeply puzzled by the rabbi's teaching. But no one ever mentioned it again.

As time went by, the monks began to treat one another with a very special reverence. There was a gentle, wholehearted, human quality about them now which was hard to describe but easy to notice. They lived with one another as men who had finally found something. But they prayed the Scriptures together as men who were always looking for something. Occasional visitors found themselves deeply moved by the life of these monks. Before long, people were coming from far and wide to be nourished by the prayer life of the monks and young men were asking, once again, to become part of the community.

In those days, the rabbi no longer walked in the woods. His hut had fallen into ruins. But, somehow or other, the old monks who had taken his teaching to heart still felt sustained by his prayerful presence.[3] □

Such, then, are the gospel stories and events. They are impacting words that toss us challenges and turn topsy turvy our accepted way of living and loving. Like all stories, the gospel stories have many levels of meaning and so provoke from each person his or her own peculiar response. But also, like all stories that have become familiar with age and repetition, they have lost their force and their ability to jar us. We think we know exactly what they mean. This is why I have tried to put them in a new setting and looked at them from a different angle. I am not alone in this, of course. For a good while now, people have been trying to get us to see and hear the word of God afresh: from Robert Short's *The Gospel According to Peanuts* to Father John Shea's retellings. One of the earliest practitioners, however, is someone who may not be familiar to Catholics, Clarence Jordan, who preached and wrote his now famous *Cotton Patch* translations of Scripture. Jordon wanted people to see and hear the Bible anew as much as he wanted them to live in a profoundly gospel way in his Christian community, Koinonia:

> As the Koinonia community endured physical violence and economic boycott [because of its espousal of racial justice: Koinonia is in Georgia], Clarence's communication grew bolder and more prophetic. He began translating his own Cotton Patch versions of the New Testament books with the hope that he could make people feel like participants in the New Testament drama, rather than like spectators. Translating the ideas more than the words of the New Testament, he set the gospel story in twentieth century Georgia and sought to recount the New Testament episodes in ways that would leapfrog centuries and confront the mind of this man Jesus. . . . To him, a failure to read the Bible with a sense of participation and imagination helped to explain

the great distance that separated the ideas of the New Testament from the activities of twentieth-century churches.[4]

If you want an example of Jordon's freshness and imagination, compare the following versions of the First Epistle of Peter. The first translation is a standard one:

Peter, an apostle of Jesus Christ. To the exiles of the Dispersion in Pontus, Galatia, Cappadocia, Asia and Bithynia, chosen and destined by God the Father and sanctified by the Spirit for obedience to Jesus Christ and for sprinkling with his blood: May grace and peace be multiplied to you.

Jordon's version:

Rock, Jesus Christ's agent, to the migrant Christians scattered through Florida, Georgia, Oklahoma, Texas and California. With his experienced eye, Father-God hand-picked you and created you in His spirit, for washing and processing by Jesus Christ. May kindness and peace bust all over you.[5]

This may jar you, but it is supposed to. It is supposed to help us all see old truths in a new, an urgent way. It is designed to catch the Christian imagination too long dulled by repetition and familiarity. It's got the flavor and the fire of this old Mississippi country preacher who prayed thus before the morning service:

Oh, Lord, give Thy servant this mornin' the eyes of the eagle and the wisdom of the owl; connect his soul with the gospel telephone in the central skies; 'luminate his brow with the Sun of Heaven; possess his mind with love for the people; turpentine his imagination, grease his lips with 'possum oil, loosen his tongue with the sledge hammer of Thy power; 'lectrify his brain with the lightnin' of the word; put 'petual motion on his arms; fill him plum full of the dynamite of Thy glory; 'noint him all over with the kerosene of Thy salvation, and set him on fire. Amen!

Amen, Indeed! And this preacher, like Clarence Jordon and many others, stands in direct line with the preacher from Nazareth who used words and language and metaphors from his environment that were earthy, basic, and full of fire. And he wove those words and figures into stories which, after two thousand years, still retain their freshness and challenge if we but look at them with new eyes.

Variations
on a
Sacred Theme

9

*T*his chapter is a demonstration chapter in which I take a Scripture passage or several related ones and then match up a story on the same theme. Obviously this is not difficult to do, but it has its points. For one thing, it reminds us that God's revealed truth is universal and must find resonance wherever human beings gather. Secondly, this demonstration continues the thrust of the past pages, namely, that of translating old familiar truths into new and compelling forms. Finally, it shows us once more the power of story.

Before we proceed, two cautions should be given. First, the stories here, and any other stories for that matter, that are associated with the Scriptures are not intended to explain exactly and perfectly a Scripture parallel. What such stories do is illumine an attitude that such Scriptures promote; we should not press them more than that. Secondly, I do not want to give the impression here (or in the rest of the book) that the Scriptures are merely one mildly relevant expression of some universal, archetypal themes that give evidence that humanity is one and that the human heart's aspirations, desires, and needs will be universal, however locally colored and expressed. Still, *this* story of Israel and Jesus, with its covenant relationships, promises, and historical centeredness stands above the rest—not over and above and certainly not in opposition to—as hope and model.

Israel's story and Jesus' story *are* everyone else's story, but, if you will, in italics. Frederick Buechner can speak of "the fairy tale of the Gospel with, of course, the one critical difference from all other fairy tales, which is that claim made for it that it is true, that it not only happened once upon a time, but has kept on happening ever since and is happening still." It's something like Walbert Buhlmann's comment in his provocative book, *God's Chosen People*:

> Not just resentment, but a sense of justice and human worth raises its hackles when one person is preferred to another as a matter of course. This is all the more true when it is done by "divine authority"—allegedly. It is either old-fashioned mythology, or a narrow ethnocentrism, to interpret the Old and New Testament idea of a "chosen people" in a way that involves the second-class status, perhaps even the rejection, of other peoples.
>
> What if election does not mean a privilege of some but hope for all? What if it means not monopoly but model?[1]

These stories, then, are a kind of natural clustering of the inclusive model of Scripture. There are eleven (random) examples presented here. I will quote the Scripture first, and then tell a secular tale that gives it a story focus we can relate to.

1. The Scripture

John 17:20-21   I do not pray for these only, but also for those who believe in me through their word that they may be one, even as we are.

   Mark 14:26-27   And when they had sung a hymn they went out to the Mount of Olives. And Jesus said to them, "You will all fall away, for it is written, 'I will strike the shepherd and the sheep will be scattered.'"

   Luke 22:31   Simon, Simon, behold, Satan demanded to have you that he might sift you like wheat, but I have prayed for you that your faith may not fail; and when you have turned again, strengthen your brethren.

The Story: The Quails and the Hunter

☐Once upon a time, a flock of quail lived near a marsh and they would fly to the nearby fields everyday to feed. The only problem was that there was a Bird Hunter who lived nearby, and of late he had gotten to snare many quail in his net to take them to a nearby market to be sold. The reason he had grown so successful in catching them was that he had learned to imitate perfectly the call of the Leader. The Bird Hunter gave the call, and the quail, thinking it was the Leader, flew to his area where he tossed his net over them and captured them.

One day the Leader called all the quail together for a conference. He said, "We are becoming decimated! Soon there will be none of us left. The Bird Hunter is catching us all. But I have found out how he does it. He learned my call and deceives you. But I have a plan. The next time you hear what you think is my call and fly to the area and the Bird Hunter throws his net on top of you, here is what you are to do: all together you stick your heads through the openings in the net, and in one motion fly up with the net and land on the thorn bush. The net will stick there, you extricate yourselves, and the Bird Hunter will have to spend all day freeing his net."

And this is what they did. The Bird Hunter came, gave the imitation call, and the quail came. When the net was thrown over them, as one body they stuck their heads through the openings, and flew away to the thorn bush. They left a frustrated Hunter trying all day to get his net loose. This went on for some time until the Hunter's wife bitterly complained that her husband was bringing home no quail to bring to market. They were becoming poor. The Bird Hunter listened to his wife, told her of the actions of the quail, and with his hand on his chin, added, "But be patient, dear wife. Just wait till they quarrel. Then we shall catch them again."

Well, it so happened that one day when the Bird Hunter made his call, all the quail rose up and flew to the area where he was. But as they were landing, one quail accidentally brushed against another. "Will you watch where you're going, you clumsy ox!" cried the one quail. The other said hastily, "Oh, I'm sorry. I really am. I didn't mean to do it. It was an accident." "An accident, was it," cried the first quail. "If you'd watch where you're going instead of peering all about, you wouldn't be so clumsy." "Well," said the second quail, "I don't know why you take that attitude. I said I was sorry, and if you can't accept that. . . ." And they got to quarrelling. Soon the others, perceiving the argument, gathered around and took sides, one for the first quail and the other for the second.

Meanwhile, the Bird Hunter had his net ready and threw it over the birds. They began to cry to one another, "Come, let us stop arguing and hurry or else we'll be caught. Let's fly over that way!" But the other quail responded, "No, we're always flying over that way. We're always doing what you people want. Come, let us fly this way!" And while they were arguing which way to go, the Bird Hunter, with a smile on his face, gathered them up in the net, brought them to market, and that day made a fine penny.☐

2. The Scripture

Luke 12:13-21   And he told them a parable saying, The land of a rich man brought forth plentifully; and he thought to himself, What shall I do, for I have nowhere to store my crops? And he said, I will do this: I will pull down my barns and build larger ones and there I will store all my grains and my goods and I will say to my soul, "Soul, you have ample goods laid up for many years. Take your ease. Eat, drink, and be merry." But God said to him, "Fool! This night your soul is required of you and the things you have prepared, whose will they be?" So is he who lays up treasure for himself and is not rich toward God.

Matthew 5:3   Blessed are the poor in spirit, for theirs is the Kingdom of heaven.

Matthew 6:19-21   Do not lay up for yourselves treasures on earth where moth and rust consume and where thieves can break in and steal, but lay up for yourselves treasures in heaven where neither moth or rust consume and where thieves do not break in and steal. For where your treasure is, there will your heart be also.

The Story: The Fisherman and His Wife

☐Once upon a time there was a Fisherman who lived with his wife in a tiny hut by the sea, and every day he went fishing; and he fished and he fished. Well, one day he sat for a long time catching nothing, until his line suddenly jerked violently. He drew it up and there was a very large fish who said to him, "Fisherman, I beg you, let me live for I am an enchanted prince turned into a fish." The Fisherman said, "Why not? Any fish that can talk deserves to be tossed back." And so he did. Then the Fisherman got up and went home empty handed. His wife said, "You have caught nothing today? What shall we do?

We shall starve! Oh, you're a lazy, good-for-nothing lout!" But the husband replied, "Yes, I did catch one fish who was an enchanted prince, so of course I let him go." "Let him go!" exclaimed the wife, "Let him go? Why did you not make a wish? You have no sense at all."

But the Fisherman said, "But what would I wish for? I am happy." "What would you wish for?" his wife replied. "I'll tell you what to wish for. I'm sick and tired of living in this run-down shack. You go back and tell the fish we want a cottage. Surely he will do that, since you let him go. Now hurry." So the Fisherman betook himself down to the sea, which was calm and smooth, and called out,

Fish of the sea, listen to me,
My wife has a wish to make of thee.
And the fish came swimming to him and asked what she wanted, and he replied, "A cottage." "All right." said the fish, "Go back home. You live in a cottage."

When the man got back home his wife was no longer in the hut but in a lovely cottage with flowers outside and a bench to sit on. "Oh," said the Fisherman, "this is quite nice. We shall indeed be quite content here the rest of our lives." "We shall see," replied his wife. Well, one week later she said, "Husband, this cottage is getting far too small for us. Go back to tell the fish that I want a mansion." "But," protested her husband, "this cottage is just fine. I can't go back so soon and ask for something else." "Indeed you can," snapped his wife. "Go, and go right now!" The Fisherman's heart grew heavy and he went back to the sea, which was getting rougher, and he called out again,

Fish of the sea, listen to me,
My wife has a wish to make of thee.
The fish came up to shore and said, "What does she want this time?" "She wants to live in a mansion," the Fisherman said. "All right," said the fish. "Go back home. You live in a mansion." And the man went back home and he could hardly believe his eyes. There was the loveliest mansion with great fireplaces and gorgeous rugs and splendid furniture. "Oh," he exclaimed to his wife, "this is beautiful. Now we shall be happy." "We shall see," she said.

Two weeks later his wife said, "Husband, this mansion will not serve any longer. Go back and tell the fish that I want to be queen! And I want to live in a castle!" "Oh my," said the horrified Fisherman, "I couldn't do that. He's already given us so much. He might get angry. I don't really think I can do that." "But you can—and you will," said the wife. "You go back and tell the fish that I want to be queen and live in a castle. And do it now!" So the poor Fisherman betook himself once more to the sea, which was churning with purple and dark green water, with heavy clouds overhead, and he called out:

Fish of the sea, listen to me,
My wife has a wish to make of thee.

The fish appeared and said, "What does she want *now*?" "Alas," said the man, "she wants to be queen and live in a castle." "All right," said the fish. "Go back home. You live in a castle and she is queen." The Fisherman went back home and there was a giant stone castle with servants and horses. The trumpeters announced his arrival and he was ushered into the great hall where there was his wife—a queen! She had on a gold crown and a gown of rubies, and a throne made of ivory inlaid with jewels. "Oh," he said, "this is magnificent! This is beyond our wildest dreams. We live in a castle and you are a queen. *Now* we shall be happy." "We shall see," said his wife.

Three weeks later his wife said, "Husband, go back and tell the fish that I want to be the pope!" The husband was thunderstruck. He was speechless. "What are you standing there for? Go, do as I say." "But I couldn't do that," he pleaded. "No, this is really quite beyond reason . . . I mean. . . ." But she interrupted. "And I mean that you should do as I say. After all, I am the queen and you must obey." And so the poor Fisherman, bent low, went back to the sea, which by this time was dark and nasty with deep green currents and the winds blowing ominously overhead. He called out over the brewing storm:

Fish of the sea, listen to me,
My wife has a wish to make of thee.

The fish came up to the shore and said, "Now what does she want?" "She wants to be the pope!" cried the poor Fisherman. "All right," said the fish, "go back home. She is pope." And he went back home and he saw that the castle had been turned into a huge cathedral. He entered and saw prelates of all kinds filling the place. There were hundreds and thousands of candles lit, and kings and emperors were on their knees kissing the hem of his wife's robe—for now she was the pope! He approached, bowed, and said, "Oh Wife, now you are pope. You cannot become anything greater now. Now we will be happy." "We shall see," she said.

Four weeks later she said to her husband, "Husband, go back and tell the fish that I want to be Ruler of the earth and the sun and moon and the stars. I want to be empress of the universe!" The Fisherman said, "No, I cannot and will not do this. It's impossible. I just can't!" But his wife badgered him day and night, screamed at him and drove him to such distraction that he gave in. Once more he went down to the sea, which by this time was a cauldron of wild waves, and thunder and lightning were sounding overhead, and the rain was pelting the sea and the ground mercilessly. He called out:

Fish of the sea, listen to me,

My wife has a wish to make of thee.

And the fish came up and said, "Well, what does she want now?" The poor Fisherman shouted over the storm, "She wants to be Ruler of the heavens and the sun and the moon and the stars. She wants to be empress of the whole universe!" "No!" shouted the fish. "And you go back home and you will find your wife in your tiny hut by the sea and there you shall live hand to mouth until you die." And he went back home. And there was the hut as the fish said. And they lived there until they died. □

3. The Scripture

Mark 8:34   What does it profit a man to gain the whole world and forfeit his life?

The Story: The Very Pretty Lady

□There was a very pretty lady once who lived all alone. She didn't have to live all alone; she was so pretty that there were many young men anxious to marry her. They hung about in her dooryard and played guitars and sang sweet songs and tried to look in through the windows. They were there from dawn to dusk, always sad, always hopeful. But the very pretty lady didn't want to marry any of them. "It's no use being loved for the way one looks," she said to herself. "If I can't find someone who will love me in spite of my face, then I will never marry anyone at all."

This was wise, no doubt, but no one is wise all the time. For the truth is that the very pretty lady rather liked the fact that she was pretty, and sometimes she would stand in front of the mirror and look and look at herself. At times like that she would be pleased with herself and would go out to the dooryard and talk to all the young men and let them go with her to market and carry home her bags and packages for her. And for a long time afterward they would all look a good deal more hopeful than sad.

But most of the time the very pretty lady stayed inside her cottage, feeling lonely regardless of all the young men in the dooryard, longing for someone who would love her as she wanted to be loved.

Now, after a while, one way or another, the Devil heard about the very pretty lady and he decided that she was the very thing he needed to brighten up his days in Hell. So he packed a satchel of disguises and went up to have a look at her.

He had heard how very pretty she was, but no one had told him that she never let anyone inside the cottage. He went disguised as a beggar, but she wouldn't open the door. He tried appearing as a preacher and then as a king, but that didn't work either. So at last he simply disguised himself as one of her suitors and hung about with the others waiting for market day.

When the pretty lady came out at last, the Devil walked beside her all the way to town, looking at her every moment, and he carried back the heaviest package. By the time she had gone inside her cottage again, his mind was made up: she was indeed exactly what he needed in Hell, and he had waited long enough to have her.

When night came and the sad and hopeful young men had all gone home, the Devil threw off his disguise and wished himself into the pretty lady's bedroom with a puff of red smoke and a noise like thunder. The pretty lady woke up at once, and when she saw him she shrieked.

"Don't be alarmed," said the Devil calmly. "It's only me. I've come to take you away to Hell."

"Never!" cried the pretty lady. "I shan't go and there's no way you can make me."

"That's true," said the Devil, "there isn't. You have to come of your own free will when you come before your time. But you'll like it so much down there—you'll be the prettiest thing in the place."

"I'm that already, right here," said the pretty lady, "for all the good it does me. Why should I go away to have the same thing somewhere else?"

"Ah, but in Hell," said the Devil, "your beauty will last forever and ever, whereas here it can only fade."

For the first time the pretty lady was tempted, and the Devil knew it. He fetched a mirror from her bureau and held it up in front of her so she could look at herself. "Wouldn't it be a shame," he coaxed, "to let such a pretty face go to waste? If you stay here, it can only last fifteen or twenty more years, but in Hell there is no time. You will look just as you do now till the stars fall and a new plan is made, and we all know that will never happen."

The pretty lady looked at herself in the mirror and felt, as she sometimes did, that it *was* rather nice to be pretty, but in the nick of time she remembered what it was she really wanted. "Tell me," she said. "Is there any love in Hell?"

"Love?" said the Devil with a shudder. "What would we want with a thing like that?"

"Well then," said the pretty lady, pushing away the mirror, "I'll never agree to go. You can beg all you want from now till Sunday, but it won't be any use."

At this the Devil grew very angry and his eyes glowed like embers. "Is that your final word?" he demanded.

"That is my final word," she answered.

"Very well!" he said. "I can't take you against your will, that's true. But I can take your beauty. I can, and I will." There was another clap of thunder and the Devil disappeared in a cloud of smoke. He went straight back to Hell and took all the pretty lady's beauty with him, and he tacked it up in little fragments all over his throne room, where it sparkled and twinkled and brightened up the place very nicely.

After a couple of years, however, the Devil grew curious about the lady and went up to see how she was getting along. He arrived at her cottage at twilight and went to peer in through the window. And there she was, ugly as a boot, sitting down to supper. But candles lit the table and she was no longer alone. Sitting with her was a young man just as ugly as she, and in a cradle near her chair lay a very ugly baby. And the strange thing was that there was such love around the table that the Devil reeled back as if someone had struck him.

"Humph!" said the Devil to himself. "I'll never understand this if I live to be a trillion!"

So he went back to Hell in a temper and tore down all the lady's beauty from the walls of his throne room and threw it away, and it floated up out of Hell into a dark corner of the sky and made itself, more usefully, into a star.[2]

4. The Scripture

Galatians 3:27-28   For as many of you were baptized into Christ have put on Christ. There is neither Jew nor Greek, there is neither slave or free, there is neither male or female; for you are all one in Christ Jesus.

The Story: The Rainbow People

☐In a beautiful meadow at the bottom of a great mountain lived a people called the "Greens." They wore green clothes, lived in green homes, drove green cars and believed that God was green.

At the top of the great mountain were another people, the "Blues." They wore blue clothes, lived in blue homes, drove blue cars and believed that God was blue.

Greens and Blues didn't speak to each other. In fact they hated each other. Green parents would teach their children to say:

"Green is happy;
Blue is sad.
Greens are good;
Blues are bad."

Blue parents would teach their children to say, "Blue is happy; Green is sad. Blues are good; Greens are bad."

Blues and Greens grew up seeing each other as "sad" and "bad." But they didn't really know each other. Some Blues went a whole lifetime without even talking to a Green. They didn't know each other because they stayed in their own territories. They didn't go to the same churches or schools.

It happened one day that a Green boy was walking with his father when he saw a Blue boy flying his kite in their meadow. When the Blue boy saw them he became frightened. He ran back toward his mountain. But in doing so he sprained his ankle and couldn't walk very well. The Green boy wanted to help him, but his father said, "No."

"Don't you remember what your mother and I taught you? Green is happy; Blue is sad. Greens are good; Blues are bad."

The Green boy still asked his dad if he could help the Blue. "Dad, how do we know this Blue is bad? All I know is that he has a sprained ankle and he needs someone to help him walk home."

When the Green boy said this, his father turned to him saying: "Blue is the color of the devil. God only loves Green. Our religion teaches us to help our own kind. I want you to do as you are told."

A few weeks later the Green boy was out playing with his pet rabbit. He chased it through the tall grass and into the open fields. He played for so long that without realizing it, he had crossed into Blue Land. He was about to catch the rabbit when the rascal jumped down a small cliff. Green went after him and in so doing caught his right leg between two big rocks. He pushed and pulled, but could not move. He called for help, hoping a Green would hear him. He worried that sooner or later a Blue would come by. This thought frightened him because he had never met a Blue.

As the sunlight faded, someone approached the trapped Green boy. It was a Blue. It was the same boy who had sprained his ankle, the boy who had been flying his kite in Green Land. The Green boy closed his eyes waiting to be hurt by his enemy.

The Blue boy stood by the Green boy for a few minutes. Then he went to a tree and broke off a branch. The Green boy said, "Don't hit me with that branch," thinking that's what Blue was about to do.

Blue answered him. "I'm not going to hit you. The branch is to pry loose the rocks that are holding your leg."

Blue pried loose the rocks. He tore his blue shirt into long strips and tied the branch to Green's leg. Then he helped Green walk home.

When Green's father saw his son's leg tied with the blue cloth, he cursed his boy. "I don't care if you were injured," he screamed. "You should have not let a Blue touch you."

Though Green knew his father was upset with him, he could not forget the Blue who had helped him. When his leg healed, he went into Blue Land to find his helper.

For a whole day Green walked in the neighborhoods of Blue Land. It took a lot of courage to do this because everywhere he went people slammed doors on him and called him names. Some young children even threw rocks at him. Finally, he found the boy who had helped him. He did not slam his door on Green. He welcomed him in his home.

Green was happy to see Blue, but he was surprised to see that his helper had clothes that combined the colors of blue and green.

"I thought you learned that green was bad. Why are you wearing green with your blue?" asked Green.

"Do you remember when I helped you when you were hurt? I tore up my blue shirt to make a splint for your leg. I figured that you became part of me, and I became part of you. In helping you and talking with you, I came to see that green is as good as blue."

"Won't the other Blues throw rocks at you when they find out you're a 'Green-lover?'" asked Green.

"I don't care what people think," said Blue. "It is right to help people whether they are blue or green."

The two boys became close friends. They often visited each other. They made up a new song which they taught to the children. It had these words:

"Green is good, but so is Blue,
Purple, Yellow and Red too —
All the children should be glad;
There is no color that is bad."

Little by little more Blues and Greens started visiting each other. Then they began going to each other's schools and churches. They even went beyond their own lands and visited the Yellows, Reds and Purples. After a while most people didn't call themselves "Greens" or "Blues" but simply "Rainbow People." And to this day their children sing, "There is no color that is bad."[3] □

5. The Scripture

Luke 9:23-24   For if any one would come after me let him deny himself and take up his cross daily and follow me. For whoever would save his life will lose it and whoever loses his life for my sake will save it.

Matthew 25:35-40   Come, O blessed of my Father, inherit the kingdom prepared for you from the foundation of the world. For I was hungry and you gave me food. I was thirsty and you gave me drink. . . .

The Story: Santoro

□ There once was a man named Santoro who was a very good businessman and very rich. He had a magnificent house, the best of food, beautiful clothes, and an exquisite garden full of exotic trees and plants. One day Santoro got sick and he called the doctor. The doctor came, treated him, and said casually as he was leaving, "Take care of yourself, Santoro. You know you're going to die someday. Don't let him come sooner than he should." When he left, Santoro began to think. He found himself saying in amazement, "Die? Die? But I don't want to die. I don't want to die!" Dejected and perplexed, he sat down on his velvet chair, put his head in his hands, and said to himself, "What shall I do?" Then it hit him. He stood up saying, exclaiming, "I know. I have heard that somewhere there is the Fountain of Youth. I shall find it, drink from it, and live forever. I shall not have to die!"

So Santoro sold all his possessions, took his riches and went in search for the Fountain of Youth. He traveled over hill and dale, asking everyone. Everyone heard of it, but no one could tell him where it was. Days passed into weeks and the weeks into months and the months into years. One day, tired and discouraged, Santoro climbed a mountain and came upon the ruin of an old temple. He lay his head on his knees and closed his eyes. When he opened them again, there was a venerable Monk, arms in long sleeves, standing before him. "Santoro," he said, "you are looking for the Fountain of Youth. I cannot tell you where it is, but would you like to go to the Land Where People Never Die?" "Oh, yes!" exclaimed Santoro, "that's what I want. Take me to the Land Where People Never Die."

The old monk withdrew his hand from his sleeve and pulled out a small paper bird and lay it on the ground. The paper bird grew bigger and bigger until it was large enough for Santoro to climb aboard his back. The bird took off over sea and dale, over mountain and rock, traveling for days until at last there was an opening in the sky and Santoro saw a lovely green island below. The bird landed. Never had Santoro seen such beauty. And there were people there. They were more or less sitting on the shoreline staring into space, but he didn't notice that. Here he was in the Land Where People Never Die.

Soon, because he was such a good businessman, Santoro once more had the magnificent house, the best of food, beautiful clothes, and an exquisite garden full of exotic trees and plants. He was very happy. And time just went on, and on, and on . . . and on . . . and on. One day Santoro said to himself, "You know, you keep thinking that something is going to happen, but it never does." It was getting to him so much that one day he again said to himself, "I know what I shall do. I shall go out into the woods and pick all those berries that my father taught me are poisonous. And I will eat them and I shall die." So he did. He picked all the poison berries and gobbled them down. But, of course, he didn't die since he was in the Land Where People Never Die. Then he decided that when the next ship came in bringing supplies he would bribe the sailors to get all the terrible and poisonous medicine out of the medicine chest and he would swallow the iodine and mercurochrome and all the rest, and so would die. He bribed the sailors, downed the poison but, he did not die because he was in the Land Where People Never Die.

Soon he too had joined all the others sitting on the shoreline staring into space. One day, dejected, bored and sad, he happened to put his arm up his sleeve. "What's this?" he said. He pulled it out and it was the paper bird! He quickly put it on the ground. It grew bigger and bigger, and he climbed on its back and off he went. He was ecstatic! At last he was free.

But while soaring over the ocean, a swift and terrible storm came up. Thunder and lightning sounded and flashed. Hard rain pelted him. The bird, being only paper, soon got drenched, crumbled, and fell toward the water with Santoro. He dropped into the pit full of water and when underneath he opened his eyes, he saw the largest White Shark he had ever seen coming straight toward him with open jaws. It opened them wider around the head of Santoro. He screamed an awful scream—and woke up.

There before him was the old monk asking, "Santoro, do you want to go to the Land Where People Never Die?" "Oh, no, no, no," responded Santoro. "I've quite changed my mind about that." "Santoro," said the Monk, "listen to me. You go home and you rebuild your magnificent house, and have the best of food and beautiful clothes and an exquisite garden full of exotic trees and plants—but instead of building these things for yourself, do them for others. Then when it comes your turn to die, they will miss you and sing your praises."

And that's what he did. And that's what happened. □

6. The Scripture

John 12:24   Truly, truly, I say to you, unless a grain of wheat falls into the earth and dies it remains alone; but if it dies it bears much fruit.

1 Thessalonians 4:13,14   But we would not have you ignorant, brethren, concerning those who are asleep, that you may not
grieve as others who have no hope. For since we believe that Jesus
died and rose again, so, through Jesus, God will bring with him
those who have fallen asleep.

1 Corinthians 15:36-44   What you sow does not come to life
unless it dies. And what you sow is not the body which is to be, but a
bare grain. . . . So it is with the resurrection of the dead. What is
sown is perishable. It is sown in dishonor, it is raised in glory. It is
sown in weakness, it is raised in power.

The Story: The Parable

☐ Once upon a time a man was told that he had an incurable illness.
The news filled him with great sadness for he had dreamed dreams
and hoped hopes, and now it seemed that they would never come
true. One day he heard that there was a wizard who could do
wonderful things for people, so he decided to visit him.

"What is it you want?" asked the wizard.

"I have dreamed dreams and hoped hopes," replied the man.

"What have you dreamed?"

"I have dreamed of a home, a home of my own to live in—a big
home with many rooms and fine furniture."

"You have but to ask," said the wizard.

With that, he snapped his fingers and at once, in the twinkling of
an eye, there stood a beautiful home. Nay, not a home, a palace—
not even a palace, a castle. The castle was far bigger, far more
beautiful than any he had ever dreamed of. There were almost too
many rooms to count, and each one was filled with exquisite furniture. The man was filled with joy as he entered his house, walked its
halls and explored its rooms.

But then, in time, he remembered the illness and again was
filled with sadness. He returned to the wizard.

"What is it you want of me?" asked the wizard.

"I have dreamed dreams and I have hoped hopes," the man
replied.

"What have you dreamed?"

"I have dreamed of food, food fit for a king. Food that would fill
all my cravings, food as I have never eaten before."

"You have but to ask," said the wizard.

And he snapped his fingers. At once, in the twinkling of an eye, the castle table was covered with fine and delicious food. Never had the man seen such food or tasted such goodness. It was food fit for a hundred kings. He was filled with joy as he sat at the banquet table.

But then, in time, he remembered the sickness and the sadness came over him again. He returned to the wizard.

"What is it you want of me?" asked the wizard.

"I have dreamed dreams and I have hoped hopes," said the man.

"Tell me, what have you dreamed?"

"I have dreamed of clothes—fine, rich, and beautiful clothes."

"You have but to ask," said the wizard.

Once again he snapped his fingers and at once the man was clothed in the finest clothes he had ever seen. His castle was filled with clothes, rich and beautiful clothes of the finest cloth imaginable. So the man walked his castle in his exquisite clothes, and sat at table to the finest of foods, and he was filled with happiness.

But then, in time, he remembered the incurable sickness, and a great sorrow overcame him.

"Why are you still sad?" asked the wizard. "Have I not fulfilled your dreams and hopes? Do you not have a castle, and clothes, and food just as you wished? Why then are you still sad?"

"Because I have an incurable illness," the man cried.

"I can cure that," said the wizard.

The man's face quickly changed to hope.

"You can cure that!" he exclaimed. "Why, if you can cure that, what do I care about the rest? If you can cure the sickness, I don't care where I live, or what I eat, or what I wear. None of that really matters if you can cure my sickness."

"You have but to ask," replied the wizard.

He than snapped his fingers, and in an instant, in the twinkling of an eye, the man was cured of his illness.

So the man walked away—away from the fine castle, away from the delicious foods, away from the exquisite clothes. He walked away from all of them—filled with joy, happier than he had ever been in his entire life.

What does this parable mean? Life is a terminal illness. When a certain man first realized that life would come to an end, when he saw the grass die, and the leaves die, and the trees die, and animals die, and his companions die, and he knew that one day he, too, would die, he was filled with a great sadness.

One day he learned of a great wizard, a wonder worker—God. So the man went before his God.

"What is it you want of me?" God asked.

"I have dreamed dreams and I have hoped hopes," replied man.

"Tell me, what is it you've dreamed?" asked the Lord God.

"I have dreamt of a house, a fine and luxurious house for me to live in," replied the man.

"You have but to ask," said God, and he snapped his fingers, and at once man had a place to live. A home of deep, rich earth with a mossy, green carpet, a home lit by the sun during the day, and the moon and the stars at night. And man made his home—homes of mud and mortar, homes of brick and stone, homes of wood and glass and steel, ranch homes and split levels, homes of one story and homes that reached into the sky.

The man in this parable was filled with joy over his home, and he walked its halls with great delight. But then, in time, he remembered he would die, and a great sadness overcame him. So he went back to God.

"What is it you want of me?" asked the Lord.

"Lord, I have dreamed dreams and hoped hopes!"

"Tell me what you have dreamed?"

"I've dreamed of food, food to fill my every yearning, food to satisfy my every hunger."

"You have but to ask," said the Lord God, and he snapped his fingers, and in an instant there was spread before the man a banquet of food, far beyond his dreams. Food from the earth was there: greens, vegetables and fruits of infinite variety. There was food from the seas, fish of every size and shape: lobster, crab, shrimps, scallops, pike, trout, and bass. Food from the land was there: beef, lamb, venison, and pork. There was, in fact, every kind of meat. Food from the heavens was there: duck, geese, quail, and pheasant. The man's banquet table was filled beyond his wildest imagining. So he ate and his heart was full of joy. But then, in time, he remembered he would die, and his sorrow returned. Again he went to his God.

"What is it you want of me?" asked God.

"I have dreamed dreams and hoped hopes," sighed the man.

"What have you dreamed?"

"I have dreamed of clothes—fine, rich, and exquisite clothes. Clothes fit for a king!"

"You have but to ask," said the Lord, and again he snapped his fingers. In an instant, the man was clothed in magnificent attire. Cloth of wool, silk, velvet, and cotton. Clothes of every size, shape, color, and fabric. Warm clothes for winter and light clothes for summer. Clothes for morning, noon, and night. Clothes fit for a hundred kings. So the man wore the clothes, and walked his castle, and ate his fill, and in his heart there was joy.

But then, once again, he remembered he must die. Again, a great sadness overwhelmed him.

"Why are you still sad?" asked God.

"Because I must die," the man cried.

"I can cure that," said God.

"You can cure that? You can cure death? Why, if you can cure death then I really don't care where I live, or what I eat or what I wear. None of that matters if you can cure death!"

"You have but to ask," said God.

With that, the Lord God snapped his fingers, and in an instant, in the twinkling of an infinite eye . . . there was Jesus!

And the man walked away. Away from the castles of stone, and wood, and steel. Away from the food, and the exquisite clothes. The man walked away from all of them as if they were nothing. Cured of death, he walked away, his heart filled with joy, happier than in any dream he'd ever dreamed, happier than he'd ever hoped, happier than he had ever been in his entire life.[4]□

7. The Scripture

1 Peter 2:22-25   When he was reviled he did not revile in return: when he suffered he did not threaten but he trusted him who judges justly. He himself bore our sins in his body on the tree that we might die to sin and live to righteousness. By his wounds you have been healed. For you were straying like sheep but have now returned to the shepherd and guardian of your souls.

The Story: The Philosopher's Love

☐Two centuries ago there lived a very famous German-Jewish philosopher named Moses Mendelssohn. Moses Mendelssohn was brilliant and compassionate—but he had one flaw. He was a small, hunchbacked man.

Hunchback that he was, he fell in love with a beautiful and charming young woman named Gretchen, the daughter of a prosperous banker. Several months after he had met Gretchen, Mendelssohn visited her father and he asked him, very cautiously, how his daughter might feel about the possibility of marrying him, for he had come to love her very much.

"Please, tell me the truth," Mendelssohn insisted. The father hesitated and then replied: "The truth is that the girl is frightened by you because . . . because . . . ." Mendelssohn finished his sentence for him " . . . because I am a hunchback?" "Yes," said the father, "because you are a hunchback."

Mendelssohn paused. Then after some silence he asked permission to see the daughter on the pretext that he wanted to say farewell to her. The father agreed. Mendelssohn went upstairs and found Gretchen in a room where she was busy with needlework.

She avoided looking at him during the conversation, which Mendelssohn eventually directed to the subject of marriage. In the course of the conversation on the topic, the young woman asked him if he really believed in that old saying that "Marriages are made in heaven."

"Of course," he replied. "And while we're on that subject, I might as well tell you that something unusual happened to me. As you know, when boys are born the angels in heaven call out for all to hear, 'This little boy is destined to have this special girl for a wife. It is decreed from all eternity and no one may change it.'

"So when I was born, the angels made the usual announcement about me and the name of my future wife was announced. But then the angels paused and added, 'But alas, Mendelssohn's wife will have a terrible hump on her back!' Then I shouted out loud before the court of heaven. I cried, 'Oh, Lord, no. No. A girl who is hunchbacked will very easily become bitter and hard, and the object of awful jokes and hurts. No, Lord, a girl should be beautiful. Oh, Lord, please . . . please *give the hump to me* and let her be well formed.'

"And you know what, Gretchen? God heard my prayer and I was glad. I am that boy and you are that girl."

Gretchen was deeply moved. She saw Mendelssohn in a whole new way and so she became his faithful and loving wife. □

8. The Scripture

Matthew 11:28   Come to me, all you who are weary and burdened, and I will give you rest.

The Story: Walking With The Lord

□One bright autumn morning, I was sitting at my breakfast table, thinking:

"I've certainly had a lot of problems lately. Troubles at work, troubles at home. . . . I really ought to take time to pray about them."

But then, all of a sudden, I sensed that someone had walked into the room behind me. I turned around and gasped:

"Lord Jesus! What are You doing here?"

The Lord Himself was standing in my doorway! I rubbed my eyes—was it really He? Yes, everything checked out . . . from the tip of the white seamless robe to the faint glimmering halo around His head. I stammered:

"That is . . . errrr . . . it's not that you shouldn't be here. I'm just not used to You dropping by in such a visible form."

This unexpected visit had unsettled me, and I vaguely wondered if I had done anything wrong. He smiled and the light in His eyes grew brighter:

"Would you like to go for a walk?"

"Uhmm . . . why . . . sure!"

And so, we walked down the little country road that leads past my home. Slowly, the truth began to dawn upon me and I murmured to myself:

"What an incredible opportunity! He has all the answers to all my problems—my relationships at work . . . my worries about the future . . . my family problems. All I need is to ask."

We walked quietly for several minutes, and then I turned to Him:

"Excuse me, Lord, but I need some advice on this very difficult problem. . . ."

But before I could finish, He had raised His fingers to His lips:

"Shhhh. . . . Do you hear it?"

At first, I didn't hear a thing. But then came the faint tumbling of a nearby brook, crisp and light beneath the autumn colors. The Lord sighed:

"Isn't that beautiful?"

"Ah . . . yes . . . I suppose so. . . ."

I was thoroughly distracted. (He had interrupted my train of thought.) I waited a few minutes to show due respect, and then—just as we walked past a rolling meadow—I blurted out:

"Lord, I've been worried about my prayer life. Things have been awfully dry. Now, according to the books that I've read. . . ."

He put His arm around my shoulder:

"Hush. . . . Do you hear it?"

Children were running through the meadow grass. Once again, He smiled:

"Isn't it wonderful?"

"Uhmm . . . yes . . . now that You mention it."

Then I added irritably:

"You know I love children."

We walked on. A horrible thought loomed in my mind: what if I lost this opportunity? Here were all the answers to all my problems, right at my elbow! He even knew the deepest mysteries of the universe: love . . . death . . . the Armageddon! As a last resort, I thought I'd talk to Him about religion. After all, that is His line of work:

"Lord, I was wondering what You think of the conflict in modern biblical scholarship between. . . ."

Again, the friendly arm came around my shoulder and I gritted my teeth. The Lord stopped and silently picked up a roadside pebble. He grinned:

"I'll bet you can't hit the top of that telephone pole."

I was bewildered. Why, of all things! And from the Lord! (This was not what I had expected from the Second Person of the Holy

Trinity. If you were God, wouldn't you be a bit more serious about it?) He casually tossed His pebble toward the pole:

It arched silently through the air.

Hmmmm. . . . He missed!

My depression was deepening, but still I stopped to pick up a pebble. What else could I do? Half-heartedly, I tossed it in the general direction of the telephone pole:

It arched silently through the air.

Hmmmm. . . . I hit it!

The Lord proudly looked at me and chuckled:

"Hey, you're good."

As we strolled on, the knots in my stomach grew tighter. Whenever I wanted to talk about anything of any importance, there would always be an interruption. Some faded blue chicory would be brushed by the wind, or a butterfly would light on a moss-covered fencepost.

At last, our walk is finished. I am so upset that I can think of nothing to say. Beneath His long black beard, the Lord has a playful smile, and as He turns to leave, the light in His eyes grows brighter.

He walks to the door, and then stops to glance at me over His shoulder:

"Stop trying so hard."⁵☐

9. The Scripture

The Kingdom of God is within you.

The Story: The Happy Man's Shirt

☐A king had an only son that he thought the world of. But this prince was always unhappy. He would spend days on end at his window staring into space.

"What on earth do you lack?" asked the king. "What's wrong with you?"

"I don't even know myself, Father."

"Are you in love? If there's a particular girl you fancy, tell me, and I'll arrange for you to marry her, no matter whether she's the daughter of the most powerful king on earth or the poorest peasant girl alive!"

"No, Father, I'm not in love."

The king tried in every way imaginable to cheer him up, but theaters, balls, concerts, and singing were all useless, and day by day the rosy hue drained from the prince's face.

The king issued a decree, and from every corner of the earth came the most learned philosophers, doctors, and professors. The king showed them the prince and asked for their advice. The wise men withdrew to think, then returned to the king. "Majesty, we have given the matter close thought and we have studied the stars. Here's what you must do. Look for a happy man, a man who's happy through and through and exchange your son's shirt for his."

That same day the king sent ambassadors to all parts of the world in search of the happy man.

A priest was taken to the king. "Are you happy?" asked the king.

"Yes, indeed, Majesty."

"Fine. How would you like to be my bishop?"

"Oh, Majesty, if only it were so!"

"Away with you! Get out of my sight! I'm seeking a man who's happy just as he is, not one who's trying to better his lot."

Thus the search resumed, and before long the king was told about a neighboring king, who everybody said was a truly happy man. He had a wife as good as she was beautiful and a whole slew of children. He had conquered all his enemies, and his country was at peace. Again hopeful, the king immediately sent ambassadors to him to ask for his shirt.

The neighboring king received the ambassadors and said, "Yes, indeed, I have everything anybody could possibly want. But at the same time I worry because I'll have to die one day and leave it all. I can't sleep at night for worrying about that!" The ambassadors thought it wiser to go home without this man's shirt.

At his wit's end, the king went hunting. He fired at a hare but only wounded it, and the hare scampered away on three legs. The king pursued it, leaving the hunting party far behind him. Out in the open field he heard a man singing a refrain. The king stopped in his tracks. "Whoever sings like that is bound to be happy!" The song led him into a vineyard, where he found a young man singing and pruning the vines.

"Good day, Majesty," said the youth. "So early and already out in the country?"

"Bless you! Would you like me to take you to the capital? You will be my friend."

"Much obliged, Majesty, but I wouldn't even consider it. I wouldn't even change places with the Pope."

"Why not? Such a fine young man like you. . . ."

"No, no, I tell you. I'm content with just what I have and want nothing more."

"A happy man at last!" thought the king. "Listen, young man. Do me a favor."

"With all my heart, Majesty, if I can."

"Wait just a minute," said the king, who, unable to contain his joy any longer, ran to get his retinue. "Come with me! My son is saved! My son is saved!" And he took them to the young man. "My dear lad," he began, "I'll give you whatever you want! But give me . . . give me. . . ."

"What, Majesty?"

"My son is dying! Only you can save him. Come here!"

The king grabbed him and started unbuttoning the youth's jacket. All of a sudden he stopped, and his arms fell to his sides.

The happy man wore no shirt.[6]□

10. The Scripture

Revelation 3:12-16   And to the angel of the church of Laodicea write: "The words of the Amen, the faithful and true witnesses, the beginning of God's creation, I know your works: you are neither cold nor hot. Would that you were cold or hot! So because you are lukewarm, and neither cold nor hot, I will spew you out of my mouth."

The Story: The Bat

□Once there was a war between beasts and birds. Bat was on birds' side. In the first battle, the birds were badly beaten. As soon as Bat saw that the battle was going against them, he crept away, hid under a log, and stayed there till the fight was over.

When the animals were going home, Bat slipped in among them.

After they had gone some distance, they saw him and asked one another: "How is this? Bat is one of the men who fought against us?"

Bat heard them, and he said: "Oh, no! I am one of you; I don't belong to the bird people. Did you ever see one of those people who had double teeth? Go and look in their mouths and see if they have. If you find one bird with double teeth, you can say that I belong to the bird people. But I don't; I am one of your own people."

They didn't say anything more; they let Bat stay with them.

Soon after, there was another battle; in that battle birds won. As Bat's side was getting beaten, he slipped away and hid under a log. When the battle was over and birds were going home, Bat went in among them.

When they noticed him, they said: "You are our enemy; we saw you fighting against us."

"Oh, no," said Bat, "I am one of you; I don't belong to those beasts. Did you ever see one of those people who had wings?"

They didn't say anything more; they let him stay with them.

So Bat went back and forth as long as the war lasted. At the end of the war, birds and beasts held a council to see what to do with him. At last they said to Bat: "Hereafter, you will fly around alone at night, and will never have any friends, either among those that fly, or those that walk."[7]□

11. The Scripture

Matthew 7:21   Not everyone who says to me "Lord, Lord" shall enter the kingdom of heaven but only those who do the will of my Father. . . .

Matthew 21:28-31   "What do you think? A man had two sons; and he went to the first and said, 'Son, go and work in the vineyard today.' And he answered, 'I will not,' but afterward repented and went. And he went to the second and said the same; and he answered, 'I will go, sir,' but did not go. Which of the two did the will of the father?"

James 2:14   What does it profit, my brethren, if a man says he has faith but has not works?

1 John 3:17-18   But if one has the world's goods and sees his brother in need, yet closes his heart against him, how does God's love abide in him? Little children, let us not love in word or speech but in deed and in truth.

The Story: Bluebonnet

☐ The Comanche People moaned aloud to the Great Spirit:
"O Great Spirit, our land is dying and we are dying too.
Tell us what we have done wrong to make you so angry.
End this terrible drought and save your people before we perish altogether.
Tell us what we must do so that once more you will send the rain and restore our land to life."

For three days the People prayed this prayer and the dancers danced the prayer. And the People waited and waited, prayed and prayed, but no rain came. And it was very hard on the little children and the old folk,

Among the few children who had not died from hunger was a small girl named She-Who-Sits-Alone. Apart from the crowd she watched her People pray and dance. In her lap she held a doll which she treasured above all things else. It was a warrior doll with a bone belt, beaded leggings and on its head were blue feathers from the Bluejay.

She-Who-Sits-Alone spoke to her doll. "Soon," she said, "the wise men will go off to the hill. They will listen to the winds which carry the wisdom of the Great Spirit. Then we shall know what to do once more to make the rains come and earth alive."

As she talked to the doll she held it close to her heart, for this doll had been made by her mother, and her father had brought her the blue feathers and her grandparents had made the leggings. But that seemed long ago. They had all died from the hunger of the land and so she sat alone. Her warrior doll was all that she had left from those happy days.

As she had told her doll, the Wise Men went to the hills to listen to winds carrying the voice of the Great Spirit. After many sunsets the Wise Men returned and the people gathered to listen to their message.

The Wise Men said solemnly, "The Great Spirit says that the people have become selfish. For years they have taken from the earth but they have not given anything back. So the Great Spirit says that they must make a sacrifice. They must make a burnt offering of their most valued possession. Then the ashes of such offerings will be scattered on the winds to the four corners of the earth. And when this sacrifice is done, the rains will come and life will return to the earth."

The People gave thanks to the Great Spirit for telling them what they must do and went back to their tents to look for their most valued possessions. One warrior said, "What shall I give? I am sure the Great Spirit does not want my new bow." A woman added, "I know the Great Spirit does not want my special blanket either." And so it went all throughout the village. Everyone had an excuse to keep what he or she valued most.

Except She-Who-Sits-Alone. She held her warrior doll to her chest and at last she spoke to it. "It is you the Great Spirit wants for you are my most valued possession." And she knew what she had to do.

Later that night, when everyone was asleep, She-Who-Sits-Alone crawled our from her blanket, took a lighted stick from the smoldering campfire and crept outside. She went to the top of a hill, placed the lighted stick in the ground, and spoke aloud: "O Great Spirit, here is my warrior doll. It is the only thing I have from my mother and father. It is my most valued possession. Please accept it."

Still holding her doll, she gathered some twigs and fanned up a fire and held her doll near it. She hesitated and tears began to roll down her cheeks. But then she thought of her parents and grandparents and her friends who had died from the hunger and thrust her doll into the fire.

When the flames died down and the ashes had cooled, she scooped them up and scattered them to the four winds. She was now tired. So on the hill she fell asleep without her doll but with a smile on her lips.

The next morning the sun awoke her. She sat up, rubbed her eyes and looked out over the hill. As far as she could see, where her doll's ashes had fallen, the ground was covered with beautiful blue flowers like little blue bonnets. They were as blue as the feathers in her doll's hair.

When the People came out of their tents they could hardly believe their eyes. They ran to the hill where She-Who-Sits-Alone was to look at the wonderful sight. There was no doubt in their minds. The flowers were a sign from the Great Spirit that they were forgiven. And then and there they sang and danced and thanked the Great Spirit. And in the middle of their song and dance a gentle rain began to fall. The land began to live again and the people were saved.

And from that day on She-Who-Sits-Alone was known by another name, the name of the One-Who-Loved-Her-People. And to this day, every spring in the land now called Texas, the Great Spirit remembers the love of the little girl and fills the valleys with beautiful blue flowers.[8] □

10   *Our Story*

*T*o be a person is to have a story.

Without my story, I have no identity. I do not know who I am, or what I am about. If you have no story, how do you know where you're going; and if you're going somewhere, how will you know when you get there?

A story is made up of the steppingstones along the footpath, markings up the side of the mountain, curves and detours along the highway of life. A story is not a fourlane "superslab" (CB jargon for highway) without stops, turns and returns. A story tells about struggle, without which life is boring. My personal story tells of the zigzags in my life—the transitions and transformations.[1]

And behind these zigzags and transformations the average storyteller tries to discern not only meaning but a Master, not only a pattern, but a Person. Somewhere, hidden in such stories, there is a "variety of religious experiences" (James), or "dimensions of ultimacy" (Gilkey), or "rumors of angels" (Berger). And that's why we tell stories, our stories: to see if Someone's there, to see if Someone cares.

We believe that Someone is there and Someone cares, and our contention in this chapter is that people, in telling their stories, are telling religious tales. They are not necessarily aware of this; they certainly do not use any kind of religious vocabulary or phrasing, but religious tales they do tell. How can we tell? Because so often they tell stories, however unconsciously, that deal with life's meaning, life's fundamentals, life's mysteries. Even when they do not realize it, people are posing ultimate questions in their storytelling. They will freely ruminate about what life is all about. Often they hold their stories, like clear crystal, before their faces and ours, as a prism to "Something more." Sometimes their stories, however casually told, are reports of ways that they have been challenged to go and see beyond themselves and to peer into hazy but seductive possibilities. What is there? Who is there? What is life all about anyway?

Because people are picking up threads of mystery in their storytelling, they tend to tell them often and tell the same story in different versions—at least the significant stories. What they are doing is trying to extract all the meanings in the happening or event that a first-time and one-time telling could not achieve. Moreover, they will interpret and reinterpret the story until it yields a configuration they can handle. And that may take years. John S. Dunne, in his intriguing book, *The Church of the Poor Devil*, tells a tale of his journey into the heart of Brazil by riverboat, a physical journey that becomes a spiritual one and whose richness is seen in hindsight.

> I remember the days of uncertainty before our voyage upriver, when I was unsure of finding passage on a riverboat, and then the richness of life I found on the voyage itself after being prepared by such a thirst for it. . . .
>
> What I actually found at the end of the voyage, instead of a cemetery of lepers, was the chapel of the Poor Devil, and that became for me the embodiment and expression of the heart's longing. At the time I did not realize the importance of what I had found. There is no mention of the chapel in my diary! It is only now, remembering it and having seen it again, that I realize how it tells rather differently than a cemetery, of the heart's desire. Bloy's pilgrim found that "the lost paradise is the cemetery, and the only way to recover it is to die." I found that it is a chapel and to recover it is to enter an imaginative space that is full of gods and saints, to let that space become still and empty like the earth in the beginning, and to let the presence of God be felt there like breath stirring the water.[2]

Notice his words: "At the time I did not realize the importance of what I had found. . . . It is only now . . . that I realize. . . ." His story (significantly a journey story) needs retelling and constant interpretation until it yields its deepest meaning.

There are in general four types of personal stories that can be considered religious even though the term "religious" may never appear nor any of its sister terms.[3] Let us examine them one by one.

First Type of Personal Story: Stories that signify self-discovery, and the questions that such self-discovery raises.

In a cassette program Robert Bela Wilhelm takes the listener on a slow and imaginative trip into the past. The listener is asked to relax, and to go back to where he or she came from. There the listener recalls the events and people of his or her story. Although on a journey of self-discovery, the listener stumbles across God. This process is very much akin to the "healing of memories" and to secular therapy. The patient in therapy is basically retelling his or her story, knowing that if the facts cannot be changed, he or she can at least change the interpretation. As the patient sits or lies there with closed eyes, the story pours forth and, often there is a moment of self-discovery. A significant realization dawns, and the person is led to exclaim, "So *that's* why I am what I am! Eureka!" Sometimes, too, from the burning bush of their self-discovery a Voice is heard, calling them by name. Sometimes, too, on their Exodus journey, a faint footstep is perceived behind them:

> I fled Him, down the nights and down the days;
>   I fled Him down the arches of the years;
> I fled Him down the labyrinthine ways
>   Of my own mind; and in the midst of tears
> I hid from Him, and under running laughter.
>   Up vistaed hopes I sped;
>   And shot, precipitated,
> Adown Titanic glooms of chasmed fears,
> From those strong feet that followed, followed after
> Deliberate speed, majestic instancy,
>   They beat — and a Voice beat
>   More instant than the Feet. . . .[4]

But whatever happens, telling one's story is to open oneself to self-discovery.

This self-storytelling becomes, as we have indicated, an essential process in finding God. People will match their stories against his, especially against the Jesus story. This is why a person's story has become a critical factor in the new Rite of Christian Initiation for Adults. When someone inquires about becoming a Catholic, it is first necessary to share one's own personal journey and the important events in it. This sharing leads to questioning, to a search for meaning to the person's story. In turn, this leads to a reflection on the stories of faith. In this inquiry the person tries to see if the Jesus story throws any light on his or her own. In brief, personal storytelling is the context for discerning God's activity and presence. In self-discovery one is likely to discover God as well.

☐One summer Saturday morning when I was twelve, I was waiting for my friend Juanita to come over. We had planned a morning together, and she was quite late. I was fretting and complaining, and generally making a nuisance of myself. In fact, I was becoming rather obnoxious to everyone else in the house. Finally, my father said to me, "Get a book, a blanket, and an apple, and get into the car!" I wanted to know why, but he only repeated the order. So I obeyed. My father drove me about eight miles from home to a canyon area, and said, "Now get out. We cannot stand you any longer at home! You aren't fit to live with. Just stay out here by yourself today until you understand better how to act. I'll come back for you this evening." I got out, angry, frustrated, and defiant. The nerve of him! I thought immediately of walking home; eight miles was no distance at all for me. Then the thought of meeting my father when I got there took hold, and I changed my mind. I cried and threw the book, apple, and blanket over the canyon ledge. I had been dumped and I was furious. But it is hard to keep up a good, rebellious cry with no audience, so finally there was nothing to do but face up to the day alone. I sat on the rim, kicking the dirt and trying to get control of myself. After a couple of hours, as noon approached, I began to get hungry. I located the apple and climbed down to retrieve it—as well as the book and the blanket. I climbed back up, and as I came over the top I noticed the piñon tree. It was lovely and full. I spread the blanket in the shade, put the book under my head, and began to eat the apple.

I was aware of a change of attitude. As I looked through the branches into the sky, a great sense of peace and beauty came to me. The clouds sat in still puffs, the blue was endless, and I began to take in their spaciousness. I thought about the way I had acted and why Daddy had treated me so harshly. Understanding began to come, and I became more objective about my behavior. I found myself getting in touch with my feelings, with the world around me. Nature was my mother, holding me for comfort and healing. I became aware of being part of it all, and I found myself thinking of God. I wanted harmony. I wanted to hold the feeling of mystery. I wanted to be a better person. It was a prayerful time, a time of deep silence. I felt in communion with much that I could not know, but to which I was drawn. I had a great sense of discovering myself as great, of seeing the world as great, of touching the holy. This sense lasted a long time, perhaps a couple of hours. I found I liked being alone, enjoyed the rich emptiness, held the stillness. It was as if I had met another person—me—who was not so bad after all.

By the time my father came to get me, I was restored. Daddy did not press me about the day. He asked no questions, and I gave him no answers. But I was different, and we both knew it. My father had dumped me into solitude and had challenged me to grow. Before I got out of the car, I thanked him. And from then on, especially during the summers, I would take a day to go off alone. I loved those times of solitude, of contemplation, of prayer. I loved the person, the world, the God I had met that day. This habit of seeking solitude has stayed with me all these years.[5] □

Second Type of Personal Story: Stories that signify an impact experience relating to mystery and its demands.

This means that there are stories that people tell that definitely indicate they have been somehow tapped by the "Sweet Mystery of Life." They tell stories that reveal they now sense that they are related to some larger Mystery. And, furthermore, it's not that they went searching for Mystery (on the contrary, they may well have been trying to avoid it) but that Mystery has noticed them first. Mystery comes impinging on them, has an impact on them; and the only way they can describe this is by rather forceful and revealing phrases such as, "You know, it suddenly struck me that. . . ." Or,

"The other day it hit me that. . . ." This kind of language indicates that the speaker is not the initiating party but is rather acted upon. By what or by whom? They and we may not know; it's a mystery and, what's more, a mystery with demands.

Rev. Bruce Ritter is a Franciscan priest who has founded Covenant House, Under 21 on New York's West 41st Street. It's a hospice for runaway teens and preteens who are easy prey for the pimps and johns of that area. There are thousands and thousands of such children pulled into prostitution and violence. Formerly Father Ritter was a high school teacher in a Catholic school. He tells the story of his impact experience and the demands it made. He says that he was describing to his class, as he often did, the terrible suffering and exploitation of the runaway kids who pile into New York from all over the country. Going on at length at the horror of it all, he was interrupted by one of his students who raised his hand and asked him why, if he thought it was all so bad, didn't he do something about it besides talk? That struck Father Ritter (that force again). It hit him, he says, came out of the blue and challenged him. He began to realize that he couldn't just go on talking about evil. He had to do something about it. He might have said something like this: "You can't live like that; I mean, you can't just be an armchair Franciscan. It's too safe and selfish. There's something more to this."

Notice that Father Ritter does not use here religious language like sin, redemption, or grace. He uses common secular language that describes his relationship to God, a relationship that carries a new demand, "Do something about it!" His impact experience (the student's challenge) and his reaction (being "hit" with the message) and the demands ("do something") are classic elements in a story that relates a person to Mystery and its demands.

Father Ritter left his teaching job and went on to found the Covenant House for runaways. And when he goes around to talk to high schoolers, he tells his story over and over again. Why not? It's his impact story and it signified God working in his life. ("There's something more to this"—with the second and third words being capitalized).

Take another sadly commonplace occurrence in American life—divorce. Because there is a fifty percent divorce rate, not only are children affected but so are the grandparents also. After a remarriage, these grandparents are often prevented from seeing their grandchildren. Some have gone so far as to sue for grandparent visiting rights. One grandfather told a congressional hearing that he went through eight years of "heartache and aggravation" to win the right to see his granddaughter. Others said that they often wait in the foliage near the schools to get a peek at their grandchildren. Another grandfather spoke of the cruelty, humiliation, and expense he and his wife went through to win the right to see their grandchild. And then he added, "This is what your life is all about. This is what you work for."

He uttered the telltale phrase: "This is what life is all about." This is always a modern response to humankind's age-old question about meaning and value. It is the modern religious statement about ultimates, about mystery and about God. Whenever anyone uses that phrase, he or she is unknowingly into the realm of religion. Here, with the grandfather, the statement is that, when all is said and done, life is about love, generativeness, intimacy, and sharing. These—all spiritual qualities—are the components that make up life's mystery. All hint of a Graciousness behind it all. Furthermore, all imply what life is *not* about: it is not about acquisition, materialism, greed, accumulation, and so on. There is "Something More" to life than these. If so, then there are demands that one should live accordingly. Once again, here's a story of an impact experience relating to Mystery and its demands. It is a religious story.

□Several years ago a group of computer salesmen from Milwaukee went to a regional sales convention in Chicago. They assured their wives that they would be home in plenty of time for dinner. But with one thing or another the meeting ran overtime so the men had to race to the station, tickets in hand. As they barraged through the terminal, one man (the one telling this story) inadvertently kicked over a table supporting a basket of apples. Without stopping they all reached the train and boarded it with a sigh of relief. All but one. He paused, got in touch with his feelings, and experienced a twinge of compunction for the boy whose applestand had been overturned. He waved goodbye to his companions and returned to the terminal. He was glad he did. The ten-year-old boy was blind.

The salesman gathered up the apples and noticed that several of them were bruised. He reached into his wallet and said to the boy, "Here, please take this ten dollars for the damage we did. I hope it didn't spoil your day." As he started to walk away the bewildered boy called after him, "Are you Jesus?"

He stopped in his tracks. And he wondered.[6]□

As he tells this story he rethinks his life and what is really of value. Somehow, although he doesn't spell it out in religious language, he dimly perceives the incident as a summary of his life. He is running, running all the time until the incident of the blind boy and his apples has an impact on him. Somewhere, unarticulated, he wonders if the blind boy with two bad eyes sees more than he with two good ones (a favorite scripture metaphor). There is repentance (his compunction) and restitution and the blind boy sees him as Jesus. The story is told because it bothers him. It is making a demand on him and he knows that sooner or later he must respond to it. He wasn't Jesus, of course—he was running too fast for that—but shouldn't he be?

These are stories of impact experiences that relate people to the larger Mystery of Life. We get the same story in a different version in the death of a friend. Looking down at the coffin and thinking to oneself that life is too short to be jealous or self-centered is an impact experience. That's a statement in nonreligious language that intimates that there must be something more. Again, such impacts are not conjured up or contrived. Something "out there" hits us. "You know, while I was looking at John in the coffin, it struck me. . . ."

Third Type of Personal Story: Stories that signify mystical experiences.

These are the kind of experiences, more or less intense, that are triggered by some event or person. The "trigger" doesn't necessarily have to be huge or tremendous. It can be quiet and subtle. So, for example, on this particular day a person suddenly experiences a lovely moment of intense friendship, a stunning sunset, Grand Canyon, or the total trust of a small child who falls asleep in one's lap. In such a mystical experience triggered by these or other events, a person is pulled out of self and feels a sense of wholeness and harmony. Everything for the moment has fallen into place. Life is not absurd at all. There really is meaning to it. It all makes sense, marvelous sense, grand sense. There is a harmony, without and within, that is quite compelling.

Some may pause in a momentary trance or a longer ecstasy (literally: to stand outside of oneself). Whatever or however it happens, there is a mystical experience best described by the code phrase, an "in and through" experience. In and through the experience there is a strong intuition that a larger Reality looms. Even more, it looms not as a kind of an overcast cloud or a static ghost-presence, but as One Who Approaches. It seems to approach a person in grace, with a keen awareness of that person, with obvious notice and love and, as might be expected, with a mission in hand. In and through the mystical experience an encounter is made. Lest the reader raise an eyebrow, surveys do show that such experiences are much more common than previously thought, cutting across all lines of sex, nationality, and creed. For obvious reasons, many people do not tell such stories openly or broadcast them, but such stories there truly are.

Carlo Carretto, the spiritual writer, relates with poetic license Francis of Assisi's mystical experience after his imprisonment and sickness at Perugia and the impact these had on him:

☐ Yes, now I saw the sun, the moon, the earth, the springs, the flowers. I had seen them before. . . .

But now they spoke to me, I felt them near, I loved them, they moved me.

In fact, I did not cease to weep when I beheld a sunset, or the meadows covered with poppies and lilies.

Everything seems new to me, ever new, and as light entered my eyes it transformed itself into joy within my heart.

I think my first real prayers were said at that time, although I had prayed with my mother so often before. In any case, I am sure my need to give thanks dates from that time.

Thanks to the sky.

Thanks to the earth.

Thanks to life.

Thanks to God.

God!

Who was God for me? . . .

What was God for me?

It is difficult to answer.

And so all I can tell you simply and clearly is that whatever God had been for me now burst upon me from without.

The "someone" that God was, so far away, whom I had known from my Umbrian childhood, was becoming very near and was beginning to speak to me with all the wonderful signs God placed in the sky and on the earth that we call creatures.

I began to grasp that God was all around me, and had sent those marvelous messengers, creatures, before his face.

I felt that he wished to speak to me. So I kept repeating, "What do you want me to do, Lord?"[7]□

Andrew Greeley quotes another story, a testimony:

□It happened in my room at Peterhouse on the evening of February 6, 1913, when I was an undergraduate at Cambridge. If I say that Christ came to me I should be using conventional words which would carry no precise meaning: for Christ comes to men and women in different ways.

When I tried to record the experience at the time, I used the imagery of the vision of the Holy Grail; it seemed to me to be like that. There was, however, no sensible vision. There was just the room with its shabby furniture and the fire burning in the grate and the red-shaded lamp on the table. But the room was filled by a Presence which in a strange way was both about me and within me, like light or warmth. I was overwhelmingly possessed by Someone who was not myself, and yet I felt I was more myself than I had ever been before. I was filled with an intense happiness, an almost unbearable joy, such as I had never known before, and have never known since. And over all was a deep sense of peace and security and certainty.[8]□

Notice the common elements: harmony, being approached, peace. People will tell these stories (those who do) that signify to them a mystical experience, a memory that will never fade and a change in their lives as they try to live out the demands of the experience. From a world that is and can be cruel, threatening, polluted, and ugly, they extract a beauty and sense a Presence. Such people easily hold the tension of the *tremens and fascinens*: the terrible and the fascinating. In and through this limited and confined world they are brought to a pervasive Beauty and Love. Perhaps no modern writer has captured the possible "in and through" tension of life as Annie Dillard. In her book *Pilgrim at Tinkers Creek* she writes:

Another time I saw another wonder: sharks off the Atlantic coast of Florida. There is a way a wave rises above the ocean horizon, a triangular wedge against the sky. If you stand there where the ocean breaks on a shallow beach, you see the raised water in a wave is translucent, shot with lights. One late afternoon at low tide a hundred big sharks passed the beach near the mouth of a tidal river in a feeding frenzy. The sharks disappeared as each wave rolled toward me; then a new wave would swell above the horizon, containing in it, like scorpions in amber, sharks that roiled and heaved. The sight held awesome wonders; power and beauty, grace tangled in a rapture with violence.

We don't know what's going on here. If these tremendous events are random combinations of matter run amok, the yield of millions of monkeys at millions of typewriters, then what is it in us, hammered out of those same typewriters, that they ignite? We don't know. Our life is a faint tracing on the surface of mystery, like the idle, curved tunnels of leaf miners on the face of a leaf. We must show how, take a wider view, look at the whole landscape, really see it, and describe what's going on here. Then we can at least wail the right question into the swaddling band of darkness, or, if it comes to that, choir the proper praise.[9]

If such a mystical experience does not compel God as an answer, at least it compels a look "beyond" to search for an answer.

□On a less serious level, there is that always delightful comic strip, *Hi and Lois*. In one episode there are three panels. In the first one Lois looks at Hi and asks "What's the matter?" He responds, "I just saw Chip walking down the road holding hands with a *girl!*" In the second panel it shows a pensive Hi saying "Our baby . . . holding hands! It makes me feel so *old!*" In the last panel Hi is sitting down, holding his head in his hand, saying, "It makes me think about the continuity of life . . . the eternal cycle . . ." and Lois replies, "I didn't know you could get so much out of holding hands."□

But some people can and do, given the right mood. They can respond to the most ordinary event and, if circumstances are right, it will trigger a response in them and pull them instantly into relationship with life's larger meaning and life's larger Mystery. There are all kinds of mystical experiences that are told in people's everyday stories.

Fourth Type of Personal Story: Stories that signify a conversion experience.

People tend to tell stories about themselves that are a kind of talking out loud about their sin and their repentance from it. Once more, of course, they do not use such terms; but they do tell, selectively, of a wrong act or judgment and their consequent movement from some position of naive innocence or pride to that of a sadder but wiser person (repentant sinner). Usually people do not go into detail; they usually mention just the clarifying event, saying where they came from (say, for example, a position of rash judgment) to where they had arrived (a new sense of their own limitations).

For example, a man who ordinarily drinks heavily (perhaps unknown to his friends and co-workers) may refuse drink. To good natured kidding he might say: "Well, I just decided. Hell, I don't need it. I feel better. My doctor says I'll live longer by knocking off the booze." Here, in a very offhand way, leaving out his real story of his bouts with drink and that he's going to AA, he is merely telling publicly about his journey from drinking (sin) to nondrinking (repentance). With all of his rationalizations, that's all his story is meant to convey: he has moved from here to there. But there is a journeying here, a real conversion. And something caused it. Here's his real story, the story of a man named Christopher:

☐Once there was a certain lawyer named Christopher who lived in Long Island. When offered the opportunity of a lucrative partnership in Jerusalem, Pennsylvania, he accepted. Uprooting and transplanting the family was a delicate matter. Two of the children were still in high school and the youngest in the third grade. Nonetheless, career advancement, prestige, higher income and a lower cost of living beckoned. Besides, Christopher reasoned, this will be a new beginning. I can start all over.

How badly he wanted that. His drinking was now out of control. The blackouts, the morning bracer, and solitary drinking had cunningly crept into his life, almost involuntarily, he felt. How many nights had he slept on the cot in the office after having what he euphemistically called a drink — a 32-ounce bottle of Scotch. His temper tantrums with his secretary were inexcusable. He knew that. Still, it was the pain in Katie's eyes that brought tears to his own. He knew his wife loved him but to learn that she had gone to an Alanon meeting last night. . . . Well, all that was behind him. Jerusalem would mark the end of the heyday of the booze, the binges and the bad blood. Jesus, he recalled, had done some memorable things in the biblical town of the same name. So would he.

Christopher did not know that he was destined to die in Jerusalem.

The family moved and he stopped drinking, cold turkey. The withdrawal had been excruciating—nausea, vomiting, diarrhea, twitching, hallucinations and finally convulsions. Katie saved his life that night. Her husband was a man of exquisite sensitivity and fierce independence. The combination allowed Christopher to defeat John Barleycorn with an iron fist in a velvet glove. All it took was will power, he daily reminded himself. Six weeks of abstinence followed —forty-two full days.

Then his senior partner absconded with the funds, certificates and stocks — bell, book and candle. The law firm collapsed in bank-ruptcy. Christopher regrouped with a double Scotch straight up. The physical compulsion and mental obsession had returned. The next two months were unadulterated hell. The children withdrew, Katie cried herself to sleep and Christopher drank himself into oblivion. His lights were out, his clock was cleaned, and there was mourning and wailing throughout Jerusalem.

On a Wednesday morning Katie said, "Chris, don't forget your appointment at noon."

"What appointment?"

"Remember, you called Alcoholics Anonymous last night and asked for help."

"Like hell I did!" Another blackout. He remembered John Chancellor on the evening news but after that. . . .

The doorbell rang. "I'm Harvey from AA. Your husband called."

Christopher escaped into the kitchen. She pursued him. "Honey, what do you have to lose? Talk with the man."

Beer in hand, he walked into the living room. "Yes, what would you like to talk about?"

"If you put down that can, I'd like to propose a new way of life to you."

For the next two hours Chris endured the drunkalogue as Harvey shared what his life as an alcoholic had been, what hap-pened and what it was now. Grudgingly Chris identified with much of the story. But finally he said, "Thank you. I appreciate what you have had to say. My wife is right. I have abused the gift of the grape.

I'll start today to cut down. Goodbye." Christopher vowed to himself that he would not take another drink until eight p.m.

Sipping slowly and triumphantly on that long awaited Scotch, he overheard his wife and eight-year-old son talking in the bedroom. "Vince, why don't you and the other kids play in the pool any more?" The boy hesitated. "I guess I'm frightened. I never know what Dad will be like and I don't want the other boys to see him."

The drink crashed to the floor. Tears cascaded down his cheeks. "Christ, what am I doing? What am I missing?"

Christopher arose from his chair and walked out the door into a new way of life.[10] □

To intimates, Christopher will repeat this story often. It's a conversion-experience story. There is no mention of God but grace and redemption are there, all the same.

The following is a gentle fiction story from the pen of Father Francis Sweeney. It catches nicely a tale of guilt and repentance and the all too evident circumstances woven in the background. It is significantly entitled "The Listener."

□ Mrs. Dowson stood in the doorway of Arthur's room and buttoned the cuff of her pink blouse. There had been a button missing but Marie had replaced it. She had found the same kind of button, a shiny pearl disk with four holes, and had sewed it on expertly, the thread criss-crossing under the fabric and not on the top of the button.

It wasn't really Marie's job. Lord knows, she had enough to do, what with ordering the groceries from Sage's, cooking, setting the table, and lifting the metal trays into the dishwasher. That and getting Mrs. Deems, the cleaning woman, to do at least some vacuuming between the recitals of failed husbands, miscarriages, rising prices at the supermarket, and the rascality of politicians. Marie was a treasure, an old phrase Mrs. Dowson's mother had used to describe cooks who worked hard for low wages and never took home steaks in their satchels.

"Marie is a treasure," Mrs. Dowson said. "I don't know what I'd do without her. It's funny. My eyes are perfect, but the one thing I can't do is thread a needle. It must be eye strain from doing too many crossword puzzles. I don't do embroidery any more, though I probably could if I put my mind to it."

She crossed Arthur's room to the mantel where a Seth Thomas

clock stood over the brown-grained marble fireplace. It was stopped at two o'clock. Mrs. Dowson opened the glass front of the dial and set the hour to five minutes after nine, to match the hands on her baguette watch. She lifted the corner of the oaken clock and set the pendulum swinging, a gold wafer catching the light. It was lost effort. The brass key which should have been under the clock was missing.

"I hope you slept well, Arthur," Mrs. Dowson said. "Toward morning I had to put on a light blanket, and I turned on the radio and listened to some foolish talk show. People were telephoning in and asking questions about flying objects. It was an hour before I got to sleep again."

She sat in a tapestried armchair near the mantel, and smoothed her oyster linen skirt over her knees. Through the open window there was a sound of lawn-mowing. Beside the house a half-acre of lawn extended to a row of Lombardy poplars. There had been tennis courts there until Arthur had grassed them over. Near the house, in the shadow of a wineglass elm, there were a white table and white wooden chairs with cretonne cushions, under a tilted blue umbrella.

A boy on the saddle of the lawn mower, his naked back glistening with sweat, drove the mower down to the poplars and back to the house. Another boy, in cut-off jeans, stood on a step-ladder and trimmed flat the top of the yew hedge. As the mower passed the hedge the boys exchanged genial abuse over the clatter of the blades.

"The days are longer," Mrs. Dowson said. "You know I like to get up with the sun, but five-thirty is too early. But how lovely to hear the first bird! Yesterday I timed the first one, a robin, I think — and it was nine minutes past four. Don't you think there are more birds this year? They say that since people have stopped using all those insecticides, the birds are coming back. I suppose we can thank Rachel Carson for that.

"Marie says the same ovenbirds that were here last year have nested in the elm. How can she be sure they are the same ones? There were some new birds at the birdbath yesterday. I should look them up in your bird book. Grosbeaks, I think. And there were gulls, dozens of them, flying in to Batton's Pond. They say gulls like to wash their feathers in fresh water.

"You remember the gulls at Boothbay and how they would fly

over a rock and drop clams to break the shells? What clever creatures they are! And all at once the whole crowd of gulls would fly off to meet a fishing boat coming back to the harbor. Strange that they would know which boat was gutting fish and which wasn't.

"I used to wish you weren't such an avid fisherman, going out each day in Cahoon's boat, even on days when the weather was so bad that the natives stayed on shore. It was lonely sometimes. Sometimes the other women would josh me and say that they were golf widows, but I was a fishing widow."

Suddenly she began to weep, the sobs rising from her chest and making her catch her breath. She took a blue handkerchief from the pocket of her skirt and covered her face. "I saw even less of you at home," she said. "It wasn't just the fishing, Arthur. It was anything that attracted you, anything at all.

"No more tears, Arthur," she said, at last, as she replaced the handkerchief in her pocket. "You don't like tears and I've tried never to annoy you. But how long will I wait for a reply? You are being cruel to me, though you are not a cruel man. But the world is cruel. Men do as they please and get away with it. But once when I was lonely, I fell. Only once, with someone who meant nothing to me except that he was gentle, and noticed my coloring and my hair, and touched my face. And he was here. He was here, Arthur, and God knows where you were, for days at a time.

"I atoned. I know God has forgiven me because God is good. But you never did. It hurt your pride. I was one of your possessions that someone had used. I don't blame you, but Arthur, how long will you make me wait for a word? One word?"

From the hall, up the echo chamber of the stairs, the D-toned bell of the grandfather clock struck ten. Mrs. Dowson dabbed once more at her eyes, went into her room and put on a grey topcoat. She spoke to Marie in the kitchen and then went out the pillared door and down the flagstoned walk. Potter was waiting with the blue Lincoln.

As they drove through the pylons at the gate of Mount Auburn Cemetery she spoke to Potter for the first time, now as she always did. "The flowers and lawns are beautifully kept," she said. Oh, there were pink begonias in the circular flower bed over Mary Baker Eddy's tomb. The forsythia were gone by, but the spirea, "bridal veil," were coming into flower.

They passed the graves she knew, and she spoke the names aloud as she saw the granite blocks and limestone urns and gesturing statues: Longfellow, Amy Lowell, Francis Parkman, Edwin Booth, Winslow Homer. They were her neighbors now; however, life had exalted them and set them apart.

At Tulip Path, Potter stopped the Lincoln at the grass verge, and came around to open the door for her. Like a verger he went ahead of her, an old man in a chauffeur's black uniform. They went up the grassy lane, by the oblong bulk of brownstone dedicated to Nathaniel Bowditch, the Salem clerk whose marvelous book, crammed with pilots' lore and tables of logarithms, had brought the ships of the nineteenth century into port.

On Orchid Path, Potter stopped at a small mausoleum, its grey blocks of Quincy granite fitted together like pieces of fondant. The brass door opened easily to the key and disclosed a narrow space lit by a small stained-glass window of Connick blue, with a red angel displaying a Latin promise from St. Paul.

The chauffeur took yesterday's roses from the shelf over the marble sarcophagus, and replaced them with a sheaf of yellow azaleas. Then he went down the path, and sat in the car.

Mrs. Dowson seated herself in the metal armchair, drew off her gloves and folded them in her lap.

"Good morning, Arthur," she said. "I am here."[11] □

Even this story of this foolish but delightful lady is replete with intonations of grace at work. But we should not get the impression that such "religious" stories in secular garb leave no room for explicitly religious accounts, those deliberately known and proclaimed in the ancient categories of sin and redemption. The gospels themselves are often catalysts for the movements of grace in people's lives. Some even use the gospel events or the parables as a foil to their own thinking and acting in order to surface something in their own lives:

> When we read the Gospels we spontaneously and unwittingly pick out from the text those parts that appeal to us. If we systematically identify those parts of the canonical Gospels that go to make up "our own gospel" we discover how much richer is the gift of God's love than our hearts could imagine.[12]

In the remaining pages of this chapter I will share precisely the discoveries of a mixed group of people from our faith-sharing meetings. Each one was asked in the course of time to tell their favorite scripture passage and why it was a favorite. The story-replies are as follows.

One elderly man said he likes that story in the gospel about the paralyzed man being let down through the roof and getting cured. He liked it because he related to it. He was always a proud man, he said, and when he had his stroke, it was humiliating for him to have others do for him. He resisted, was angry and nasty. Until one day when he read this scripture and it took on a whole new meaning for him. He identified with the paralyzed man, a man who had likely four others to lower him with a rope tied to each corner of a stretcher. He realized that this was a parable of himself. As long as he tried to reach the Lord alone, he failed. But when he let go, first physically and then emotionally and spiritually, to the help of others who loved him, then he found that Jesus entered his life. Like the man in the gospel, he was let down with others' help through his roof of anger and hostility, down to Jesus himself. There is no doubt that for others this gospel story is but another episode, but for this man it is forever *his* story.

An adolescent of about 19 said his favorite passage was somewhere in St. Paul's letters. It's the place where Paul is saying goodbye to a lot of people and happens to mention one person who was at the imperial court. The young man was very impressed with this. Did we know what was being said here? (No, we didn't). Well, he answered in response to our ignorance, in Paul's time the imperial court was that of Nero, and so it was as wicked a court as could be imagined. And yet, for all of that, there was a Christian not only living there but living the gospel there! Well, this young man resonated with that. It was tough living at his college where his roommate often had his girlfriend in overnight forcing him to sleep in the lobby, and where dope and booze were commonplace. But what sustained him, he said, was the thought of that Christian hacking it spiritually in Nero's court. And if he could do it, so can I—or at least give the gospel a try on campus.

One lady claimed to have the strangest gospel passage; it was the one where Jesus came down from the mountain and called his twelve apostles. Could anyone in the room name all twelve? Could anyone tell what happened to them or where they went or how they ended their days? We did very poorly, which, I suspect, is about average. But this pleased her. It pleased her because she could identify with the twelve. She herself was rather shy and had always lived a kind of put-down life. No one really knew her, either. And yet, yet Jesus picked the little, unknown people to do his greatest work. And she felt that she too was chosen, called. No talent, no name, no qualifications—just called by the Lord as were those others, whoever they were.

One very vocal man in our group, a diamond in the rough as they say, had no trouble identifying his favorite passage in the gospel. It was the story of the tribute to Caesar. He said, "If those jerks were so upset about that damn coin and hated it so much, then what the hell were they doing with it? You noticed that as soon as Jesus asked them to show him the coin of tribute which they were supposed to hate, they all reached down into their damn trousers and pulled out a whole pocketful! I think the Lord had a smile on his face when they brought them out, and I think they knew they had been caught. They were phonies! Hypocrites! And every time I see or hear about some sanctimonious son o' a bitch pretending to be so holy and above it all, I think of this and laugh out loud. The Lord keeps us honest." I don't know how good a commentary this is on scripture or how accurate his exegesis, but for him this story carries an implicit demand to be open and honest himself with others and, above all, with the Lord.

In reading these stories you might have thought that the people in this sharing group might have tapped into the obvious stories: Ah, they were betraying Peter, scarlet Magdalene, doubting Thomas, the Prodigal Son, unsocial-minded Dives, and all the rest. Indeed, there were such stories but I have shared these more unusual ones to show that different gospel events will appeal differently to different people and that the rich gift of the Lord is varied.

At this point let me insert a little fiction piece on that passage from the Acts of the Apostles (9:10) involving Ananias, the one sent to the blind Paul to cure him. It's one of those stories that might not get told out loud in a prayer group or anywhere else for that matter, but whose final lines might speak volumes of meaning and encouragement to many. It's the kind of story, in endless variations, that could be told in a parish by the little people who "only stand and wait."

☐Along a cobblestoned alley of ancient Damascus, there once lived a shoemaker named Ananias. Like others of his scattered nation, the little cobbler went to his synagogue each week to pray for the birth of the Messiah:

"How long, Adonoi? How long is a little while?"

But then one Shabbat evening, some Galileans arrived at the synagogue door. Though dusty and tired from their long desert journey, the newcomers lifted their hands high above their heads:

"Brothers! We bring glad news! God has raised Jesus of Nazareth from the dead, that we might return to God!"

There was an ugly silence. One of the scribes murmured:

"The chief priests of Jerusalem have sent word: 'Beware of rabble-rousers who claim that a poor crucified carpenter is the Messiah!' "

Then an old man stood up:

"You are a disgrace to the people of Israel!"

Ananias sat on his crowded workbench and watched the porters throw the men outside. A great sadness crept over the little shoemaker—when would the Messiah come? He slipped out the back door and found the Galileans lying in a nearby gutter, laughing. Ananias suggested timidly:

"If I were you, I might not be so happy to be tossed into a gutter."

One of the men wiped a gash on his forehead and smiled:

"Now that the Messiah has come, I wouldn't mind being tossed headfirst into a manure pile."

There was something about these men that the poor shoemaker liked.

"Tell me more about this Messiah. . . ."

And so, after he had listened, Ananias became one of the brotherhood.

What an exciting time to live—the news of the empty tomb still rang freshly in the ears of men and women! With each passing day, new miracles broke through:

"Did you hear? Joseph the weaver has believed in the Messiah, and his whole family has received the Holy Spirit!"

"Incredible news! The blind man who begs by the old stone well—he can see!"

Yet, miracles never visited Ananias. He stitched strips of leather on his workbench and mused:

"After all, I'm only a simple cobbler who can hardly read the alphabet. A shoemaker must be content to sew sandals for the glory of God. . . ."

Ananias' times of prayer were also very ordinary. There were no startling revelations—only a quiet gentle Presence. But then one noontime, just as he set down his awl, something very unusual happened. A whisper rose within his heart:

"Ananias!"

The startled shoemaker tripped over his workbench. Then he remained still on the clay floor and listened to the silence, but the only sound was the wild pounding of his heart. But just as its beat began to calm, the voice came again:

"Ananias!"

This time the little cobbler knew who had spoken. He glanced upward:

"Here I am, Lord."

The voice came with a deep quiet authority:

"Arise and go to Straight Street, and at the house of Judas ask for a man from Tarsus named Saul. He will be praying. In a vision he has seen a man named Ananias. You are to place your hands on him so that he may see again."

Ananias winced. Forgetting to whom he spoke, the poor cobbler scrambled to his feet:

"Lord! Many people have told me about this man, about all the terrible things he has done to your people in Jerusalem. And now he has come to Damascus to arrest anyone who even calls upon your name!"

There was a long silence. Ananias looked upward:
"Lord?"

Silence. The shoemaker awkwardly shuffled his feet and cleared his throat:

"Ahem. . . Lord?"

Ananias sighed and bowed his head. Then the voice spoke again:

"Go, because I have chosen him to be my servant, to carry my name to Gentiles and kings, and to the people of Israel. I myself will show him all that he must suffer for my sake."

Ananias stumbled down his dirty alleyway. As in a dream, he wandered toward the wealthiest quarter of Damascus. Then the shoemaker knocked timidly on the door of Judas and waited until the huge gate opened a crack. A skeptical servant peered out.

Ananias pushed past him with a clumsy dive:

"Please, sir! I must see a man by the name of Saul!"

At first the servant was startled by the frantic little shoemaker, but he quickly recovered:

"See here! The servants' entrance is around the back . . . of all the nerve!"

He planted his palm squarely in Ananias' face and pushed the poor man out toward the street. The struggling cobbler screamed:

"No! I must splee a man by the nab of Salb . . . Pleeb, I must splee. . . ." (It is difficult to be articulate when someone has his hand in your face.)

Just as the servant slammed the door, Ananias swung his leg into its path. This actually worked in the shoemaker's favor, since the volume of his screams markedly increased. They echoed throughout the neighborhood:

"Ahhhhhhhhhggrrrr! My leg!"

Then there came a deep troubled voice from the inner courtyard:

"Wait! I had a vision about that man!"

Ananias panicked and forgot everything:

"Oh, no! . . . He had a vision about me! Now I'm really in trouble. . . ."

The angry servant grabbed the shoemaker's belt and jerked him back into the courtyard. There, under an aging olive tree, a sightless man lay on a mat. The shoemaker's fear quietly melted away:

"Saul, I have been sent by the Lord Jesus whom you met along the way. He sent me here that you might see again and be filled with the Holy Spirit."

Ananias reached out for the sightless eyes. For a quiet moment, human history rested beneath the hands of a cobbler.

When it was finished, a man named Saul had become Paul.

Some time passed before Paul began his ministry, and many more years fled by before the world realized its tremendous impact. And so, the little shoemaker never knew what came of the day when he stretched out his hands beneath that aging olive tree.

At the very end of his life, Ananias lay on his deathbed. He looked upward to the desert skies and whispered:

"I haven't done much, Lord. A few shoes sewn . . . a few sandals stitiched. . . . But what more could be expected of a poor cobbler?

But then, once again, that same voice rose quietly within his heart:

"Don't worry, Ananias, about how much you have done—or how little. You were there when I wanted you to be there.

And that,

> my little shoemaker of a saint,
> is all that really matters."[13] ☐

And this message is beautiful and comforting and a true one that will mean much to many.

It should be noted that these Jesus stories are offering people another option in life, another way of acting and living. That is, the old man could remain in his pride, the adolescent could go along with the crowd, the shy woman could retire into self-pity, but the gospel is giving them options, a graced way of responding to life. It offers them possibilities and invites them to different perspective. Of course, we must not be naive here. As soon as any of them choose not to float with the mainstream, conflict will arise. A faith stance always brings conflict. Which is why faith people need community. They need to tell their stories among believers to have them validated and, above all, to measure them against the Greatest Story Ever Told. Our liturgical year retells the great events of Father, Son, and Spirit precisely to keep the Great Story before our eyes as a living, ongoing resonance in our lives. And as encouragement.

A wholesome and genuine way that the Jesus story is mediated for many is the cycle of the saints weaving within the larger seasonal cycle. This is why it is so important to restore the tradition of saint stories. These are the flesh-and-blood interpreters of the gospel for each age, the pacesetters, the endurers in conflict. Who, for example, would not be impressed and moved by playwright Robert Bolt's version of the life of Sir Thomas More, *A Man For All Seasons*. In this scene, Henry VIII is trying to coax More, his Chancellor, to agree to his divorce of Catherine. They are in the garden and Henry is speaking:

□. . .You must consider, Thomas, that I stand in peril of my
soul. It was no marriage; she was my brother's widow. Leviticus:
"Thou shalt not uncover the nakedness of thy brother's wife."
Leviticus, Chapter eighteen, Verse sixteen.

More: Yes, Your Grace. But Deuteronomy—

Henry: Deuteronomy's ambiguous!

More: Your Grace, I'm not fit to meddle in these matters—
to me it seems a matter for the Holy See—

Henry: Thomas, Thomas, does a man need a Pope to tell him
when he's sinned? It was a sin, Thomas; I admit it; I re-
pent. And God has punished me; I have no son . . . .
Son after son she's borne me, Thomas, all dead at birth,
or dead within the month; I never saw the hand of God
so clear in anything . . . . I have a daughter, she's a
good child, a well-set child—But I have no son. It is my
bounden *duty* to put away the Queen, and all the Popes
back to St. Peter shall not come between me and my
duty! How is it that you cannot see? Everyone else does.

More: Then why does Your Grace need my poor support?

Henry: Because you are honest. What's more to the purpose,
you're known to be honest . . . . There are those like
Norfolk who follow me because I wear the crown, and
there are those like Master Cromwell who follow me
because they are jackels with sharp teeth and I am their
lion, and there is a mass that follows me because it
follows anything that moves—and there is you.[14]□

Anyone who hears this gospel interpretation is made uneasy. Could
that inverted praise be said of us, "And there is you"? Do we find
ourselves more aligned with Norfolk, Cromwell, and the mass of
mindless people who follow slogans and commercials? Sir Thomas
challenges us to a lived and not intellectualized gospel.

    Our stories, then, need not always be in explicit religious terms
like the stories above, and usually they are not. Still, the perceptive
listener will sense grace at work, especially as people tell those stories
of self-discovery, impact, mystical experience, and conversion. But
for believers, the Scripture story will still be the normative one. They,
more openly than others, will use the sacred themes and the sacred
vocabulary to celebrate the "something more," the mystery that has
a name: Abba. And the Abba has a synonym: Jesus.

11

Story,
Theology,
and Church

A t this point in our book, drawing to a close as it is, it might be well to put aside for the moment the direct story and illustration (to be resumed, however, in the final two chapters) and briefly list ten propositions of a theological nature. This exercise will, I hope, not be heavy or obtuse. It will serve as a means of extracting, for the sake of clarity and reflection, the theological implications of what has been stated here and there in the past chapters. So this is a very brief chapter—an interlude really—and is intended as a kind of theological summary, an overall view of how stories relate to theology and the structures of the church.

First Proposition: Stories introduce us to sacramental presences.

Stories are designed to force us to consider possibilities. To that extent they are grounded in hope. Even the most outlandish fairy tales, for example, raise possibilities and tease our hopes. The biblical stories do the same, only more overtly. Their whole point is to coax us to look beyond our limits and experiences of limitation and to suggest, through the wonderful, Wonder itself. Stories hint that our taken-for-granted daily realities may, in fact, be fraught with surprise. There are "rumors of angels" and grace abounding in our world. If a frog might be a prince, a lost sailor an angel, a pilgrim the Christ, then all of creation may be a sacramental presence pointing to "Something More." Stories declare that this just might be the case.

Second Proposition: Stories are always more important than facts.

Facts, in relation to story, are inert. It is the genius of story to arrange the facts and proclaim the good news about them. For example, the pivotal "fact" of the resurrection is fundamentally less important in its description and verification as a statement of Jesus of Nazareth rising from the dead than as a central proposition of hope. What counts are the implications the resurrection story has for us in our living and in sustaining our outlook on life and death. Otherwise you have reportage, not gospel.

Third Proposition: Stories remain normative.

We have seen in the first chapter of this book that all of theology is but a reflection on the original story. To test a theology, we must always go back to the pristine material (and its subsequent unfolding). To this extent the biblical stories will always remain normative. There is a serious caution, however. Some may go back to the original story and make an idol of it; that is, they will take it as a rigid and finished document, detach it from its history, contemporary and subsequent, and force it to remain compressed and restricted. This is the fault of literalists or fundamentalists.

Fourth Proposition: Traditions evolve through stories.

Traditions evolve through stories: that's the nature of important and critical stories. People "caught" by the story, its hero or heroine and its message, want not only to share an experience but to share an experience *faithful* to the original story. Hence tradition arises that has two functions: preserving and protecting. Preserving is "handing on," which is what the word tradition means literally. Protecting may need more explanation.

Because stories are really extended metaphors, they are open-ended. They are freely adaptable and can easily be recast and retold. Details, names, and locales are easily accommodated to different audiences and places. We detect this even in the short span of the writing of the four gospels. Still, a boundary is implicitly set beyond which flexibility may not go and still be true to the founding story. To take a secular example: Santa Claus may be metamorphosed throughout the centuries easily enough. He can be tall or short, smooth faced or bearded, clothed in purple or green, rotund or as slim as Ichabod Crane. But Santa can never be a child abuser. After all, he derives from St. Nicholas, who derives from the Christ Child, who derives from the Father of all gifts. The core tradition would not permit a connection between Santa and harm when his whole point is benevolence and kindness. Along the way somewhere, tradition would protect the image from intrinsic contradiction. The biblical stories about Jesus evoke the same process of protection. This is where church tradition fits in. And since the stories of Jesus are varied, varied traditions will not only arise but will be quite legitimate.

Fifth Proposition: Stories preceed and produce the church.

This we noted early on. The story exists first, then people are caught by it, savor it, reflect on it, retell it, preserve it, and pass it on (tradition). When many people are caught by, believe in, and celebrate the same story, you have a church.

Sixth Proposition: Stories imply censure.

This proposition is a logical outcome of the preceeding two. If you have a tradition dedicated to preserving and passing on the core story, and if you have a church to live by and celebrate the core story, then those of the group who at any time might radically contradict the essential story must be dealt with. This is quite commonplace in all walks of life. Here is where we get—in any religion, government, or university—the censure, the reprimand, the excommunication. Wide latitude may be allowed, but not beyond contradicting what the story stands for. A civil liberties group could not, for example, tolerate an overt bigot. Of course, as history has shown, people tend to be far more restrictive of what they perceive to be the "true" tradition than may be accurate. One person's orthodoxy may be another's heresy, depending on who wields the power. But that is beside the point here. The point is that when story gives rise to tradition, and tradition to a church, then censure is implied sooner or later. (Quite soon, in fact, as we learn from Paul's epistles).

Seventh Proposition: Stories produce theology.

Reflection on and conclusions from the Jesus stories began early in the church. We see this in the church's earliest writings, the epistles of Paul. When you reflect on the story, make associations, and draw conclusions, you have a theology. We can see this easily, for example, in the faith trajectory concerning the nature of Jesus. In a very special way the story tells us that he is God's man. If he is God's man, then maybe he is his spokesman. If he is his spokesman, then maybe he is his very word. If he is his word, then maybe he has a special relationship with the Father. If he has a special relationship with the Father, maybe he is his son—and in a unique way. If God's son, then maybe he is his equal. If equal, maybe he is God in the flesh. Theology is a putting of pieces together and discovering richer conclusions than might first be grasped.

Or we might put it this way. Theology arises because there is always more to the story than even the tellers either realize or intend. We have a classic example in John's gospel (11:49-52): "But one of them, Caiaphas, who was high priest that year, said to them, 'You know nothing at all; you do not understand that it is expedient that one man should die for the people and that the whole nation should not perish.' " John then goes on to give his reflection and expansion concerning these words (theology): "He did not say this of his own accord, but being high priest that year, he prophesied that Jesus should die for the nation, and not for the nation only, but to gather into one the children of God who are scattered abroad." Time and hindsight often reveal deeper and richer motifs to stories. Theology grabs onto this and draws it out. Theology is rooted in and flows from the story.

Eighth Proposition: Stories produce many theologies.

The Jesus stories themselves are varied and obviously reflect different traditions. Even a casual reading of the four gospels demonstrates this. Since this is so, we expect that such varied story-traditions will give rise to varied theologies. No one system is made absolute—nor should it be. The normative stories themselves, after all, are not only open-ended but conditioned by the assumptions and frame of references of their times. There have been and will continue to be many systems of theology in the church. Although there has been a drive in modern times to reduce all systems to one, in the history of the church there has been a wide tolerance of diversity.

Ninth Proposition: Stories produce ritual and sacrament.

We must remember that the experience of Jesus came before reflections about him. This is a way of saying that life came before thought, and that story came before theology. The experience of Jesus was indeed, as we have seen, enshrined in stories, but it must also be noted that it was simultaneously enshrined in ritual and in celebration. Signs, actions, gesture, and symbol also became part of the overall story. Ritual itself is a story line in action. So right away there arose rituals reenacting the death, burial, and resurrection of Jesus. Paul calls this baptism. Then there was a ritual meal breaking bread and sharing a cup, signs of the very givingness of Jesus. In short, there were also lived and shared stories we have come to describe as celebrating the mysteries of God or have come to call simply the sacraments. Story (word), celebration (festivity), and ritual (sacrament) all go together.

　　Of course, it can happen and has happened that a ritual can lose its story connection through routine, boredom, and repetition. When this happens, people often continue the ritual out of rote, but no longer remember the story it was attached to or expressed. To revitalize or recast the ritual we must go back and remember the story. Church renewals are basically an exercise in this.

Tenth Proposition: Stories are history.

Since stories are open-ended, they cannot be or must not be literalized. Stories have a life of their own and each age extracts from and adds to the story in a kind of symbiotic relationship. The result is a profound enrichment. History is the bridge from which we view the story in all its forms and in all its aspects of truth. Ideally, history saves the story from the twin dangers of idolatry and irrelevance.

12

Spirituality and Story

After our brief didactic summary on story and theology in the last chapter, let us end our book with a similar chapter on spirituality and story. But here we reenter our storytelling pattern by beginning with a story, in this case, the old legend of St. Christopher. It goes like this.

☐ Christopher was a mild and gentle giant of a man who served the king of Canaan faithfully. Though he cared deeply for his lord, the king, he dreamed of serving the strongest master in the world. Taking leave of Canaan, he traveled until he came to the castle of the one said to be the greatest ruler in the world. When the king saw the size and strength of Christopher, he made him second in command and invited him to dwell in his court.

One day when a minstrel was entertaining the king, he sang a song about the devil. Whenever the name of the devil was mentioned, the king made the sign of the cross. Christopher asked the king about his actions.

"It is to ward off the devil," the king answered.

"Do you fear his power?" asked Christopher.

"Ah, yes," said the king, "he has great might."

Christopher shook his head sadly. "I must leave you, my lord, for I have a great desire to serve the most powerful one in this world. It seems the devil is that one."

Christopher began his search for the devil, wandering until he met a great company of knights. The leader of the knights, a man who appeared cruel and horrible, approached him and asked him what he wanted. "I am in search of the devil to be my master," said Christopher evenly.

"I am the one you seek," said the terrible knight. Christopher immediately bowed before the devil and promised his allegiance.

A bit later, as the company of knights walked together, they came upon a cross standing at an intersection. Immediately the devil turned to the side, taking his followers in a circuitous route until he finally came back to the highway.

"Why did we take this route?" asked Christopher.

At first the devil was reluctant to answer, but Christopher persisted. "There was once a man called Christ who was killed on a cross," the devil explained. "When I see his sign, I am afraid and attempt to avoid it."

"Then he is greater and more powerful than you," said Christopher. "I see that I have yet to find the one who is the greatest lord on the earth. I will leave you to find Christ, whoever he is."

Christopher began a long search for the one people called Jesus, the Christ. At last he came upon a pious hermit who welcomed him and began to teach him about Jesus. One day the hermit spoke to Christopher. "You are not ready to serve Christ. In order to do this you must fast."

Christopher said, "It is most difficult for me to fast. Ask me to do something else."

"You must wake early in the morning and pray long hours each day," the hermit said.

"Please," said Christopher, "find me a task more to my ability. I am not a man who can pray for long periods of time."

The hermit thought for a moment before he spoke again. "You are indeed tall and strong. You shall live by the river and carry across anyone who comes in need. In that way you will serve Jesus. I hope that our Lord Christ will one day show himself to you."

So Christopher began his life of service at the river, where the current was strong. There, with the help of a huge pole, he carried rich and poor alike over the treacherous river.

One day as he slept in his lodge by the river, Christopher heard the voice of child calling, "Christopher, come carry me over." When he looked outside, he saw no one. Back in his lodge, he again heard the voice call. Again his search was unsuccessful. The third time he went outside, he found a child who begged Christopher to carry him over the river.

The giant took the child on his shoulders and began his walk across the river. As the water rushed against his body, the weight of the child was almost too much to bear. The farther he walked, the more the water swelled, and the heavier the child rested on his shoulders. For the first time in his life, the giant Christopher was gripped with a fear of death. At last, using all his might, Christopher reached land and put the child down.

Lying nearly exhausted, Christopher spoke to the child. "I was in great trouble in the water. I felt as if I had the weight of the whole world on my shoulders."

Then the child spoke. "Indeed you have borne a great burden, Christopher. I am Jesus Christ, the king you serve in your work. This day you have carried not only the whole world, but the one who created the world. In order that you might know what I say is true, place your staff in the earth by the house, and tomorrow it will bear flowers and fruit." Then the child disappeared.

The next morning Christopher walked outside, and there he found his staff bearing flowers, leaves, and dates. Christopher now knew that he served the greatest and most powerful master in the world. □

Among the principles of spirituality embedded in this story is the one of finding God where you are. Here is a man who could not fast and could not pray for long, but in his own gifts he found the Christ. He found his sanctity, as we would say, where he was planted. He uncovered his story where he was. In turn, he became a story for us to live by.

Story and sanctity, then, go hand in hand, and here I would like to share six links between them. I would like to make six suggestions that provide the connection.

First Suggestion: Learn the story.

Learning the story has a twofold target. It means learning the larger story of revelation, of God and his movement in history. Then it means learning the smaller story of ourselves, of God's movement in our own personal history. As for the first, we are speaking of the necessity of catechesis, of study, of spiritual reading. We are speaking of all the ways our tradition passes on the God story. There are great teachers and mystics who know the story well and who can teach us, and we must listen to them. Learning, study, "adult education" if you will, are important, as we saw it is in the Jewish tradition. Sometimes people are suspicious of too much learning but it was Frank Sheed, himself a devout and prayerful Catholic, who remarked that surely God will not be loved less for us knowing him more. We must learn God's story, our tradition. It is one of our woes today that so many young people do not know elementary concepts and language and even personalities that characterize our tradition. Knowing God's story is a prerequisite for knowing our own.

Furthermore, the God story often provides the key for our own. Too often we do not perceive any pattern in our lives. We are too close to ourselves and our environment. It is often only in hindsight that we detect a scheme. Frequently a crisis forces a design upon us, helping us suddenly to discover the "wonderful works of God" in our lives.

☐A poor but honest jeweler was arrested for a crime he never committed. He was placed in a high and well-protected prison in the center of the city. One day, after he had been imprisoned for months, his wife came to the main gate. She told the guards how her husband, the poor jeweler, was a devout and prayerful man. He would be lost without his simple prayer rug. Would they not allow him to have this single possession? The guards agreed that it would be harmless and gave him the prayer rug. Five times daily he would unroll his rug and pray.

Weeks passed, and one day the jeweler said to his jailers: " I am bored sitting here day after day with nothing to do. I am a good jeweler and, if you will let me have some pieces of metal and some simple tools, I will make you jewelry. You could then sell what I make in the bazaar and add to your low salaries as jailers. I ask for little—just something to fill the idle hours and keep my skill in practice."

The poorly paid jailers agreed that it would be a good arrangement. Each day they brought the jeweler some bits of silver and metal and some simple tools. Each night they would remove the tools and metal and take home the jewelry that he had made. Days grew into weeks, weeks into months. One bright morning when they came to the jeweler's cell, they found it empty! No sign was found of the prisoner or of how he had escaped from this well-protected prison.

Some time later, the real criminal was arrested for the crime the poor jeweler had been falsely accused of. One day in the city's bazaar, long after that, one of the guards saw the ex-prisoner, the jeweler. Quickly explaining that the real criminal had been caught, he asked the jeweler how he had escaped. The jeweler proceeded to tell the amazing story.

His wife had gone to the main architect who had designed the prison. She obtained from him the blueprints of the cell doors and the locks. She then had a design woven into a prayer rug. Each day he would pray, his head would touch the rug. Slowly, he began to see that there was design, within a design, within another design, and that it was the design of the lock of his cell door. From the bits of leftover metal and his simple tools, he fashioned a key and escaped![1] □

Like the jeweler, we must look closely for a pattern of God's grace in our lives. We must explore our personal history for his presence. Some keep a journal trying to sense some movement and growth, where they've been and where, by the grace of God, they are.

Second Suggestion: Own your story.

To own one's story means to accept the whole of it, the whole of our lives, the light side and the dark. In short, owning the story is to give ourselves the total acceptance that God gives us. There is no room for self-hatred in our own story. This was the regret that George Bernanos in *Diary of a Country Priest* had the dying priest utter when he cried out that he wished he had shown himself the same compassion and understanding and forgiveness that he gave other members of the mystical body of Christ. In accepting our dark, shadow side we learn who we are and what God's grace means. It's an "amazing grace" that "saves a wretch like me." In owning our story we learn to make friends with our shadow side, for only then can we know the redemptive love of Jesus who overcame the powers of darkness in his own life.

In our tradition, then, an essential part of owning our story is the fruitful celebration of the sacrament of reconciliation. Here there is a more explicit acceptance of our story placed deep within the governing mercy of the Father. In the sacrament of reconciliation we proclaim and own our story, loud and clear. There is here real dialogue, real connection, between the two stories, God's and ours. We tell our story of infidelity and sin, and Jesus tells his of prodigal fathers and redeemed Magdalenes. An exchange is made.

Third Suggestion: Contemplate the story.

In order to sense God working in our stories, we must give time to looking at them. We must move into contemplation in order that we might better see the patterns of grace and sharpen our perception of the spirit. Here's an old African tale retold by Laura Simms that says the same thing:

☐There was once a man who owned black and white cattle. They were no ordinary cattle and he tended them as if they were his children. He took them each day to graze in green pastures and they gave white frothy milk. But for three mornings, when the man went to milk his cows, their udders were empty and withered and they gave no milk. So he decided to stay up at night and watch them. And he did.

In the middle of the night he saw a rope come down from the sky. Women descended from the sky with calabashes (large gourds). They were sky people. They placed their calabashes on the earth beneath his cows and milked them until the gourds were overflowing with the white frothy milk. Then they began to ascend the rope.

He saw one woman more beautiful than the others and he wanted her for his wife. So he caught her. The other women ran away. She struggled, until he cried out to her, "I want to marry you." She stopped struggling and said, "Mortal, I will marry you on one condition: I have a finely woven basket. Promise not to open it until I give you my permission. If you open it too soon, harm will befall us." He promised. She married him.

She placed the basket by the door of their house. She was a good wife. She even tended his black and white cattle. But as time passed, the man grew curious. "What does she keep in the basket?" One day he thought, "What harm will it be if I look? And after all, isn't she my wife and isn't it then my basket too?" So when she was tending his cattle, he opened the basket.

The man began to laugh, for he saw nothing in her basket. So he closed it, putting the lid carefully onto the bottom. Just then the wife returned home. "What did you do today?" she asked. Laughing, the man answered, "I looked into your basket." "What did you see?" she asked sadly. "I saw nothing. It was empty," he said laughing.

The woman picked up the basket and put it on her knees. "You saw nothing. But the basket was full. I kept all the beautiful things of the sky in the basket for you and me. If you had waited, I would have taught you to see." She left. The woman who came from the sky went back to the sky. □

It is the same today. Mankind still thinks the things of the spirit are empty.[2]

Wondering about our story helps us to see the things of the spirit.

Fourth Suggestion: Pray the story.

To contemplate our story is to learn to see the things of the spirit; to pray our story is to dialogue about it in the presence of God. Prayer links our story and God's. Prayer moves our ongoing conversation with God. It helps us against the powers of darkness. We can take a lesson from Gandhi:

> I am neither a man of letters nor of science but I humbly claim to be a man of prayer. It is prayer that has saved my life. Without prayer I would have lost my reason a long time ago. If I did not lose my peace of soul, in spite of many trials, it is because the peace came to me from prayer. One can live several days without food, but not without prayer. Prayer is the key to each morning and the lock to every evening. Prayer is the sacred alliance between God and man, in order to be delivered from the clutches of the prince of darkness. We have to choose either to ally ourselves with the forces of evil or on the other hand with the forces of good. This is my sacred teaching: let every one try this experience and he will find that daily prayer will add something new to his life, of which there is no equivalent to be found anywhere.[3]

Fifth Suggestion: Share the story.

Sharing our story is a threefold process. First we share with a confidant, a spiritual director, a "soul friend" as the English mystics put it.

Sharing our story is part of the process of discernment: to know God's will, to hold holy conversation about our story and God's story, to assess spiritual movements within both stories. This is a key ingredient in the spirituality of story.

Secondly, sharing our story and the story of God is a part of evangelization. To tell the Good News, to be an open witness, even perhaps to teach religious education or whatever, all are parts of sharing the story of salvation, our story and God's.

Finally, sharing our story means tapping into social justice. No one can simply "pray" passively or be a part of a religious community or parish and not be alert to the excruciating needs of the poor. There is an urgency to right injustice, to be more than comfortable armchair Christians. Else we'll be a part of this parable:

□Once there was a farming town that could be reached by a a narrow road with a bad curve in it. There were frequent accidents on the road especially at the curve, and the preacher would preach to the people of the town to make sure they were Good Samaritans. And so they were, as they would pick the people up on the road, for this was a religious work. One day someone suggested they buy an ambulance to get the accident victims to the town hospital more quickly. The preacher preached and the people gave, for this was a religious work. Then one day a councilman suggested that the town authorize building a wider road and taking out the dangerous curve. Now it happened that the mayor had a farm market right at the curve on the road and he was against taking out the curve. Someone asked the preacher to say a word to the mayor and the congregation next Sunday about it. But the preacher and most of the people figured they had better stay out of politics; so next Sunday the preacher preached on the Good Samaritan Gospel and encouraged the people to continue their fine work of picking up the accident victims—which they did.[4]□

Writing from Bolivia, spiritual writer Henry Nouwen talks of spirituality and living in the midst of the poor, being a kind of hermit in their midst. He says true prayer always includes becoming poor. He asks, "Who will be the St. Francis of our age? . . . Who will lift up the world of today to God and plead for His mercy? . . . When the Lord looks down on us what does He see worth saving? He sees His son Jesus, in the faces of the few who continue to cry out in the valley of tears . . . ." So spirituality and our story must include many paragraphs of concern for our brothers and sisters in justice.

Sixth Suggestion: Celebrate your story.

Any true spirituality must be liturgical. We must be a part of a larger, witnessing and worshipping community that meets to celebrate salvation by our God. The liturgy is storytelling at its best. It has the great Scriptures proclaimed and meditated on, the normative sourcebook of God's story. It has the narrative of Jesus' own Last Supper, his work, passion, death and resurrection. The liturgy brings God's people together in a community of faith, hope, and love. We remember and are remembered at the church's liturgy. We are celebrants of a great mystery.

The liturgical year gives us seasons that, like paragraphs, move us from episode to episode in the life of Christ. Our verses, our songs, our vestments, our decorations are all trappings for our on-going celebration of God's redemptive story and ours. We know we have been touched with grace; we are bound to celebrate our story.

Such are the six connections between spirituality and story. Let me end with a true story from Brennan Manning that incorporates all six suggestions in a moving way. It's a story of sin, grace, repentance, sharing, and celebration.

☐A few years ago, I lay desperately sick on a motel floor in a southern city. I learned later that within a few hours, if left unattended, I would have gone into alcoholic convulsions and might have died. At that point in time I did not know I was an alcoholic. I crawled to the telephone but was shaking and quivering so badly that I could not dial. Finally, I managed one digit and got the operator. "Please help me," I pleaded. "Call Alcoholics Anonymous." She took my name and address. Within ten minutes a man walked in the door. I had never seen him before and he had no idea who I was. But he had the Breath of the Father on his face and an immense reverence for my life. He scooped me up in his arms and raced me to a detox center. There began the agony of withdrawal. Anyone who has been down both sides of the street will tell you that withdrawal from alcohol can be no less severe than withdrawal from heroin.

To avoid bursting into tears, I will spare the reader that odyssey of shame and pain, unbearable guilt, remorse and humiliation. But the stranger brought me back to life. His words might sound corny to you, like tired old cliches. But they were words of life to me. This fallen-away Catholic who had not been to the Eucharistic table in years told me that the Father loved me, that He had not abandoned me, that He would draw good from what had happened (*etiam peccatis*). He told me that right now the name of the game isn't guilt and fear and shame but survival. He told me to forget about what I had lost and focus on what I had left.

He gave me an article from an American Medical Association journal explaining alcoholism as a bio-psychological sickness, that an alcoholic is a biological freak who cannot stop drinking once he takes the first drink. The stranger told me to feel no more guilt than if I were recovering from some other disease like cancer or diabetes. Above all else, he affirmed me in my emptiness and loved me in my loneliness. Again and again he told me of the Father's love; how when his children stumble and fall, He does not scold them but scoops them up and comforts them. Later I learned that my benefactor was an itinerant laborer who shaped up daily at Manpower, a local employment agency. He put cardboard in his work shoes to cover the holes. Yet, when I was able to eat, he bought me my first dinner at MacDonald's. For seven days and seven nights, he breathed life into me physically and spiritually and asked nothing in return. Later I learned that he had lost his family and fortune through drinking. In his loneliness he turns on his little TV at midnight and talks to John Wayne, hoping he will talk back. Every night before bed he spends fifteen minutes reading a meditation book, praises God for his mercy, thanks him for what he has left, prays for all alcoholics, then goes to his window, raises the shade and blesses the world.

Two years later I returned to the same southern city. My friend still lived there but I had no address or telephone number. So I called A.A. In one of life's tragic ironies, I learned that he was on Skid Row. He had been twelve-stepping too often (i.e., the twelfth step of the A.A. program is bringing the message of recovery to practicing alcoholics). There is a buzz word with the A.A. community— HALT. Don't let yourself get too hungry, angry, lonely or tired or you will be very vulnerable to that first drink. My friend was burnt out from helping others and went back on the sauce.

As I drove through Skid Row, I spotted a man in a doorway whom I thought was my friend. He wasn't. Just another drunk wino who was neither sober nor drunk. Just dry. He hadn't had a drink in 24 hours and his hands trembled violently. He reached out and asked, "Hey man, can you gimme a dollar to get some wine?"

I knelt down before him and took his hands in mine. I looked into his eyes. They filled with tears. I leaned over and kissed his hands. He began to cry. He didn't want a dollar. He wanted what I wanted two years earlier lying on the motel floor—to be accepted in his brokenness, to be affirmed in his worthlessness, to be loved in his loneliness. He wanted to be relieved of what Mother Teresa of Calcutta, with her vast personal experience of human misery, says is the worst suffering of all—the feeling of not being accepted or wanted. I never located my friend.

Several days later I was celebrating Eucharist for a group of recovering alcoholics. Midway through the homily, my friend walked in the door. My heart skipped. But he disappeared during the distribution of communion and did not return. Two days later, I received a letter from him which read in part: "Two nights ago in my own clumsy way I prayed for the right to belong, just to belong among you at the holy Mass of Jesus. You will never know what you did for me last week on Skid Row. You didn't see me, but I saw you. I was standing just a few feet away in a storefront window. When I saw you kneel down and kiss that wino's hands, you wiped away from my eyes the blank stare of the breathing dead. When I saw you really cared, my heart began to grow wings, small wings, feeble wings, but wings. I threw my bottle of . . . wine down the sewer. Your tenderness and understanding breathed life into me, and I want you to know that. You released me from my shadow world of panic, fear and self-hatred. God, what a lonely prison I was living in. Father Brennan, if you should ever wonder who Ben Shaw is, remember I am someone you know very well, I am every man you meet and every woman you meet. . . . Am I also you?"

His letter ends, "Wherever I go, sober by the grace of God one day at a time, I will thank God for you."[5]□

It's the "Hound of Heaven" retold, the perennial retelling of the story of Abba's redemptive love.

13 A Postscript of Stories

*T*he dying man, Morris, was talking to his wife. "Jennie, be sure to put David in charge of the store when I'm gone." "David?" she asked, "Why not Nathan? He's a smart boy." Morris nodded weakly. "Okay, but give Isaac the station wagon." "But Benny needs it for his family." "All right," Morris said, "give it to Benny. But let Becky have the country house." "Papa," said his wife, "you know Becky hates the country. Give it to Rosalie." "Mama," the old man groaned, "who's dying, you or me?"

Every family has its stories that they will tell for generations until they become that precious thing, a tradition. Some families preserve their traditions in albums, recipes, festivals, customs and mementos brought from the old country. But it is chiefly the stories that entice and enthrall. Children in particular love to hear stories of their parents' youth, their meeting, their courtship. It is instructive to know where their grandparents came from, their early struggles in a new country, and all the rest. Knowing the family story certainly helps explain certain traits and characteristics.

Families with a religious tradition can gain much from a common reflection on the Bible. The Joseph story of Genesis with its betrayal, hurt, struggle, jealousy, and its themes of forgiveness and

213

reconciliation are well understood by any family. The Cain and Abel story of sibling rivalry, the perplexed and hurt father of James and John as they left him for Jesus, the wife of Zacchaeus flabbergasted by his over-compensation and seeing her house money dwindle, the Martha/Mary tension—all are family themes. All invite family reflection, even to the point of uncertainty:

> That Mary chose the better part is not
> Debatable. The Word is healthy fare,
> And Jesus served it rich and piping hot;
> So Mary simply hungered for her share
>
> And let her sister cook the evening meal.
> But worried Martha, standing in the door,
> Could see the need for sustenance was real,
> And knowing bread was more than metaphor,
>
> Let slip her single, overworked complaint:
> She needed help to serve the food and drink!
> Then Jesus spoke; and yet that sermon grates
> A little on my soul: I've met some saints
> In kitchens too! And so I like to think
> As Jesus lectured her, He also set the plates.[1]

Admittedly, in these days of high mobility, split families, and alternative lifestyles, it is hard to find enough stability to locate and tell the family story. Still it is important. Aided by tape recorders and cameras the old folk can be encouraged to tell their stories for the future.[2] All can contribute to the general fund of tradition, to the storytelling that not only binds us to one another but to God. And our stories can not only validate our values, but can also give food for thought for future generations. Sr. Jose Maria Hobday has one such story that illustrates a value she learned from her parents. Telling it invites us to consider our own life's values:

☐ As a sister in a religious community, I have taken a vow of poverty. But what that freedom is all about first came to me through my parents. I learned the heart of this vow from a strawberry-ice-cream evening.

We were rather poor during the 1930's; not desperately so, but poor enough to feel the lacks and to live on the edge of insecurity. One Saturday evening I was working late on my homework. I was in the living room, my brothers were outside with their friends, and my parents were in the kitchen, discussing our financial situation. It was very quiet, and I found myself more and more following the kitchen conversation, rather than attending to my homework. Mama and Daddy were talking about what had to be paid for during the week, and there was very little money—a few dollars. As I listened, I became more and more anxious, realizing that there was not enough to go around. They spoke of school needs, of fuel bills, of food. Suddenly, the conversation stopped, and my mother came into the room where I was studying. She put the money—a couple of bills and a handful of change—on the desk. "Here," she said, "go find two or three of your brothers and run to the drugstore before it closes. Use this money to buy strawberry ice cream."

I was astonished! I was a smart little girl, and I knew we needed this money for essentials. So I objected. "What? We have to use this to pay bills, Mama, to buy school things. We can't spend this for ice cream!" Then I added, "I'm going to ask Daddy." So I went to my father, telling him what Mother had asked me to do. Daddy looked at me a moment, then threw back his head and laughed. "Your mother is right, honey," he said. "When we get this worried and upset about a few dollars, we are better off having nothing at all. We can't solve all the problems, so maybe we should celebrate instead. Do as your mother says."

So I collected my brothers and went to the drugstore. In those days you could get a lot of ice cream for a few dollars, and we came home with our arms full of packages. My mother had set the table, made fresh coffee, put out what cookies we had, and invited in the neighbors. It was a great party! I do not remember what happened concerning the other needs, but I remember the freedom and fun of that evening. I thought about that evening many times, and came to realize that spending a little money at that time for pleasure was not irresponsible. It was a matter of survival of the spirit. The bills must have been paid; we made it through the weeks and months that followed. I learned that my parents were not going to allow money to dominate them. I learned something of the value of money, of its use. I saw that of itself it was not important but that my attitude toward it affected my own spirit, could reduce me to powerlessness or give me power of soul.[3] ☐

But enough of the stories. You, the reader, are by now full of them; and I, by now, am in danger of becoming addicted and in need of a cure:

☐ Once long ago, in Holy Russia, there lived a villager whose wife was passionately fond of fairy tales. At first, the man thought this was a harmless foible and made no objection to her indulging her taste by asking everyone she met to tell her new stories. But at last her appetite for them grew to such an extent that she would no longer have any of her friends or her husband's cronies in her house, because they had already told her all the tales they knew, and nothing would satisfy her but ones she had never heard before. So she filled the house with passers-by, many of whom, drawn there by rumors of the woman's weakness, made their stay as long as possible, eating greedily and keeping her husband awake all night with their fantastic chatter.

One cold winter night, an old man knocked on the door and asked for shelter.

"Can you tell fairy stories the whole night through?" asked the villager. "For unless you can, I am sorry to say that my wife will not allow you to stay."

The old man eyed the warm stove within and felt the bitter wind on his back.

"I can tell stories for a hundred nights," said he, "for I am the greatest of all storytellers. But there is one condition: I am serious about my art, and I must not be interrupted, or I shall not go on."

"If I interrupt you," cried the wife, delighted, "may I never listen to another story in all my life!" She gave the old man a good supper and a comfortable place near the stove, and settled herself to listen. The old man began.

"There was once an owl that flew into a garden, sat down on the well and drank . . . . There was once an owl that flew into a garden, sat down on the well and drank . . . . There was once an owl that flew into a garden, sat down on the the well and drank . . . . There was once an owl . . . ," and over and over he repeated the same words. At last the woman could stand it no longer and cried out: "What kind of story are you telling me? I have heard about your owl and the well; get on with what happened next, for the love of Heaven!"

The old man flew into a rage. "You have interrupted me!" he cried. "This is the way this story begins and you have spoiled it with your impatience. Do you understand nothing of the importance of repetition in fairy stories? Now I cannot go on!"

The husband, delighted with this turn of affairs, grabbed his wife and raised his fist. "You broke your promise!" he shouted, "and now we shall never hear the end of this fascinating tale. And I shall see to it that you abide by your vow never to listen to another story if you interrupted this one. Now this old man shall sleep here in peace tonight, and hereafter my house shall welcome friends without requiring any storytelling in payment for our hospitality."

So he beat his wife a little to convince her and while she was sobbing and promising to be good, he winked gratefully at the old man and slipped a silver coin into his hand.[4] □

Before you beat me to convince me to end this book, like the punster who must tell one more as though his life depends on it, I must end with one more story. But it's a delight and, in its own way, a fitting postscript to this book and an expression of everything that I've tried to say in it. It is called *The Little Tin Box*[5] by contemporary storyteller, Ed Hayes.

□ The long gravel driveway that led up from the highway was filled with cars and pickup trucks. The two-story, white farmhouse and large barn were surrounded by tractors and other farm machinery, together with furniture and a variety of household articles. The farm had been in their family now for two generations and, like so many other Midwestern farms, it had been sold recently to some European businessmen. Today, Tom and Mary would sell their furniture and all of their farm machinery. After trying different solutions, even a part-time job in town, Tom was giving up at attempting to make a living from farming.

The farm auction had attracted neighbors and strangers alike. The farmers gathered in small clusters, chatting about the price of cattle or recent futile efforts of the government to help farm prices. Their wives exchanged local news and gossip, but the general mood was sad. The auctioneer, a fat man wearing a white cowboy hat, stood on the haywagon and began the auction with gusto. The furniture went first. The antique oak dining room table and Victorian picture frames were purchased by strangers. After the furniture and

antiques came the machinery. The large, orange Allis Chalmers trac-
tor, the combine, and cultivator changed hands to the Morse code of
the auctioneer's chant. Most of the sale items had been sold when
the auctioneer held up a small tin box and began his usual spiel:
"How much do I hear for this small tin box?"

Before a single bid could be placed, Tom shouted, "Sorry,
friends, the tin box is not for sale . . . everything else is, but not
that!" He came forward and took the tin box from the auctioneer's
hand saying, "Sorry, it must have gotten mixed up with the sale
things by mistake." Tom walked away through the crowd smiling,
with the battered tin box under his arm. The remaining items went
quickly; the auction was over.

The day also began to quickly disappear as the long shadows of
afternoon crisscrossed the old white farmhouse and the barnyard.
The pickup trucks slowly rolled down the gravel driveway, the life
possessions of Tom and Mary stacked on them or being towed
behind. The ladies of the VFW auxiliary, who had served the sale
with a lunch of sandwiches, donuts, and coffee, gave Mary some of
the leftover food and drink. She carried them into the kitchen as
Tom settled with the auctioneer, who echoed the sympathies of their
neighbors about having to sell. He placed his fee into a worn-out,
brown billfold and drove down the drive . . . the last car.

Mary was alone at the kitchen table as Tom entered the back
door. The glare from the single bare lightbulb (the antique glass
shade had brought a good price) made that once cozy room now
seem as stark as a morgue. The house was empty except for the kitchen table and three chairs, and the large, old bed upstairs. The antique bed had belonged to Tom's parents and was solid walnut. It
and the table were not included in the sale, but had been given to
one of their sons. Tomorrow he and his wife would pick them up.

Tom and Mary had planned on leaving the farm that night.
Their suitcases and a pile of cardboard boxes stood ready by the
door. The couple sat in silence at the kitchen table sharing the unsold
ham sandwiches and coffee. The tin box had a place of honor in the
center of the kitchen table. Mary was the first to speak: "They almost
sold your little tin box."

"Yeah, that was close, wasn't it?" said Tom, as he slowly
opened the lid of the box. To the average eye the box appeared to be

empty, but in reality it was filled almost to the top. The old battered tin box was filled with memories. Mary opened a suitcase and removed a small tin box that could have been a twin to Tom's. Slowly, one after another, they took out memories from their tin boxes and passed them to each other. One memory would awaken another one or be the leader of an entire parade of memories: "Remember the first night we stayed here after we were married . . . or when Dick came home from the Army . . . or that Christmas day in the 50s when we and the kids were snowbound?" Their little tin boxes held memories that went back to their early childhoods. In one corner of Tom's box was a memory of him and his friends, when they were young men, swimming in that deep pool down the creek, the one that's surrounded by the giant cottonwoods.

These small tin boxes were what made Tom and Mary the richest people in the county. Early in life they had learned a great secret from Tom's grandfather. "The purpose of any possession," the old man had said, "is to make memories! The only purpose of money—only purpose—is to make memories. Things and possessions only rust and age, but memories, Tommy, memories are like fine wine . . . they grow in value with time." Now that the farm sale and auction had completely dispossessed them of their belongings, they knew the wisdom of what grandfather had said to them in his funny, broken German accent.

Tom returned the last memory to his tin box. He had to rearrange some memories for it to fit. He closed the lid and looked at his watch. They had visited over their memories so long that it seemed too late now and too much trouble to drive into town to their new apartment. Instead, they decided to spend just one more night at the farm. Mary unpacked some sheets from one of the cardboard boxes by the door and made the bed. By now the moon had risen and the wind blew waves of moonlight through the open windows. With no curtains or pictures, the bedroom was empty of things but full of pale, white moonlight. Tom placed his little tin box on the windowsill as he climbed into the ancient great bed. Their last night on the farm was one of the most beautiful of their lives. Mary was asleep as Tom arose and stood by the open window. The fields, the barn, the windmill and, off in the distance, the cottonwoods along the creek were all silent but beautiful, bathed in the light of the giant moon.

Tom smiled as he opened, once again, his little tin box and gently placed inside it the memory of this beautiful night. He attempted to close the lid, but it wouldn't close; the box was so full. Gently he rearranged the memories so they would all fit. Then he closed the lid. As he did, it made a strange click that he had never heard before. Tom placed the old tin box on the windowsill and slowly laid back on the bed. He closed his eyes and was asleep almost at once. The next morning, when she awoke, Mary found him sleeping peacefully in the gentle arms of death.

The following days were hectic. The arrangements for the funeral, the arrival of their children and relatives, and the visits of friends and neighbors took Mary's time. Three nights later, accompanied by the family, she went to the funeral home. As they entered, the lobby was filled with many of the same farmers who, only a few days before, had stood in their yard on that auction day. They stood in small groups, discussing how selling the farm had been just too much for Tom. As she passed, Mary overheard their comments. She smiled to herself as she walked down the aisle toward the casket in the center of a sea of flowers, for she knew that selling the farm had nothing to do with Tom's death. Dressed all in black, she was regal in her serenity as she stood by the casket, looking down at her husband. Tom looked peaceful, his weatherworn face relaxed, his hands folded across his chest. His fingers still had tiny grease-darkened lines from all the years of hard work. Intertwined among his fingers was a black rosary. Mary opened her handbag and then, reaching down, she removed the rosary from Tom's hands and placed it in her bag. She then took from the handbag the little tin box and placed it in Tom's hands. The parish priest, who had been standing by the foot of the casket, stepped forward and, with his authoritarian but hushed voice (the one that came from years of speaking in the confessional), said to her, "Mary, Mary . . . you can't do that!" He started to reach down to remove the tin box from Tom's hands.

"Leave it there, Father Cryziski," Mary said, in an equally authoritarian voice, "that's Tom's rosary. Hardly a day would pass that he wouldn't take some memory out of that box and be filled with gratitude. He was a holy man, and he understood what poverty and prayer were all about. No, Father, the box remains because it's the only thing he's taking with him to heaven."

The priest began to object, but Mary outwitted him. She turned to the crowded funeral home, filled with people wall-to-wall, and said in a loud, clear voice, "Father Cryziski is now going to lead all of us in the rosary"; and with that she knelt beside the casket. The priest was trapped . . . and so, forced to kneel beside her, began, "In the name of the Father, and of the Son . . . ."

When the wake was over, and family and friends had all departed—even the Polish pastor who, while unhappy about the seeming sacrilege, had decided to let it go without further discussion—Mary returned to her apartment. Her black dress hung on the back of the bedroom door as she sat on the bed and smiled, thinking of how much Tom would have approved of what she had done that night. Then she carefully took out her own little tin box and opened it. She placed the memory of the wake—the many, many kind words about Tom, even the expression on Father Cryziski's face—all of it, into her little tin box. That memory fit perfectly on the very top of the full box. As she closed the lid, it made a strange little click. Mary smiled and lay back on the pillow. She was asleep, peacefully, almost at once.

Click.

Endnotes

Introduction

1. Rosemary Haughton, *Tales From Eternity* (New York: Seabury Press, 1973), 14.

2. Anthony Padovano, "Aesthetic Experience and Redemptive Grace," *Aesthetic Dimensions of Religious Education*, ed. Gloria Durka and Joanmarie Smith (Ramsey, N.J.: Paulist Press, 1979), 6.

3. Andrew M. Greeley, *Religion, A Secular Theory* (New York: Free Press, 1982), 103.

Chapter 1

1. Modified from Jakob J. Petuchowski, *Our Masters Taught* (New York: Crossroad, 1982), 37.

2. Elie Wiesel, *The Gates of the Forest* (New York: Schocken Books, 1982).

3. Amos Wilder, *Theopoetic: Theology and the Religious Imagination* (Philadelphia: Fortress Press, 1976), 2.

4. Thomas Driver, *Patterns of Grace: Human Experience as Word of God* (San Francisco: Harper & Row, 1977), xxiii.

5. Sallie McFague, *Metaphorical Theology* (Philadelphia: Fortress Press, 1982).

6. Eugene LaVerdiere S.S.S. and John Gartner S.S.S., "Through Cultural Eyes," *Emmanuel*, January/February 1983, 7.

7. Jake Empereur, *Modern Liturgy*, Vol. 10 No. 2 (March 1983), p. 12. See also Patrick W. Collins's excellent work *More Than Meets the Eye* (Ramsey, N.J.: Paulist Press, 1983).

8. John Navone, S.J. and Thomas Cooper, *Tellers of the Word* (New York: La Jacq Publishing, 1981), xvi. For a different view of the emergence of mystical and imaginative, see Kathleen Agena's article "The Return of En-chantment." The author sees "The Return of Enchantment" as a reaction to the breakdown in Western thought and the social stresses growing out of the technological revolution, and the complexity and size of bureaucratic and government institutions. She contends that the return of enchantment and story are attempts to fill the void in the face of the collapse of a coherent world. But she also sees the danger of a real but subtle authoritarianism as people look to larger-than-life heroes to save them, heroes to whom they are ready to give blind allegiance. Ms. Agena misses, I think, some other valuable insights, but her views are worth noting. *New York Times Magazine* (November 27, 1983), 66 ff. See also an incisive and telling commentary on the Agena article in *Commonweal*, the editorial "Fantasy, Theology and Mysticism," Jan. 27, 1984, 35.

9. See, for example, Wesley A. Kort's *Narrative Elements and Religious Meaning* (Philadelphia: Fortress Press, 1975).

10. Petuchowski, 2.

11. Elie Wiesel, *Night* (New York: Farrar, Straus & Giroux, 1960), 75-76.

12. Maria Harris, "Enlarging the Religious Imagination," Pace, 13 (1982), 1.

13. Lewis Thomas, *The Medusa and the Snail* (New York: Viking Press, 1979), 9.

14. Quoted by Maria Harris, 1.

15. Sallie McFague, 34.

16. Ann Faraday, *The Dream Game* (New York: Harper & Row, 1974), 5.

17. James Hillman, "A Note on Story," *Parabola*, Vol. IV, No. 4 (November 1979), 43.

18. Flannery O'Connor, *The Habit of Being* (New York: Farrar, Straus & Giroux, 1979), 100.

19. Joseph Campbell, a commentary in *The Complete Grimm's Fairy Tales* (New York: Pantheon Books, 1944), 860-61.

20. Anne Morrow Lindburgh, *Gift From the Sea* (New York: Pantheon Books, 1955), 58.

21. Carl Jung, *Modern Man in Search of a Soul* (New York: Harcourt Brace Jovanovich, 1955), 107.

Chapter 2

1. Petuchowski, 51.

2. Ray Bradbury, *Fahrenheit 451* (New York: Ballantine Books, 1953), 163.

3. Thomas Buckley, "Doing Your Own Thinking," *Parabola*, Vol. IV, No. 4 (November 1979), 34.

4. Buckley, *Parabola*, 33.

5. Italo Calvino, *Italian Folk Tales* (New York: Harcourt Brace Jovanovich, 1980), xvi.

6. Campbell, 846.

7. Harold Goddard, *The Meaning of Shakespeare*, Vol. 2 (Chicago: University of Chicago Press, 1965), 208.

8. William R. White, *Speaking in Stories* (Minneapolis: Augsburg Publishing, 1982), 118.

9. White, 119.

10. Willa Cather, *Obscure Destinies* (New York: Alfred A Knopf, 1930), 136.

11. David McCord, *One At A Time* (Boston: Little, Brown and Co., 1961).

12. Frederick Buechner, *The Sacred Journey* (New York: Harper & Row, 1982), 68.

13. T.S. Eliot, "The Dry Salvages, " Stanza V, *The Four Quartets* in *The Complete Poems and Plays* (New York: Harcourt, Brace and World, 1971), 136.

14. Buechner, 32.

15. Coventry Patmore, "The Toys," in Elizabeth Goudge's *A Book of Comfort* (New York: Coward-McCann, 1964), 94.

Chapter 3

1. Antoine de Saint-Exupéry, *The Little Prince* (New York: Harcourt Brace Jovanovich, 1943), 17, 18.

2. Chaim Potok, *The Chosen* (New York: Fawcet Crest, 1967), 264.

3. Bruno Bettelheim, *The Uses of Enchantment* (New York: Alfred A. Knopf, 1976), 27.

4. Karl Rahner, *Theological Investigations*, Vol. IV (Baltimore: Helicon, 1961), 365.

5. Edward Lear, *The Illustrated Treasury of Humor for Children* (New York: Grosset and Dunlap, 1980), 26.

6. Poems by Sister M. Pamela Smith, SSCM, in *Waymakers* (Notre Dame, Ind.: Ave Maria Press, 1982).

7. Dennis and Matthew Linn, *Healing Life's Hurts* (Ramsey, N.J.: Paulist Press, 1978), 76.

8. Barbara Leahy Shlemon, *Healing the Hidden Self* (Notre Dame, Ind.: Ave Maria Press, 1982), 26, 32.

9. Retold by Belden C. Lane on his tapes, "Story Telling: The Enchantment of Theology" (St. Louis: Bethany Press, 1981).

10. Italo Calvino, xviii.

11. Kathleen R. Fischer, *The Inner Rainbow* (Ramsey, N.J.: Paulist Press, 1983), 135.

12. Paul Reps, *Zen Flesh, Zen Bones* (Rutland, Vt.: C.E. Tuttle, 1957), quoted in *Let's Pray/2* by Charles Reutemann, FSC, (Winona, Minn.: St. Mary's Press, 1982), 74.

Chapter 4

1. Matthew Fox, *Whee! We, Wee All the Way Home* (Santa Fe, N.M.: Bear and Co., 1981), 10-11.

2. Adapted from Petuchowski, 40-41.

3. John Powell, *Unconditional Love* (Allen, Tex.: Argus Communications, 1978) 110-18.

4. Petuchowski, 40-41.

Chapter 5

1. Again I am indebted to Belden Lane for the topical outline.

2. This and the two stories following are from Benedicta Ward, *The Desert Christian: Sayings of the Desert Fathers* (New York: Macmillan, 1975).

3. Joan Windham, Introduction to her three volumes *Story Library of the Saints* (Chicago: The Catholic Press, 1974).

4. Joan Windham, Introduction to her *Sixty Saints for Boys* (New York: Sheed and Ward, 1955).

5. Windham, *Sixty Saints for Boys*.

6. C.S. Lewis, *The Lion, the Witch and the Wardrobe*, Book One in *The Chronicles of Narnia* (New York: Collier Books, 1950), 74.

7. Rosemary Haughton, *The Passionate God* (Ramsey, N.J.: Paulist Press, 1981), 2.

8. C.S. Lewis in the introduction to George MacDonald's *The Fantasy Stories* (Grand Rapids, Mich.: Wm. B. Eerdmans, Co., 1980).

9. James Hillman, *Parabola*, Vol. IV, No. 4 (November 1979), 45.

10. Franz Kafka, *The Penal Colony* (New York: Schocken Books, 1948).

11. Howard Schwartz, ed., *Imperial Messages: One Hundred Modern Parables* (New York: Avon Books, 1976), 326.

12. John R. Aurelio, "The Search," *Gather Round* (Ramsey, N.J.: Paulist Press, 1982), 43 ff.

13. C.S. Lewis, *The Lion, the Witch and the Wardrobe*, 75-76.

Chapter 6

1. Robert Alter, *The Art of Biblical Narrative* (New York: Basic Books, 1981), 3.

2. Frederick Buechner, *The Hungering Dark* (New York: Seabury Press, 1969), 51 ff.

3. Paul Hofmann, *Rome: The Sweet Tempestuous Life* (New York: Congdon and Lattes, 1982), 222.

4. John H. Westerhoff, "Contemporary Spirituality: Revelation, Myth and Ritual" in *Aesthetic Dimensions of Religious Education*, 23.

5. Raymond E. Brown, *The Birth of the Messiah* (Garden City, N.Y.: Doubleday & Co., 1977), 8.

6. Brown, 8.

7. Sandra M. Schneiders, I.H.M., "The Paschal Imagination: Objectivity and Subjectivity in New Testament Interpretation, " *Theological Studies*, Vol. 43, No. 1 (March 1982), 67-68.

8. Robert Alter, 23, 32.

9. See Raymond E. Brown's *The Critical Meaning of the Bible* (Ramsey, N.J.: Paulist Press, 1981).

10. William Barclay, *The Gospel of John* (Revised) (Philadelphia: Westminster Press, 1975), 103.

11. George W. MacRae, *Invitation to John* (New York: Doubleday & Co., 1978), 48.

12. Eugene LaVerdiere, S.S.S. with John Gartner, S.S.S., "Engaging in Imagination," *Emmanuel*, December 1982, 605 ff.

13. John Shea, *Stories of Faith* (Chicago: Thomas More Press, 1980), 89.

Chapter 7

1. Andrew M. Greeley, *Religion: A Secular Theory* (New York: The Free Press, 1982), 44.

2. Nathan Mitchell, "Exorcism in the RCIA," *Christian Initiation Resources*, 3 (1981), 163.

3. Sallie McFague, *Metaphorical Theology*, 20.

4. I am indebted to John Shea for the following topical outlines I have developed here. See especially his article "Jesus the Savior," *Chicago Studies*, April 1983, 3 ff.

5. John Shea, "Storytelling and Religious Identity," *Chicago Studies*, Vol. 21, No. 1 (Spring 1982), 39-41.

Chapter 8

1. Martin Bell, "Arnold," *Nenshu and the Tiger* (New York: Seabury Press, 1975), 30 ff.

2. Shakespeare, *Henry VIII*, Act Three, scene 1.

3. Francis Dorff, "The Rabbi's Gift," *The New Catholic World*, March/April 1979, 53.

4. Clarence Jordon, *The Substance of Father and Other Cotton Patch Sermons* (New York: Association Press, 1972), 8.

5. Clarence Jordon, *Letters From Partners* (Americus, Ga.: Koinonia Farm, 1969), 1.

Chapter 9

1. Walbert Buhlmann, *God's Chosen People* (Maryknoll, N.Y.: Orbis Books, 1982), xiii.

2. Natalie Babbitt, *The Devil's Storybook* (N.Y.: Farrar, Straus & Giroux, Bantam Skylark, 1974), 9-15.

3. Lawrence Castagnola, S.J., *Parables for Little People* (San Jose, Calif.: Resource Publications, 1982), 15-18.

4. John Aurelio, "The Parable," *Story Sunday* (Ramsey, N.J.: Paulist Press, 1978), 35 ff.

5. David Juniper, "Walking With the Lord," *Along the Water's Edge: Stories That Challenge and How to Tell Them* (Ramsey, N.J.: Paulist Press, 1982).

6. Italo Calvino, *Italian Folk Tales*, 117.

7. Susan Feldmann, ed., *The Storytelling Stone* (New York: Dell Publishing, 1965), 250.

8. My own retelling of the many versions of this classic Indian tale. For another gracious story on this same theme, see Ann Ashford's *If I Had A Wistful Unicorn* (Atlanta: Peachtree Publishers, 1978).

Chapter 10

1. Tom Downs, *A Journey to Self Through Dialogue: An Excursion of Spiritual Self-Discovery for Individuals and Groups* (Mystic, Conn.: Twenty-Third Publications, 1977), 66.

2. John S. Dunne, *The Church of the Poor Devil* (New York: Macmillan Publishing Co., 1982), 93.

3. Again I am indebted to John Shea for the category suggestions.

4. Francis Thompson, "The Hound of Heaven."

5. Sister Maria Jose Hobday, *Parabola*, Vol. IV, No. 4 (November 1979), 6, 7.

6. Brennan Manning, *A Stranger to Self Hatred* (Denville, N.J.: Dimension Books, 1982), 95.

7. Carlo Carretto, *I, Francis* (Maryknoll, N.Y.: Orbis Books, 1982), 6.

8. Andrew Greeley, *Death and Beyond* (Chicago: Thomas More Press, 1976), 90.

9. Annie Dillard, *Pilgrim at Tinkers Creek* (London: Jonathan Cape, 1975), 8-9.

10. Brennan Manning, 69-71.

11. Francis F. Sweeney, *It Will Take a Lifetime* (Boston: Charles River Books, 1980), 53 ff.

12. Navone and Cooper, 154.

13. David Juniper, 63.

14. Robert Bolt, *A Man For All Seasons* (New York: Random House, 1960), 54-55.

Chapter 12

1. Retold by Edward Hayes in *Twelve and One-Half Keys* (Easton, Kansas: Forest of Peace Books, 1981), 9.

2. Retold by Laura Simms in *Psychology Today*, March 1983, 16.

3. Quoted in *Let's Pray/2* by Charles Reutemann, FSC, 81.

4. Francis X. Meehan, "Ministry in the Church: A Structural Concern for Justice," *Review for Religious*, January 1978.

5. Brennan Manning, *The Wisdom of Accepted Tenderness* (Denville, N.J.: Dimension Books, 1978), 60 ff.

Chapter 13

1. Christopher P. Durney, "Mary and Martha," *The Bible Today*, Vol. 19, No. 2 (May 1981), 167.

2. See Joan and Mary Thiry's *You Must Tell Your Children* (Chicago: Chateau Thierry Press, 1978).

3. Sister Maria Jose Hobday, *Parabola* Vol. IV, No. 4 (November 1979), 5.

4. Retold by D.M. Dooling, *Parabola*, Vol. IV. No. 4 (November 1979), 39-40.

5. Edward Hayes, "The Little Tin Box," in *Twelve and One-Half Keys*, 139 ff.

Resources

Recordings

Baumer, Fred. *Preacher: Storyteller of God*. Kansas City, Mo.: National Catholic Reporter, 1981

Friedman, Greg. *Storytelling in Ministry*. Notre Dame, Ind.: Ave Maria Press, Modern Cassette Library, 1982.

Lane, Belden C. *Storytelling: The Enchantment of Theology*. St. Louis: Bethany Press, 1981.

Manning, Brennan. *The Parable of Willie-Juan*. Notre Dame, Ind.: Ave Maria Press, Modern Cassette Library, 1981.

Newland, Mary Reed. *How to Tell Bible Stories*. Kansas City, Mo.: National Catholic Reporter, 1976.

        Storytelling to Teach Religion. Kansas City, Mo.: National Catholic Reporter, 1976.

Shea, John. *The Stories of Jesus in Pastoral Ministry*. Kansas City, Mo., National Catholic Reporter, 1980.

Wilhelm, Robert Bela. *Storytelling for Self-Discovery*. Kansas City, Mo.: National Catholic Reporter, 1977.

Collections

Aurelio, John, ed. *Gather Round*. Ramsey, N.J.: Paulist Press, 1978.

Calvino, Italo, ed. *Italian Folk Tales*. New York: Harcourt, Brace, Jovanovich, 1975.

Doherty, Catherine de Hueck. *Not Without Parables*. Notre Dame, Ind.: Ave Maria Press, 1977.

Feldmann, Susan, ed. *The Storytelling Stone*. New York: Dell Publishing, 1965.

Hays, Edward. *Twelve and One-Half Keys*. Easton, Kansas: Forest of Peace Books, 1981.

Juknialis, Joseph J. *When God Began in the Middle*. Saratoga, Calif.: Resource Publications, 1982.

Schwartz, Howard, ed. *Imperial Messages: One Hundred Modern Parables*. New York: Avon (A Bard Book), 1976.

The Complete Grimm's Fairy Tales. New York: Pantheon, 1944.

Story Library of the Saints (3 volumes). New York: Catholic Press (Delair Publishing Co.), 1974.

Books and References on Storytelling and Imagination

Bauer, Caroline Feller. *Handbook for Storytellers*. Chicago: American Library Association, 1977.

Crossan, John Dominic. *The Dark Interval: Toward a Theology of Story*. Niles, Ill.: Argus Communications, 1975.

de Bello, Anthony. *The Song of the Bird*. Chicago: Loyola University Press, 1982.

Eisner, Elliot, W. *The Educational Imagination*. New York: Macmillan Publishing Co., 1979.

Fisher, Kathleen R. *The Inner Rainbow*. Ramsey, N.J.: Paulist Press, 1983.

Harrell, John and Mary. *To Tell of Gideon*. Berkeley, Calif.: (Box 9006), 1975.

Millman, Lawrence. *Our Like Will Not Be There Again*. Boston: Little, Brown and Co., 1977.

Navone, John, S.J. and Thomas Cooper. *Tellers of the Word*. New York: LeJacq Publishing, 1981.

Samples, Bob. *The Metaphoric Mind*. Reading, Mass.: Addison-Wesley Publishing Co., 1976.

Sawyer, Ruth. *The Way of the Storyteller*. New York: Viking Press, 1965.

Shea, John. *An Experience Named Spirit*. Chicago: Thomas More Press, 1983.

   Stories of Faith. Chicago: Thomas More Press, 1980.

   Stories of God. Chicago: Thomas More Press, 1978.

White, William R. *Speaking in Stories*. Minneapolis: Augsburg Publishing, 1982.